GRACE

ELEANOR McCALLIE COOPER
AND WILLIAM LIU

INTRODUCTION BY CHARLES RUAS

GRACE

AN AMERICAN WOMAN IN CHINA: 1934–1974

Published by

Soho Press, Inc.

853 Broadway

New York, N.Y. 10003

Library of Congress Cataloging-in-Publication Data

Cooper, Eleanor, 1946–

Grace : an American woman in China, 1934–1974 /

Eleanor McCallie Cooper and William Liu.

p. cm.

ISBN 1-56947-314-5 (alk. paper)

1. Divine, Grace McCallie, 1901–1979—Journeys—China.

2. China—Description and travel.

3. China—Social life and customs.

I. Title: American woman in China, 1934–1974.

II. Liu, William, 1941–   III. Title.

DS710 .C714 2002

951.05'092—dc21   2002070784

10 9 8 7 6 5 4 3 2 1

Designed by Pauline Neuwirth, Neuwirth & Associates, Inc.

To Grace's four granddaughters,
Yanhui (Julia),
Yancui (Tracy),
Yanyu (Ellen),
and Yun (Annie)

· INTRODUCTION ·

I REMEMBER GRACE as my mother's close friend and the mother of my playmates when I was growing up in China but I had not seen her since. Soon after my return to New York from completing a Fulbright stint that took me back to China for the first time in over forty years, I was surprised by a call from Eleanor McCallie Cooper in Tennessee who contacted me to discuss the life of her relative Grace, whose story she wanted to write with Grace's son, William Liu. She had learned from him that I had spent two years teaching in the city of Tianjin where I was born and where Grace had lived. While there, I located the surviving members of Grace's family. When we met, our conversation conjured up for me the elusive image of the young Grace—thin, her face pale-complexioned, with bright, penetrating grey eyes and a kindly expression, framed by wavy dark hair. She spoke decisively in a lilting American accent. Eleanor knew the American side of Grace's story but had not yet gone to China to do research; I knew the Chinese side but not the American. I said how important I felt it was to tell the whole story, because Grace in her straightforward and unassuming way had lived her life by crossing racial, cultural, and political barriers. Her life exemplified what is now called "multiculturalism," which was then unknown in the United States. Her story has been told here with profound sympathy and lucid understanding by her son, William, and her cousin, Eleanor.

From the first letter sent home by the young American, we see through her eyes that exotic China of the Foreign Concessions in the 1930s before the Second World War. Beijing was still surrounded by medieval walls and one of the most beautiful cities in the world; further south Shanghai was the fleshpot of the East. For me it was especially interesting because Grace is describing life in Tianjin, the center of colonial power in Northern China, the city my French grandfather helped to develop and where my father was an engineer in the Water Works, as well as the city where my brothers and I were born. The thirties was an exciting time of foreign clubs, jazz bands, international high finance, and military power mixed with the political struggles of the new Chinese Republic and the nascent Communist Party. The foreign concessions protected Westerners along with Chinese of every political persuasion including the families of warlords who menaced the city.

Grace had followed her Chinese husband from the United States back to China where she witnessed the sweep of history from before the Revolution through the struggles to build a new China. She is one of only a handful of Americans who chose to stay in China after the Communist Revolution; she not only survived the Cultural Revolution but also outlived Chairman Mao himself. Reading this book was especially fascinating to me because through Grace's letters home I learned about events that affected my family—the great flood of 1939, and my father's brave efforts to supply drinking water to the city resulting in the infection that would prove fatal to him. My brothers and I had known little about the circumstances surrounding the death of my father as it was a subject my mother could never bring herself to mention.

WHENEVER WE DISCUSSED CHINA as I was growing up in New York City, my mother always had an unanswered question: What happened to Grace? I recalled that Grace and her children, Nini, Ellen, and Willy, were planning to leave Tianjin sometime after we did in 1946. In preparation for our departure my mother took us to have a passport picture made of herself surrounded by her three children. Grace followed suit and brought all her children to the photographer as well. She wanted them pictured on her new American passport to establish their nationality because the two youngest had been born in China. Later we learned that Grace had postponed her departure and communication became increasingly difficult during that unsettled period of our lives. Down came the Bamboo Curtain and the ensuing silence lasted for years.

Before leaving China, Grace told my mother that if they ever lost touch with each other, to write her brother Tom who would always know where to find her. When my mother received a terse answer to an inquiry that she sent Tom saying that he knew of no such person in China, she understood that she had to stop trying to find Grace. My mother had joined the staff of the newly organized United Nations in New York, while Tom worked for the Manhattan Project atomic research center in Oak Ridge, Tennessee, which required top security clearance. This was at the height of the McCarthy era witch hunt for communist sympathizers inside the government and any link to Communist China was a dangerous liability.

When I returned to China in 1992 to teach at Nankai University, one of the first questions I asked Prof. Zhang, the chairman of the English Department, was how I could find the Water Works Company where my father had been an engineer. I wanted to see how his name was written in Chinese characters so I could learn to write mine. I also hoped to find traces of "Grace Divine," my Mother's old friend. Prof. Zhang told me that there had been a teacher at the university named Grace Liu whose husband worked at the Tianjin Water Works. At first I thought it a strange coincidence, not realizing that this Grace Liu might be "Auntie Grace." It never occurred to any of us that she had remained in Tianjin. It turned out that she developed the English Department at the university and trained some of the professors who were now my colleagues. After all these years I had finally returned to Tianjin and landed in the same department as Grace, only to learn that she had died in 1979.

MY DEPARTMENT HELPED TO locate Grace's daughter, Nini, and her family in Tianjin. The departmental secretary, Miss Chen Jing, was delegated to assist me. It was after work and already dark when she came for me and we set out on the downtown bus to a residential neighborhood of now dilapidated town houses on a dimly lit street. Miss Chen Jing told me that Grace's son, William, was in the United States, that Ellen had died of cancer many years ago, but that Nini was in Tianjin and we were going to her home. Once there, we entered a building in total darkness, climbed up the rickety stairs, carefully made our way through piles of wood, bags of coal and boxes, and down a hallway. We knocked at a door showing a sliver of light. Liu En-hua opened the door and invited us into the sitting room. He was Nini's husband and this was their home. He introduced me to his daughter, Liu Yun, a tall pretty girl with long black hair who was a student at Tianjin University. Grace's grandaughter was a perfect combination of two worlds: completely Chinese, studying to be an engineer like her grandfather, with Chinese as her first language. Yet I felt there was something about her, whether in her physiognomy, her movements, or her facial expressions, that was typical of an American teenager.

Miss Chen Jing and I were embarrassed and confused when Nini's husband informed us that Nini had died of asthma a few years back. It seemed such a terrible waste to me; she could have been treated for asthma had she been in the States. We talked about all of Grace's children—Nini, Ellen, and Willy. I explained that we had grown up together in the old days (before the Communist Revolution). My older brother Franklin was Nini's age, I was born a month after Ellen, and Willy was a year younger than my brother Alex. But it was not until Liu En-hua brought out some family albums that we could put all the pieces of the puzzle together. I don't know how they saved these precious photographs from the Cultural Revolution, a time when people burned everything that connected them with the past. But here was a photograph of three children wearing straw coolie hats walking along a beach, and I recognized Nini in the lead and my brother Franklin trailing behind— an idyllic moment at Beidaihe the summer resort for Beijing and Tianjin on the coast just below where the Great Wall comes to an end at the sea.* But most moving to me was a photograph of three young women in masquerade costumes at a party at the country club. One was in Arab robes, but I immediately recognized the other two as Auntie Grace and my mother wearing long Chinese dresses.** All three women were smiling radiantly at the camera, caught in the moment, utterly unaware of the future. Seeing our parents when they were young brought home the realization that Nini's life was over. Her life might have been my brother's or mine had my family chosen to remain in China. It raised the question once again, "What made Grace choose to stay in China?" Eleanor McCallie Cooper and William Liu's eloquent book captures all the nuances of this courageous life: the innocence and love that made Grace take her child from New York City to go live on the other side of the world; the commitment and passionate faith that made her want to build a life in a revolutionary society; and the fortitude and courage to live out the choices she made.

CHARLES RUAS
New York, 2002

---

*See page 66, infra.
**See page 65, infra.

· FOREWORD ·

G RACE DIVINE LIU was one of only a few Westerners who lived in China during the Cultural Revolution; we know of no other foreigner who was condemned publicly on stage before jeering crowds. Grace was witness to a social transformation that few foreigners and no members of the media saw from within. Her perspective is unique, not just for the duration of her stay—from the semi-colonial period through the Cultural Revolution—but because she was both insider and outsider, a foreigner married to a native, with neither political nor religious affiliations. Grace followed her heart, educated herself, challenged wrongs, spoke her mind, and changed over time. Her personal transformation is gradual, yet dramatic, allowing others to make that journey with her.

I first heard of Grace in 1968 when I was heading West to go East. On my way to Japan to teach English, my aunt in California told me I was not the first in my family to go to the Orient: In the 1930s my father's first cousin had "married a Chinaman" and lived in China ever since. No one knew then if she was still alive. I imagined she must have met some cruel death under the Communists. Although China was not open at that time, I determined to go there someday and find Grace—or at least what remained of her— and tell her story.

As it transpired, Grace found me. In 1974, out of the blue, a letter arrived in Chattanooga from Grace herself. Her survival was amazing news. After reconnecting with her family, Grace accepted her brother's invitation to return to America for the first time in forty years. In late 1974 she arrived with her son, William Liu, and was reunited with her family in Tennessee.

I lived with Grace and William the last year of her life in Berkeley, California. It was then she began writing her life story. When she became ill, her daughters, Nini and Ellen, came from China to help with her care. Grace died of cancer in 1979 and we put her unfinished work in a box. William took the box with him to Wellesley College where he had accepted a teaching position. Nini and Ellen returned to China with Grace's ashes, and I returned home to Tennessee. It was there, in her hometown and mine, that I realized the significance of the story she had told me.

For many years I kept hearing Grace's voice muffled in that box, feeling her push against the cardboard and try to peek through the cracks. Years later, when William and I reopened the box, Grace's presence poured out. Her voice on the tapes was clear and strong, her letters fresh and full of details, her writing brimming with information about her life in China. In those intervening years, both Nini and Ellen had died. William was Grace's only surviving child. He and I knew this story had to be told, and as much as possible in Grace's own words.

Grace's records in China had been destroyed on two occasions —once when she and her husband burned their own documents as Japanese troops attacked during the Second World War and later when she and her son were arrested and their house ransacked by Red Guards during the Cultural Revolution. Her only papers that survived were those that were sent home.

When we began writing this book, I called Grace's sister-in-law, Mary Hills Divine, who had saved Grace's letters over the years. Mary Hills, then in her nineties, couldn't remember where she had put the box of letters. She feared someone had thrown it out while cleaning. Sometime later her daughter, Elinor Benedict, called to tell me she had found the box of letters—did I still want it? Yes, I replied, but where had it been? Under her mother's bed, she said.

The box arrived, full of old letters, many yellowed. Some were bundled and held together with an old rubber band that had practically melted. Others were loose, handwritten in flowing script or typed, refolded, and stuffed back in their envelopes, loaded with stamps or stamps torn off, postmarked fifty, sixty, some seventy, years ago. The letters were addressed to different people—brothers, aunts, cousins—anyone in the family who had received a letter from Grace and sent it on to Mary Hills. Then I found one dated August 4, 1934—"Dear Mama and Everybody, Well, I'm here at last . . ." The first letter from China! Following came another one dated a week later . . . and another, the next.

Correspondence between Grace and her family stopped in the 1950s. During the McCarthy era, receipt of Grace's letters from "Red China" became threatening to her brother who was employed in a high security position at Oak Ridge, Tennessee, one of the sites involved with atomic bomb research. It is a tribute to him and his wife that they kept these letters intact despite that threat.

In order to present the story in Grace's own words, we drew on four sources: letters, articles written by Grace from 1949–59, interviews conducted from 1976–79, and Grace's unfinished memoir. When she provided two or more renditions of the same event, we chose details from each of them to give the most complete picture.

In 1998, thirty years after I first heard about Grace and determined that someday I would go to China and uncover her story, I finally made that journey. I flew into the bustling city of Beijing and was met by Grace's granddaughters. I stayed with my Chinese cousins and saw their lives inside China. They took me to places where Grace had lived. I met and talked with her former students and colleagues at the university where Grace taught. I found people who were grateful to a woman who had contributed to their lives under the most adverse circumstances. I, in turn, am grateful to them.

Grace's story, as well as the survival of the papers, is a testament to the power of relationships. Love for one man drove Grace to defy cultural norms, to leave her family and her nation and face

· GRACE ·

nearly insurmountable odds. Her family—which found it hard at first to accept her marriage—were ultimately reunited with her after twenty years of silence and forty years of separation. In a real sense, it is a story about the ordinary people who live through history in all its contradictions and complexities, tending to their families, and carrying forward a renewed commitment to each generation.

ELEANOR COOPER
Chattanooga, January 2002

· NOTE ON CHINESE/ENGLISH ·

ALL BOOKS THAT take place in historical China face the problem of spelling Chinese names and places in English. Grace used the traditional Wade-Giles system then standard. To avoid confusion, we do the same, indicating the contemporary *pinyin* spelling in brackets the first time the word is used or as needed for clarity. Commonly accepted spellings, such as Shanghai and Chiang Kai-shek, are used throughout. We use *pinyin* in the last part of the book (from Chapter 15 on) when it became the accepted form.

GRACE

Grace, center, as Princess Ting Ling, in Chinese operetta (all female cast), Tennessee, 1926.

ONE

ONE DAY IN late February 1974 an unusual letter arrived at a boys' school in Tennessee. It identified no one as recipient, bore no street address or postal code. It was addressed simply to "McCallie School, Chattanooga, Tennessee, USA." In a finely written script, it gave a return address of Tientsin, China.

The secretary who found the letter in the morning mail took it immediately to the headmaster, Dr. S. J. McCallie, exclaiming about the beautiful Chinese stamps. Neither of them could imagine who had sent the letter. Communication with China had been cut off for years; the missionaries had left, no tourists traveled to China, and there were no student exchanges.

Dr. McCallie opened it and read this simple note handwritten on plain rice paper:

· GRACE ·

February 12, 1974

To the Management of the McCallie School:

Since I have been completely out of contact with
anyone in or concerned with Chattanooga for nearly
twenty years, I do not know which elder members of my
family are now living. I shall be very grateful if someone
will send me some information about the elder living
members of my family—both Divine and McCallie—who
would remember me. When I last heard from Chattanooga,
my uncle J. P. McCallie was living and headmaster of the
McCallie School. But that was twenty years ago! I would
particularly like to hear about my brother, Thomas
McCallie Divine, who used to live near Kingsport.

We are all well here and I am working with English
language teachers at Nankai University.

I will appreciate very much whatever you can do to help
me get in touch with my family in Tennessee or wherever
else they are.

Very sincerely,

Grace Divine Liu

"I am amazed!" Dr. McCallie exclaimed. He turned to his secretary.
"Get Tom Divine on the the phone immediately. His sister is alive!"

Grace Divine Liu, a native of Chattanooga, had lived in China
since 1934, when she left to join her husband F. C. Liu, a Chinese
engineer who had studied at Cornell. The shocking news of her
marriage to "a Chinaman" years ago had been surpassed many times
by her startling and fascinating letters from China.

This was not the first time that one of Grace's letters brought
news that she was still alive when presumed dead. Once before,
after four years of silence during the Second World War, a U.S.
Marine found her and personally delivered a letter to her family.
But this time it had been twenty years since anyone had heard from
her and she had long ago been given up as dead.

Then in 1972, President Richard Nixon and Mao Zedong's historic visit opened the doors between the two nations. A year later when a U.S. liaison office opened in Beijing, Grace, then seventy-two years old and living in Tianjin (Tientsin), discussed with her children the possibility of contacting her family in the United States. Not knowing anyone's address, she sent a letter to the school that her uncles had founded, unaware that the incumbent headmaster would be her own cousin.

How had this American woman survived so many years of China's tumult? Since arriving in China in 1934, she had experienced floods, near starvation, the Japanese invasion and occupation, the ascent of the Communists, and the storming of the Red Guards. Why had she chosen to stay when other foreigners left? What had happened to her during the long years of silence? To comprehend Grace Liu's story, one has to understand that what brought her to China in the first place was love. It all happened because of a coincidental meeting in an elevator—

IN 1926, GRACE DIVINE was teaching music at a girls' school in Chattanooga, Tennessee. Since childhood she had been known for possessing a voice like "the sound of silver bells" and she had long dreamed of being an opera singer. One day at a concert, someone in the audience who heard her sing recommended her for a music scholarship. At the end of that school year, she boarded a train for New York. She had a trim figure and long brunette hair pulled back and tied at the nape of the neck. Her strong chin was held high and her gray eyes glistened as she waved good-bye to her mother.

A year earlier, on the other side of the world, Liu Fu-chi, a serious-looking student, with a stocky build and a soft, round face, boarded a ship from China. No mother or father waved good-bye to him from the dock. He came to America to study engineering

at Cornell University. After graduating at age twenty-four, he decided
to gain some practical experience before returning to China. He took
a job with a civil engineering firm in New York and found a room in
an apartment house on West 112th Street.

New York in 1928 was the ideal place for a young engineer. Following the First World War, New York had emerged as the commercial and artistic center of the world. American technological
innovation was everywhere visible as buildings rose higher than any
civilization had dared to erect. The Empire State Building, which
symbolized the skyscraper, would soon be under construction, and
many of the other art deco buildings of this era—the Chrysler
Building with its graceful spire, the Waldorf Astoria Hotel bringing
elegance to Park Avenue, and the Irving Trust Company building on
Wall Street were being built. The construction that fascinated him
the most was the George Washington Bridge crossing the Hudson
River. This dramatic expansion of steel over water was the largest
suspension bridge ever built and was later claimed to be the most
beautiful bridge in the world. The newly built subways were another
feat of American engineering. Over water, in the air and even underground, New York was breaking the limits of the past.

Grace, on the other hand, hardly noticed this construction in
progress. Her days were filled with music lessons, auditions, singing
engagements, Broadway shows, concerts, and opera. Her teacher,
Franz Proschowsky, who had come to New York from Berlin after the
war, pronounced her voice "one of the easiest he has ever undertaken
and its qualities most wonderful," or so it was reported in a Chattanooga newspaper. He had trained many well-known opera singers of
the day, and Grace fully intended to be one of them. Even the stresses
of the big city were exciting to her, as Grace recalled in her memoir:

> My first weeks in New York were delightfully hectic.
> Everything came fully up to my expectations, especially
> the subway rush hour—hordes of people shoved,
> squashed, and squeezed into a tiny space and hurled at
> terrific speed from place to place. Once I had a shoe
> literally squeezed off my foot when I made a precipitate

entrance. It finally reached me, traveling overhead from
hand to hand, at the other end of the car.

At first Grace lived in a boardinghouse for music students, but
it was not long before her mother decided to keep house for her.
Although Grace was twenty-seven years old, to be single and alone
in the big city was not considered proper for a young lady. The
move from Chattanooga suited Mrs. Divine because her husband
had died, leaving her some rental property for income, and her five
sons had all married and left home. Mrs. Divine brought along her
sixteen-year-old granddaughter, Julianne, and found a place close
to Grace's conservatory just two blocks off Broadway in an apartment house on West 112th Street.

It was her mother who first struck up a conversation with the
quiet, bespectacled young man in the elevator of their apartment
building. When Mrs. Divine discovered he was alone and had no one
to cook for him, she invited him to dinner, and it wasn't long before
he became a frequent guest. At first Grace was preoccupied with her
own interests, not paying much attention to someone she considered
just a foreign student. She wrote later of her impressions of Mr. Liu:

> At first I was merely interested and intrigued by his talk,
> his speech full of original and amusing imperfections,
> his opinions and his stories of his home province,
> bedeviled with rival warlords and bandits, and his
> participation in the big anti-Japanese student movement
> of 1919. But gradually as his English became more fluent
> with practice, his unusual intellect and character
> impressed me and his calm self-confidence without
> conceit won my respect and admiration.

Through her mother's probing questions and the resulting conversations, Grace gradually came to learn a great deal about this
young man from a distant world:

> Mama, Julianne, and I all three listened, fascinated, to
> Mr. Liu talk about China and his home province of

Shensi [Shaanxi], called the "Cradle of Chinese
Civilization." A part of Shensi, we learned, was the
ancient feudal state of Chin [thus, "China"], which
eventually conquered the other feudal states in 221 B.C.
Nearby Sian [Xian], then called Changan, was the
capital of the first emperor of China more than 2,000
years ago.

He had grown up in West Liu Village, located in a fertile river
valley in Central China and made up of about one hundred families, most of them named Liu.

He told us all about the Lius, a well-to-do peasant
family. They did their own farm work but there were
teachers, doctors, and even merchants among them. He
was brought up in the strict Confucian ethics of his
family. This interested Mama tremendously and she
enjoyed discussing Confucian teaching with him. It
differed little, she thought, from the strict Calvinist
upbringing of her own youth.

His father died before he was born and he was brought
up under the strict supervision of his three uncles. At an
early age, he was set to memorizing Confucian classics—
in parrot fashion as was the custom of the day. He said it
was the teaching and training from his uncles that molded
his character and shaped his life. This training emphasized
the traditional moral concepts and high principles of the
Chinese people: honesty, discipline, hard work, education,
and respect for family and authority.

Grace pondered how different, and yet how similar, their worlds
sounded. His village had a written history of eight hundred years,
her hometown was barely a hundred years old. But her family, once
farmers, also played many roles in the community. Her uncles,
mostly preachers and teachers, had been influential in her life and
they emphasized the same values that his uncles had. How could
two people from opposite ends of the world, she wondered, have
such seemingly similar values?

Mr. Liu said that as a young boy he had seen many alarming events. Millions of peasants died in devastating floods near his home, Manchu officials were brutally murdered in nearby Sian when the emperor abdicated, and rival warlords and roaming bandits rampaged the countryside. He later came to under-stand that his childhood was a time of intense political and social ferment.

For over two thousand years China had enjoyed a relatively stable civilization managed by a Confucian code of order and a systematic bureaucracy that survived even when dynasties collapsed and emperors died. But by the nineteenth century, the system had become cumbersome and the population had grown faster than its ability to respond. Pressure to change was building from within at the same time that foreign powers were applying pressure from without. With a weakened imperial system of government and a feudalistic social structure in the countryside, the nation could not long withstand these pressures.

Mr. Liu recalled a gruesome tale from his childhood. One of his uncles was a schoolmaster in Fu-ping county. Every day young Liu walked the distance from his village to his uncle's school and back:

> He was going home to the village from his school one
> late afternoon. He was taking his time along an old
> familiar road when, on tree branches just ahead of him,
> he saw human heads hanging like some monstrous fruit.
> After one frozen moment, he covered the remaining
> miles to the village on wings of terror. At home he
> heard about the capture and execution of marauding
> bandits, their severed heads hung up in trees along the
> roadside.

He told his uncles that China must change and that he must study to find solutions to the nation's problems. His uncles knew that without a father, his future depended on having a good education. At that time each province in China selected two boys a year for scholarships provided by the Boxer Indemnity funds. (Following

the Boxer Rebellion of 1900, the United States returned its portion
of the indemnity funds to China in the form of scholarships.)

> When he was thirteen, Fu-chi won a scholarship to
> Tsing Hua [Qinghua], a school just outside Peking
> [Beijing]. It was then a high school with two years of
> college. At graduation it was stipulated that the students
> should come to America to complete their college
> course at the American university of their choice.
>   At first things proceeded normally at Tsing Hua. He
> played on the basketball and track teams and even
> learned American baseball. He was short and squarely
> built but tough and fast enough to make a name for
> himself in sports. I learned this from his classmates who
> came to visit in New York. An American girl taught him
> English and judging by the results I heard ten years
> later, I would say that she was an exceedingly poor
> teacher. But she did teach him to read English, which
> opened up a new world to him.

During the long summer vacations, young Liu was unable to go
home because the trains did not go all the way to his home village
and the territory in between was considered a "no-man's land,"
beset with conflicting warlords and bandits. The young student
spent many hours reading under the trees on campus. Again Grace
was struck by the similarities in their backgrounds: "I was surprised
to discover that he had read books by so many of my favorite
authors—James Fenimore Cooper, Robert Louis Stevenson, Sir
Walter Scott, Charles Dickens, Mark Twain, Victor Hugo, and
other books young people used to read."

Conversations between Mrs. Divine and Fu-chi, as she came to
call him, moved from the past to the present: "Mama and Fu-chi
had long philosophical discussions, going back to Confucius, Men-
cius, and the Greek philosophers, on up to John Dewey whom
Mama didn't like."

Confucian values, Mrs. Divine agreed, may have been the basis for
a stable social order for centuries in China but, she argued, they were

not Christian. Precisely, Fu-chi explained to her. In China a religious basis for government was not necessary. Besides, the youth of China wanted to cast off the past; they believed that Confucianism ran counter to what they wanted for a new society in China.

Mr. Liu was familiar with American philosopher John Dewey because his writings had been translated into Chinese by Hu Shi, a Boxer Indemnity Fund scholar who had studied under Dewey at nearby Columbia University. Mrs. Divine didn't like John Dewey because he debunked religion. Fu-chi appreciated his emphasis on pragmatism, on social reform, and on education for change. Young people in China, like himself, were torn between wanting to free China of feudalism and imperialism and to replace it with something more than nationalism. Many of them studied in Japan and Europe and the United States to learn all they could from the West and bring it back to China. He wanted to find a way to replace the old Confucian bureaucratic system with a practical, scientific, and progressive social order that was continuous with his own culture and conformable with civilization worldwide.

Grace listened as if waking from a dream. She knew nothing of these things. She had once starred as Princess Ting Ling in an operetta set in imperial China, and as far as she knew China was still an ancient land veiled in romantic mystery. How surprised she was to find out that the Emperor had abdicated in 1912 and the imperial court no longer existed, that China's revolution of 1911 establishing a constitutional republic had only partially succeeded leaving China in a vacuum, torn by the militaristic ambitions of provincial warlords and political factions of different parties.

She had heard from missionaries of the poverty and suffering but she was unaware of the fact that Western nations themselves had dismembered China, extracting territories called "concessions" where they claimed right to govern under their own jurisdiction, immune from Chinese law. The United States, a latecomer as an imperialist claimant to China, held no territories but moved freely among the foreign concessions of others. China's disillusionment with the West intensified after the First World War.

As a student in Peking in 1917–18, Fu-chi watched as Chinese troops set off to aid the Allies in the war in Europe. He celebrated with others the defeat of Germany at the end of the war and expected the German held territories to be returned to China.

But on May 4, 1919, word reached China that at the signing of the Treaty of Versailles, the Western powers had agreed to transfer Germany's former territories in China to Japan. Outrage in China was boundless. Protests erupted throughout the country. Thousands of students gathered at Tiananmen Square in front of the Forbidden City and marched toward the foreign Legation Quarter, carrying banners and shouting protest slogans. In the clash with the police, several students were injured and one killed. Grace recounted Fu-chi's experience: "A terrific blow from the butt of a police rifle sent Fu-chi limping back to school, unable to sit down for several days."

The years following the 1919 protests witnessed an outpouring of intellectual exuberance and questioning that had not been seen previously in China and rarely in the world. Known as the "May 4th Movement," it engaged all levels of Chinese society in a quest to determine where the country was heading. Study groups, socialist clubs, and new periodicals and magazines, written in the vernacular rather than in classical style, attempted to redefine China's culture and its role in the world. Students and workers of all ages were affected by these debates. China delved into a period of exploration of every form of political and social organization that promised transformation. Different approaches were advocated; some opposing Western ways, some adulating the West. There were pragmatists and radicals, but the spirit of "China for the Chinese" galvanized the youth.

Liu was attracted neither to the political radicals nor to the militarist isolationists. His pragmatism led him to choose a practical path of reconstruction. Through education, engineering, and structural reform, he thought, China could solve its devastating problems and ameliorate the social disorder he had witnessed in his youth. Grace described his quandry: "Fu-chi said that for a while he couldn't decide whether he would be more useful as a doctor or as an engineer. Finally engineering won out over medicine and he chose Cornell as the best school for his purpose."

After graduation, Fu-chi came to work for Allan Hazen in New York, a specialist in flood control and water filtration, who wrote many of the texts Fu-chi had studied at Cornell. In the winters he drew plans and did design work, and in the summers he worked as a surveyor on construction sites in New Jersey and the Catskills. In China, an engineer was considered an intellectual, often remaining aloof from workers. Fu-chi disabused himself of these old notions and learned a great deal from the construction workers including, Grace said, "a large vocabulary of choice American invectives."

> When he was not working outside the city, Julianne and I often went with him to movies and plays, going afterward to have a Chinese dinner. It was a delightful and rewarding friendship for the three of us. His background of ancient civilization and culture, his modern education, both Chinese and Western, his pleasant courtesy, poise, and quiet assurance all made him a fascinating and stimulating person to know.

Grace described their budding relationship, not as a sudden infatuation, but as a gradual growing of respect and admiration for each other. At one point, Grace thought that he was attracted to her niece, Julianne, because she was younger and prettier. But quite the contrary was true—he watched Grace's every movement, keeping his distance, respectful of her career, but even more because he feared that she would be hesitant to become involved with a foreigner. Both of them, she said, resisted valiantly any urge to fall in love—until a night at the opera.

It was one of the rare times that Grace was alone with Fu-chi. Neither her mother nor Julianne accompanied them. Grace wanted to show him the music that she was studying with the very best voices in the finest venue that New York offered. The Metropolitan Opera House on Broadway with its curving horseshoe auditorium in ivory and gold radiated glamour, a perfect backdrop for top hats and long gloves, jewels and flowers.

Rosa Ponselle emerged on the stage of the Met that night with a haunting beauty and a sumptuous voice in the leading role in Bellini's *Norma*. If Grace wanted to show off the operatic voice, she picked the right event. The role of *Norma* was acknowledged among performers to be a cruel test of a singer, requiring the full range of three octaves as well as agility in the fast-paced coloratura passages. In her anxiety lest Fu-chi not like the opera, she had forgotten that the story of *Norma* is one of illicit love between two people of different cultures. In this case, a noble Druidess—who is living in a country conquered by the Romans—is caught in a love affair with a Roman soldier, contemplates murdering her two children, and is, finally, heroically burned at the stake. The story and the music had such a mesmerizing effect on them both that they left the theater in a daze: "The music had made Fu-chi so absentminded that he forgot his hat and when we went back to find it, he said, 'I think music like that could make people a little crazy.'"

In the evenings after dinner at home, Grace would often sing while accompanying herself on the piano. She was uncharacteristically small compared to most opera singers and she had a thin face. Her hair was now cut in a stylish bob and her clear gray eyes sparkled when she sang. Soon after the opera, she noticed something different in his gaze:

> When I sang, he had the habit of standing beside me
> and leaning his elbow on the piano. Although he was
> usually very circumspect in speech and manner, I caught
> an unguarded look that put me in a turmoil of
> conflicting thought and feelings. I began to realize that
> my feelings were getting beyond the safe "respect and
> admiration" stage. Was I ready to challenge all the
> prejudices of race, religion, culture, and customs?

Interracial marriage was illegal in Grace's home state of Tennessee, and although the law was intended to prevent union between whites and blacks, it applied to Chinese as well. It would have been considered shocking to marry across any racial lines. Even in New York with its polyglot of languages and cultures, such a marriage was not common. Her family would have been against it as much for religious reasons as racial ones. Mr. Liu was not a Christian and therefore "unsaved."

Throughout her acquaintance with Fu-chi, she had remained comfortably in her own cultural context. Seldom did she venture outside of her world except for an excursion into Chinatown or a Chinese restaurant. Consequently her cultural habits, customs, and ways of thinking and doing had not been challenged yet.

> I knew it was Fu-chi's plan to go to Germany in the fall to study hydraulics a year there with a well-known professor in Karlsruhe University. He would go back to China through Russia and Siberia and not return to New York. That should settle the matter.
>
> As the sailing date neared, I thought, "Yes, this is the wisest way." But being wise did not console me. Fu-chi was going through the same struggle. He could not let anything, no matter what it meant to him personally, jeopardize his longtime purpose to devote his life and work to the Chinese people. So we were both silently and unhappily determined to let wisdom prevail.
>
> And so it did until our farewell on the *Queen Mary* the night she sailed revealed what we really felt. Thinking we would never see each other again, what did it matter if we dropped the mask this one time?

When Fu-chi departed on the *Queen Mary*, the dock must have been full of people hugging and kissing, waving farewell, and trying to get in one last embrace before separating, the horns and noise of the port so loud, that an embrace would have been the only way to communicate. If it was their first embrace, it was one of farewell, not one of beginnings. Or so Grace thought.

Days followed when I felt my heart was utterly broken and my life desolate. Mama was sympathetic. She was fond of Fu-chi and thought he was quite a wonderful person, but—I could tell that she was glad he was gone.

For three months he wrote impersonal letters, addressed to the three of them, about his life in Germany.

Then came a letter for me, saying he had made up his mind—he was coming back. He said he'd written to the Chinese Education Mission in Washington, the organization that had charge of the Chinese scholarship students in the United States, telling them he was disappointed in the course and wanted to come back to New York and continue working. The Mission, knowing well his real reason, refused to give him permission to return to New York but told him to do as he had planned and go back to China via Russia and Siberia. "I told them," Fu-chi wrote, "that I was coming back no matter what they said and I asked them to transfer my allowance to someone else. It's no use my staying here. I'm just wasting time. I can't study. I see your face on every page. On the bank of the Rhine, I hear you singing."

While in Germany, Fu-chi had the courage to free himself from a major commitment, the last barrier to his relationship with Grace. He wrote his uncle to break the engagement arranged for him when he was twelve with a girl from his home village whom he had never met. When his uncle refused, he wrote the girl directly telling her that she was educated in the old school and he in the new, and they would never be compatible. The girl wrote back that she would try to adapt herself to his life. He insisted he did not believe in the old customs anymore and he must choose his own course.

All Grace knew was that he was coming back:

> I came to life again. Julianne was delighted. And
> in spite of her doubts and fears, Mama was pleased,
> too. She was a romantic soul and I knew she liked
> Fu-chi's daring.
>
> Not long afterward, he was back in New York, and I
> heard his voice on the telephone say, "Can you meet me
> on the corner of 113th Street and Morningside Drive
> tomorrow morning at nine?"
>
> I walked the two and a half blocks the next morning
> on clouds. The first words he said were, "I'd forgotten
> how beautiful you are!" *What love can do to the eyesight!* I
> thought. Aside from being in good health at the time,
> young and happy, I hadn't the slightest claim to beauty.
>
> We walked down to 110th Street and got on the
> upper deck of a Fifth Avenue bus and rode to
> Washington Square and back again. Maybe we did it
> twice, we had a great deal to discuss and to decide.
>
> All doubt and hesitation were gone now, for both of
> us. I knew that this was the one man I wanted now and
> forever to live with and be with, to face life with
> whatever the years might bring.
>
> I asked Fu-chi what made him decide to defy all
> warnings and advice against a foreign marriage. All of
> his friends—but one—and the education ministry had
> warned him against the relationship. He said that what
> gave him the final confidence to go against all of their
> advice was the fact that I was the daughter of my
> remarkable mother.

They thought it would take only a little time for Mrs. Divine to
get used to the idea. They planned to stay in New York a little
longer before they married, then wait for the proper time to leave
for China together. But this plan was not so easily carried out.

Liu Fu-chi (center front) as Deputy Chief Engineer with Department of Sanitation, Nationalist Government, Nanjing (Nanking), 1933.

點水蜻蜓款款飛行帶長落

紅吹不定幽趣在濠梁

TWO

BY THE TIME Fu-chi returned from Germany, the Great Depression had taken hold. The stock market crash of October 1929 left many homeless and unemployed on the streets of New York. When the Empire State Building opened in 1931, it was unable to find tenants.

Mrs. Divine's small income from her property in the South dwindled to almost nothing. To keep their apartment, she and Julianne went to work at The Johnny Cake, a tea room opened by a Swedish friend. Mrs. Divine helped in the kitchen and Julianne, vivacious and energetic, served the customers. Grace, too, put her voice to work in a new venue, singing opera on the radio.

Mr. Liu arranged to get back his old job but was unable to get his apartment back. Mrs. Divine, whom Fu-chi now called by her first name, Julia, or her nickname, Juie, invited him to sublet a room in their apartment. The arrangement, she thought, would solve two problems, but the hospitable gesture caused far greater ones.

It was not unusual in that age for a girl's family to prevent a marriage. Mrs. Divine's brothers had opposed her younger sister's engagement to a young minister whom they considered inadequate. She had no doubt what they would think of this union. She thought their objections might be lessened if Mr. Liu were Christian. As Grace observed: "After Fu-chi moved into our apartment Mama couldn't give up the idea of converting him."

Not far from their apartment was the headquarters of a popular African-American evangelist who shared the same last name. Drawn to Father Divine's mission to feed the poor and save souls, Mrs. Divine volunteered to be a server at the mission's "Feast." Every day sumptuous free meals were served to the hungry and downtrodden, followed by singing and a sermon. One day Mrs. Divine took Fu-chi with her through the heart of Black Harlem, down wide, bustling 125th Street, past the famed Apollo Theater where many jazz musicians had made their appearances, to a storefront that bore the sign, "The Kingdom of Father Divine."

There was an economic side to Father Divine's mission that would have interested Fu-chi. The growing number of his followers formed many small cooperative businesses—restaurants, groceries, barbershops, fresh food vendors, and laundries—which in the Depression created a source of income other than welfare. It is unlikely that Fu-chi observed the economic side of the mission or saw past the religious overtones. Grace said he listened docilely to the long sermon, but when they returned home, he said to her mother, "It's of no use, Juie. I'm just a born heathen."

Fu-chi claimed that he had no religion. Growing up in the countryside, in addition to Confucian teachings, he had heard stories of ghosts and other spirits, but these were just folktales and superstitions to him. They had nothing to do with God. He always resented it when a priest or other leader tried to manipulate these tales to control people's behavior. His religion, he tried to explain to her, was of a more practical nature. What he believed was manifested in what he did. He didn't have to have a religious reason, it was just important to him to be a good man, to use his reason, and to follow his inner direction.

A letter from Fu-chi best illustrates his religious or philosophical point of view at the time. The letter was written to Mrs. Divine's brother, the Reverend Thomas S. McCallie, himself a Presbyterian minister in Chattanooga and the son of a minister whom Grace described as "thoroughly Calvinistic and deeply evangelical in his views." Fu-chi had loaned Mrs. Divine some money, which her brother felt was his duty to repay. By this time, Grace's liaison was undoubtedly known at home, and Mrs. Divine was being held accountable. Fu-chi felt called upon to defend Mrs. Divine and, boldly yet humbly, to speak his own truth. This is the only letter from Fu-chi:

New York City
August 10, 1931

My dear Dr. McCallie:

I thank you so much for your kind letter and the check. What I did for Mrs. Divine is so little it should never be mentioned.

Now I have the honor and opportunity to write you, a dear brother of Mrs. Divine who, I am absolutely sure, loves her dearly and always has full sympathy with her, no matter what course she follows.

Sometimes in our life, things good or bad happen to us beyond our expectation. I do know—anybody is helpless in such a case. I do not know how some people can better it, which they think is unwise, or foolish.

I am heathen. I do not want to judge other people with my own yardstick, which may be ridiculous and sometimes full of ignorance. There is one thing, which I think is true [of] all peoples. May I say "Truth"?

I never saw anyone who lives up so true to the teachings of Christianity as Mrs. Divine. As I know, the main teaching of Christianity is to please God. It does look very simple,

but it is impossible to all peoples. In the present day, with
the results of the bad practices of the old churches, the
unbelievable development of industry and science, and the
backwardness in the social, political, and economical
practices and reforms, all religions are in a dark period. In
the States, people generally live with a philosophy of "do as
I please, nobody's business." In Europe people ask God's help
with hatred, jealousy, and national pride. I think, the
Western world can only be saved by the true practice of the
teachings of Christianity. But it is still a test.

May I at the same time quote what Confucius said once,
"I do not murmur against Heaven. I do not grumble against
men. My studies lie low, and my penetration rises high. But
there is Heaven,—that knows me!"

I traveled in Asia, America, and Europe. I saw bad people
are bad ones; good ones are good ones; fact is fact; and
truth is truth. I do not want to bother you anymore by my
useless writing. May I thank you again for your kind letter.

Respectfully yours,

Fu-chi Liu

Grace had not counted on her brothers' interference with her
plans to marry Fu-chi. First the youngest of Grace's five brothers,
Edward, came to check out the situation. When he found Fu-chi living in the same quarters, he contacted his older brother Robert, the
father of Julianne. Although Robert had been unable to support
Julianne and had left her to the charge of his mother, he now indignantly entered the scene, yelled at his mother for exposing
his daughter to such indecency, and threatened to have Fu-chi
deported.

Shortly thereafter, two plainclothes investigators entered Fu-
chi's office and demanded to see his papers. They pummeled him
with questions—why had he not left after he graduated, why
had he returned from Germany, and where was he living? Finding
all of his documents in order, they left without evidence to support deportation or cause for further disturbance. But the event

confirmed Grace's resolve to proceed with her plans—only more quickly.

In a letter to her younger son, Tom, Mrs. Divine wrote in May 1932: "I do not know what is before us—I cannot tell. Grace looks wonderfully well. She weighs about 125 pounds wholly due to the persistent milk diet—." (The milk diet was her mother's way of trying to fatten her for the stage.) But her mother soon learned that Grace's weight gain had to do with more than a milk-enhanced diet.

Grace described her simple wedding in happy terms:

> Soon after the incident with the plainclothesmen, we went down to City Hall and were married, with Julianne and a clerk as witnesses. Julianne was delighted with her important part in the procedure and was in high spirits. A walk over to nearby Chinatown and lunch in a Cantonese restaurant was a suitable and lively celebration.

On June 29, 1932, The Chattanooga Times carried the headline: MISS GRACE DIVINE WED TO FU-CHI LIU: WEDDING SOLEMNIZED YESTERDAY IN NEW YORK—BRIDE FORMER CHATTANOOGAN. The article also listed her five brothers and her five uncles, all well-known in the small Southern town.

The Depression was in full swing by the time they married. Breadlines were prevalent and shanty towns had sprung up in Central Park. Political unrest began to ferment. A riot broke out in Union Square with thousands of Communists and sympathizers fighting the police. The elections in the fall brought Fiorello LaGuardia to the mayoralty of New York and Franklin D. Roosevelt to the presidency. These two men, although of opposite political parties, joined in their efforts to turn the tide. Millions of dollars of federal relief began to flow into New York. Grace wrote in her memoir:

> Fu-chi knew that his office must soon be letting people go. He felt he must begin preparing immediately to go back to China.
> "You can find another job," pleaded Mama.

"Impossible, Juie. And I mustn't waste any time hunting. I must go quickly before my bank account begins to shrink."

There was no question of my going with him. My baby was due in December and Fu-chi's situation was too uncertain. There was no job waiting for him in China. His search to find one would take time.

It was his plan to leave me his money in the bank and travel to China very cheaply—to Seattle by Greyhound bus and third-class passage to Shanghai. He would get a job and save every penny, and when the baby was big enough to travel, he would send for me.

In the last week in September the inevitable happened. Fu-chi was called in—"We are terribly sorry, Liu, but, you see how it is . . ." There was very little in the way of preparation left to do, and on October 4, 1932, he left New York on the five-day bus trip to Seattle.

I remember the afternoon I said good-bye to Fu-chi at the door and watched him as he walked down the hall with his two old schoolmates who were seeing him off. At the elevator he turned, raised his hand, and smiled at me. I did not cry. I was very brave until I went in and closed the door.

Perhaps Grace was the only one who had absolute faith that this plan would be carried out successfully. She waited, hoping, while others waited, fearing. Grace recalled the first letter after Fu-chi left:

I answered the doorbell one afternoon to find our landlord standing there with a letter in his hand. He bowed and made me a little speech.

"I am very glad," he said, "to be the one to bring you this first news," and he handed me the letter with the Seattle postmark. I tried to thank him.

"Ah," he smiled with sympathy and understanding. "I knew it would make you happy."

As I turned back inside and shut the door, Julianne came running, snatched the letter, and ran back to the kitchen where Mama was ironing.

"Juie, Juie, the letter has come!"

"Julianne," I pleaded. "Give me my letter! It's for me!"

"No, no, it's not just for you. Juie and I must hear it, too. I'll read it aloud." She began to tear it open begging Mama to be on her side. "Juie, can't I read it to all of us? She would leave something out, I know."

Mama smiled. "Let her read it, Sister," she said to me.

So I sat and listened to my letter read aloud. Julianne read with emotion, interrupting herself several times to exclaim, "Oh, Juie, isn't that wonderful?"

Toward the end when there was a sentence about the "baby angel for whom we've had this separation," Mama's tears fell sizzling on the hot iron.

There were other letters, one every week. He had landed in Shanghai with five dollars in his pocket, he wrote, and was staying with an old school friend while he looked around for a job. Grace knew he had no wealthy or influential family or friends, none of the "pull" that was so important in China of that day. But his confidence and self-assurance were high. He felt he could make his way solely on his ability. Another letter said there was nothing suitable in Shanghai—he was going on to Nanking (Nanjing), further inland.

From Nanking he wrote of success. He was now the deputy chief engineer of sanitation for the municipal government. The chief engineer was an American whom he liked immensely. He would be paid the highest salary a Chinese in that position could get, but it was only a third of what a foreigner would be paid—evidence of China's semi-colonial condition.

His weekly letters arrived usually on Friday afternoon or Saturday mornings. Grace was so excited to get them that she hesitated to open them. Even the longest ones were too brief and no matter how slowly she read them they were gone too fast and she would have another long week to wait.

On Christmas eve, December 24, 1932, a cable from New York to Nanking announced the good tidings, "Mother and daughter doing well." At Fu-chi's suggestion, Grace named her daughter Ju-lan, which in Chinese meant "Little Orchid" but in English sounded like her mother's name, Julia. Her mother, however, said the baby looked just like Fu-chi and called her "Fuchina."

With Mrs. Divine and Julianne working each day, the house-keeping, as well as baby care, fell to Grace, as she described later:

> I was exceedingly tired but glad to be so busy, and if I had not had the baby I don't know how I would have made it. Ju-lan's daily outings in her carriage made us a familiar sight on Broadway and Amsterdam, the Columbia University campus, and the grounds of St. John's Cathedral. Dressed in a short, short dress and wearing a little pink bonnet, she looked exactly like an animated doll. The nurses at the New York hospital where she was born had called her "the China doll." When she went with me to the fruit store on Broadway, everybody—men, women, and children—stopped to stare and exclaim. I wrote to Fu-chi that his daughter was a sensation on Broadway.

Despite her lightheartedness, Grace was torn between two worlds, knowing the inevitable separation that was ahead. She wrote to her sister-in-law, Mary Hills Divine, on January 10, 1934: "Now I am between the 'devil and the deep blue sea.' As crazy as I am to go I can't stand to think of leaving Mama. She loves the baby to death, and the baby loves Mama better than she does me. I know they will feel terrible when I go. It is very painful to be so torn."

When the baby was more than a year old, Grace heard from Fu-chi that his situation had changed:

> Fu-chi began writing me about the negotiations he was having with the Tientsin-Water Works Company. It was then a British-Chinese company registered in Hong Kong and had a Danish chief engineer. Patriotic Chinese directors of the company were trying to oust the British and reorganize as a Chinese company registered in Nanking. According to new Chinese government regulations the

chief engineer must be Chinese. The Chinese directors were having difficulty finding a suitable Chinese to take the chief engineer's position.

In the search for one they heard about Liu Fu-chi. He seemed to be just what they needed and the two top Chinese directors came to Nanking to talk to him.

The American chief engineer had gone home on a short leave and Fu-chi was the acting chief in his place. This looked most impressive to the Tientsin men and they were anxious to get Fu-chi to come to Tientsin.

"I have a good job here," he told them. "I like it and I'm satisfied with my work here, but there's nothing I'd like better than to help you take your company from British hands." The arrogant, colonial British were the most disliked foreigners in China.

But when he named the salary he wanted, they were horrified, just as he knew those wealthy North China industrialists would be. For it was considerably more than a Chinese engineer was ever paid. When they said as much, Mr. Liu replied, "It's much less than the foreign engineer is paid."

They tried to argue, but Fu-chi implied politely that they could take it or leave it. He was perfectly satisfied where he was. They left saying they must discuss it with the other Chinese directors.

A telegram came within a week saying all the Chinese directors agreed to the salary Fu-chi named and asked him to come as soon as he could. But now, the American chief engineer in Nanking had returned from his home leave and protested Fu-chi's leaving. He tried to persuade him to stay, offering more money and the promise of going to the States for further study. But to Fu-chi the prospect of ousting the British was more appealing.

He would soon be leaving Nanking, he wrote, and when he settled in Tientsin, he would borrow the money and wire for me and the baby to come.

Now Grace quickly set about the troublesome task of getting her passport and papers in order. The court house in Tennessee had burned, destroying her birth certificate. She had to ask one of her uncles to sign a statement attesting to her birth on February 23, 1901. She took Ju-lan to the Chinese division on Ellis Island where she was fingerprinted and footprinted. Then they took a passport picture together, booked their steamship passage, and went shopping for clothes to wear on their arrival.

Mrs. Divine and Julianne moved south at the end of June. Grace followed a little later with her eighteen-month-old daughter and a ticket to China.

Grace's whirlwind visit home was big news in the Southern town. *The Chattanooga News* carried a front-page headline on June 22, 1934: CHATTANOOGA GIRL WHO BROKE RACIAL TIES AND MARRIED CHINESE ENGINEER PAYING VISIT HERE. Wishing to dispel all doubt about her marriage, Grace was quoted in the article:

> "I married him because I loved and admired him and wanted to more than anything I ever wanted to do," said Mrs. Liu Fu-chi, when asked why she had chosen for her husband one of the Chinese race. But Grace Divine didn't marry Liu Fu-chi simply because there was a deep infatuation for this man of the East. She married him because he was the man of her dreams, because as she expresses it, he seemed to possess all of the good qualities of every man whom she had ever known. She married him after cool deliberation and has never regretted her action "for one single moment."
>
> And so it is that Mrs. Liu Fu-chi will sail July 14 for China to make her future home with her husband taking with her their little daughter who will meet her father for the first time.

Beside the article ran a photograph of Grace and Ju-lan, holding a globe of the world. The caption read: "'East is East and West is West and never the twain shall meet.' But for Grace Divine Liu, a Chattanooga musician, the twain have met."

Grace's aunts hosted a reception in her honor, indicating publicly their acceptance of Grace, if not her marriage. She stayed with her brother, Sam Divine, and visited her brother, Tom, and his wife,

Mary Hills Divine. Tom described later how he felt when he first saw his sister and her "mixed" baby: "My sister Grace came in the door of our house with her chubby little black-haired baby toddling along beside her. She [the baby] had never seen me before, yet she stretched out her arms to me and ran to greet me. Grace hugged me and all my resentment of her marriage melted away."

Mary Hills Divine wrote to her own mother the day after Grace departed and said, "Grace left yesterday morning for China and I feel sorry for her traveling with that lively, cute fifteen-month-old [sic] baby . . . I saw a picture [of her husband] and he doesn't look at all Chinese."

Years later Grace described her departure from Chattanooga without sentimentality:

On a scorching hot mid-July day in 1934, I stood in the big railway station in Chattanooga, surrounded by my family. We had spent a week in my brother Sam's home, seeing and greeting relatives and friends again, some for the first time since I'd left Chattanooga eight years before, and at the same time saying good-bye—a sort of "hail and farewell" visit.

While waiting for the train to come in, everyone was giving me last-minute advice, suggestions, and warnings.

"And don't lose your passport," said Uncle Park. "Have you got it in a safe place?"

My passport! It hit me with a blow.

"No, no," I almost shrieked. "I've left it. It's on the dining room table in Sam's house!" I wailed, wringing my hands in despair.

"All right, all right," said Sam, "Don't have a fit. I'll get it."

Mama, Uncle Park, Aunt Hattie, and my brother Tom were quite speechless. Aunt Hattie shook her head in consternation. I knew they were thinking, "If she begins like this, how will such an absentminded addlepate get herself and her baby safely halfway round the world?"

Sam took his car on two wheels around corners and was back with the passport just as the train pulled into the station.

It was hay fever weather in Tennessee and my last words of farewell were lost in fits of sneezing and weeping. A miserable start to my long journey.

My emotions were mixed. It was heartbreaking to leave Mama and all the family and yet there was the deep happiness and excitement of being on my way at last.

First, to the Chicago train station, then three days and three nights to Vancouver, ten days across the Pacific and four days across the China Sea, before I reached my new home—

No one, not even Grace, dreamed it would be forty years before she saw this country again.

Saturday, August 4, 1934

Dear Mama and Everybody,

Well, I'm here at last. I got to Tientsin Tuesday afternoon at two o'clock. I thought I would write back right away but I have been completely exhausted. I had absolutely reached the end of my endurance and I just collapsed. The last part of my journey was quite interesting and very beautiful but with no chance at all to rest a second. I guess I'd better go back to where I left off in my last letter.

When the train reached Vancouver, some of my fellow passengers, a kind man carrying Fuchina [Ju-lan] for me and another one taking my bags, got us safely on to the *Empress of Asia*. It was just an hour to sailing time. When Uncle Park took me to the train station in Chattanooga, he had scolded me for leaving so little leeway between the train's arrival and the sailing of the boat: Only diplomats and important people travel like that. Any unforeseen accident could make a train several hours late, he said. I was thankful that the cow on the tracks hadn't held us up any longer than it did and happy to be unpacking in my cabin when I felt the ship's impatient throbbing and thumping to be off.

Life on the boat was pretty much what it had been on
the train except there was a lot more room for Fuchina to
run around and more places for her to explore. When the
weather was fine and the sea was calm, I spent most of the
day walking her around the deck and swinging her in one
of the swings. We made friends with cabin boys and fellow
passengers. On cloudy or stormy days we investigated
everything below we could get into. No wonder I lost ten
pounds by the time I reached Tientsin.

One night there was a big storm. The ship seemed to
roll almost over on its side and back again. The waves
dashed and banged against the porthole. I heard the cabin
boy going around knocking on doors. I sat up quickly,
fearing the worst, but when he got to my door, he just
asked to come in and lock the porthole securely. He
explained that the porthole might come open during such
strenuous rolling and banging and the sea would rush in.

I had planned to get off the *Empress* in Kobe and take a
Japanese boat through the Yellow Sea to Tangu. But as we
neared Japan, I began having a sore throat and the thought
of being ill in Japan where I knew no one was alarming.
Better stay on the *Empress* for the next four days to
Shanghai, I decided. That would give me time to recover.
Mr. Liu had friends in Shanghai who would put me on the
train to Tientsin. I promptly cabled Mr. Liu to have me met
in Shanghai instead of Tangu.

But by the time we reached Kobe, I felt fine. Now I was
anxious to follow my original schedule, and when Mr.
Buckberough, the Canadian Pacific agent, came on board I
told him what I'd done and that I had changed my mind
again. I feel perfectly well, I said, so I want to get off here
and take a Japanese boat to Tangu.

Fine, he agreed, there's a boat leaving tomorrow at noon
Get your things together and we'll get right off. I'll send
your husband a cable, get you settled in a hotel and put you
on the *Chuan Maru* tomorrow.

Just as easy as that. And I had been so worried about
how troublesome this change of plans might be. We were
soon off the boat, in my hurry leaving behind a stack of
music with some of my favorite songs which has caused me

much regret. I also forgot Fuchina's beloved woolly monkey and little chair made on Lookout Mountain.

Mr. Buckberough said his assistant would take care of my cable to Mr. Liu. He took us to dinner and bought Fuchina some powdered milk and other things to use on the Japanese boat. He was wonderful to me and carried Fuchina everywhere for me. The next morning he checked us out of the hotel and gave me a cable that had come to the *Empress of Asia* in the night from Mr. Liu in answer to my first cable, saying that Mr. Tung would meet me in Shanghai. At eleven o'clock he sent me to the boat in his car with his assistant Mr. Shimada to see that I got on all right.

The *Chuan Maru* was a much smaller ship than the *Empress*, of course, but it was a pretty good-sized boat, bigger that a river boat and it was very clean and nice. As it was a last-minute cancellation, my accommodations were not the most choice. The cabins were quite small with four berths and a very narrow hard sofa. There were two other women in the cabin with me and three grown women and a baby in such little space is anything but comfortable. The berths were so narrow that I couldn't possibly sleep with the baby, so I put a chair and two pillows down at the lower part where there was a railing and let her sleep by herself and I slept on the narrow little sofa. I was so tired at night that I slept in spite of its hardness.

We sailed from Kobe at twelve o'clock Friday. Sailing thru the little Japanese islands was perfectly beautiful. The weather was marvelous and the water as smooth as glass. Saturday morning we stopped at Moji and Japanese officials came on board. Most of the passengers seemed to be nervous about the inspection and that made me nervous. It was my first encounter with Japanese officialdom. However they showed me only the most kindly and friendly interest and paid much more attention to Fuchina than to me.

The weather was so beautiful that we stayed out on deck all day long and I really had a good time in spite of the wild little Fuchina. Everybody was simply crazy about the baby. There was an awfully attractive French couple from Paris, the Count and Countess de Chevegnac, on board. Madame de Chevegnac wanted to take care of Fuchina an hour or two every day for me. They all thought I had accomplished a remarkable feat in keeping the baby so well all through such a long trip. She really looked grand. We sat at the captain's table, and Col. and Mrs. Drysdale of the American Legation in Peking sat next to me. Anybody who thought that I would be cut off and ostracized by people was certainly mistaken. I was treated marvelously by everybody. Mrs. Drysdale begged me to come visit her at the Legation in Peking.

The nights were like something out of a picture, with a full moon shining on the smooth water and the graceful little Japanese sailboats with their little lanterns. Those nights on the Yellow Sea, I watched the fishing boats drifting across the moon's path in the water and thought happily that the long trip would soon be over and the long separation ended. We would be two more days reaching Tangu which is only an hour's train ride away from Tientsin.

Monday afternoon the day before we landed was the most beautiful of all. We were out of Japanese waters and were nearly to China. The water looked just like green jade and we saw the Chinese junks floating around. It didn't even look real. We docked at Tangu the next morning at five o'clock; I was up long before that watching the sunrise. I put on the new outfit I'd bought in New York specially for my first appearance. I woke up Fuchina at 5:30 and put on her new dress and bonnet. We went out on deck to see if Mr. Liu had come to meet us. It was raining, a nice soft shower that looked awfully pretty coming down on the green fields. The boat was surrounded by little Chinese boats with coolies in blue suits and funny pointed hats. There were lots of people on the dock. Men in long gowns, coolies, soldiers, and all sorts of people. But I didn't see a soul I knew.

We walked up and down the deck for a long time and I looked carefully at each new arrival on the wharf. Suddenly I noticed a man facing away from the boat. There was something familiar about his back view—the height, the build—but to my horror, I felt an instant dislike for this person whose back I was staring at! It was a shocking moment. Had I followed across the world a man I didn't like? Fortunately the man turned around before I could work myself into a panic and I saw beyond doubt that he resembled no one I'd ever seen before.

I need food, I thought, faint with relief, and hurried off with Fuchina to join the Colonel and his wife at breakfast, but I was so excited I couldn't swallow a bite. I thought that Mr. Liu would be down later, but seven, eight, nine o'clock and still he hadn't come. Most of the people on board were going up to Peking on the 12:45 train, so everybody stayed on board as it was still raining. At nine I went and asked the purser if any message had come for me. He said no. Col. Drysdale said perhaps Mr. Liu would come down on the 10:00 train. When he didn't come on that train, the Colonel asked me if I didn't want him to take me ashore to telephone or telegraph. So we went to the telegraph office and sent Mr. Liu a telegram saying I would arrive in Tientsin at 1:45. The Colonel said that they would take me with them. He said he was sure Mr. Liu had misunderstood my second cable or it was possible that he never got it at all. On the way back to the boat it started pouring down rain and I got soaked. The rain didn't hurt my dress but it ruined my big white hat.

At lunch time I couldn't eat a thing again. Mrs. Drysdale begged me to eat just a little soup. She said I mustn't worry that they would take care of me. After lunch, we left the boat and walked slowly to the train. I expected Mr. Liu to appear at any minute, but he didn't. The minutes went by and the train was ready to leave. We had to get on.

Col. Drysdale bought my ticket and I went in their compartment with them. Mrs. Drysdale said she is crazy about the Chinese and has lots of Chinese friends. She said I mustn't feel strange at all, that there were at least a hundred American girls in Peking married to Chinese. Col. D. was evidently putting the worst construction on Mr. Liu's non-appearance. He finally said, If anything has gone wrong, you must come to us in Peking. You have our address and phone number. Promise you will. I promised, but I was not at all worried. I was sure that changing my mind and sending two cables had caused some confusion.

During the one hour's ride to Tientsin, the glimpses I had of the countryside from the train window did not fit my idea of Chinese scenery. This flat, flat land with nothing higher than grave mounds and no trees at all jolted my preconceived notions of graceful willow trees and fantastic misty mountains. The Colonel explained that most of this land was "filled in" land, that the seashore used to be much further inland.

When we reached Tientsin the Colonel got off the train with me. We stepped down into the midst of a great crowd milling noisily around with the bewildering sound of Chinese shouted in chorus—passengers calling to friends or for transportation, rickshaw men and taxi drivers shouting for customers—adding to the confusion. We looked anxiously in every direction. The Colonel had to raise his voice to ask me if I saw my husband. I shook my head and stood as tall as possible so I could be readily seen, but there was nobody looking for me.

We had only a few minutes before the train went on to Peking, so according to the arrangement we'd made on the train, the Colonel put me and Fuchina in a taxi with all my baggage and told the driver to take me to the Water Works Co.

We rode through streets that looked neither American nor Chinese. Along the main street high brick buildings with white porticoed fronts intimidated the neighboring stores and shops. Rickshaw men, running in the hot summer sun, pulling complacent-looking passengers, didn't seem to fit in with the Late-Victorian Western style of the buildings. A short ride brought us to the front of a large building beside a walled compound with a sign on the gatepost—the Tientsin Native City Water Works.

Here I was at the end of my long journey. What a way we'd come, Fuchina and I! From New York to Tennessee— then across the United States to Vancouver, across the Pacific to Japan and across the China Sea to Tientsin.

I was so excited I just handed Fuchina to the taxi driver and hurried through the big gate of the compound, past stacks of pipes and groups of workmen and up some steps into a side entrance. I stepped immediately into a big room. I had the impression of heads being raised and of many eyes staring at me in amazement.

I asked the room at large where I could find Mr. Fu-chi Liu. Most continued to stare. There were actually only five or six men writing at desks and one of them got up and came over to me. He said very politely and in good English that Mr. Liu had gone out on some business that morning and hadn't come back yet. But he said I could go into his office and wait.

As we stepped out into the hall, I heard Mr. Liu's voice and saw him coming down the hall with a tall European-looking man.

"Well, there you are!" he said, heavy accent on "there" with both relief and reproof in his voice.

"Yes, *here* I am and I got here all by myself. Why didn't you meet the boat at Tangu or the train in Tientsin?" I felt as if we were speaking lines in a play. We sounded as if we had parted only last week instead of a year and eight months before.

"I didn't know you were on that boat or on the train. I just this minute found your second cable." He had it in his hand.

The whole thing was a terrible mix-up due to the stupidity of Mr. Buckberough's assistant. All he put in the cable was, "Sailing instead Chuan Maru." It didn't say where I was landing or when, so Mr. Liu naturally thought I was still going to Shanghai. Mr. Tung had cabled him that I was not among the passengers leaving the *Empress of Asia*. He said he had the China Travelers Association looking for me. He was just about to take an airplane to Shanghai himself to try to find out something about me.

Mr. Liu then introduced me to the gentleman with him, Monsieur Ruas, the Water Works' French engineer, and I felt sure the sentimental Frenchman was shocked and disappointed at not witnessing a more touching scene of reunion. But I knew better than to commit such a *faux pas*— a public display of that sort would not be considered proper behavior. However, Mr. Ruas did what he could at least to add some ceremony to the welcome. He bowed elegantly and kissed my hand and assured me that monsieur, my husband, had been so longing for my coming.

Suddenly Mr. Liu realized that something was missing. "The baby!" he exclaimed, "Where is the baby?"

We rushed out and found the taxi man standing on the sidewalk holding her and a lot of Chinese workers standing around looking at her. She wasn't a bit afraid of all the strange people. She knew her daddy right away and went right to him. She was used to seeing his picture and calling it "Daddy," so he probably looked familiar to her.

As we drove off in a big car, waiting with its chauffeur in the compound, to the apartment Mr. Liu had been preparing for several weeks, he turned to me and said very seriously, "I'm sure when Ruas heard you speak, he had never heard such a beautiful voice before in his whole life." And into that blunt statement I could read a whole declaration of love and welcome.

Mr. Liu had rented an apartment, but the furniture hadn't come, so Tuesday night we stayed in a hotel. Fuchina had to sleep with us of course and she had either eaten too much or was too excited, for she rolled around all night long and cried and jumped from one side to the other and from the head to the foot, so we didn't get much rest. Mr. Liu was a wreck from worry and loss of sleep and I was exhausted so we are both just now recovering somewhat.

We went to the apartment Wednesday afternoon. It is in the French concession and is a darling place. The apartment house doesn't open on the street as ours do but onto a courtyard. We have three rooms and bath, a bedroom, living and dining room combined, and kitchen. It's awfully pretty. I'm crazy about it. The bedroom opens out on to a little balcony and it has three big windows with shutters. The living room furniture doesn't come till Monday, but we have all the bedroom furniture. Fuchina has a nice little white iron bed with a mosquito net over it. The first night here the mosquitoes almost ate her up. With mosquito net all over her bed, she looks like a little bear in a cage.

I certainly am a lady of ease and luxury now. We have a boy who cooks, cleans, shops, and does everything. His name is Sun Pao-san and he certainly is a marvel compared to American servants. He is a grand cook. He cooks American food marvelously. I don't have to think of what to eat, buy it or go get it. All I do is to eat it when it is ready. Yesterday for lunch we had omelettes and tomatoes stuffed

with shrimp and mayonnaise. Sun makes grand mayonnaise.
Ordinarily I hate shrimp but these were delicious. Last
night for dinner we had a half small chicken apiece with
deliciously cooked potatoes and lettuce salad and ice cold
watermelon. I have two qts. of milk every morning from a
Chinese dairy. It's not nearly so rich of course as your all's
milk but it is very good. Sun cleans the house, fixes
Fuchina's food too, and does all the shopping, and you
should see how spotless he leaves the kitchen when he is
through cooking. I don't need a nurse. I would have
nothing to do for all our dirty clothes are sent to the
laundry. We are going to rent a piano soon so I can
continue my music.

I haven't seen much of Tientsin yet as I have been too
tired to go out. We did go to the French Park the other
night about six. It was very interesting to see the Chinese
men in their long white, blue, or lavender silk gowns and
the pretty Chinese girls and cute children. Fuchina had a
grand time. She ran her daddy all over the park. I had a
hard time keeping up with them. They look so cute
together—the big one and the little one.

Mr. Liu was very shy with her at first. But now they are
very crazy about each other and the first thing she says in
the morning is "Dada." He is going to spoil her rotten. He
can't stand for me to spank her and he cries if she cries.
Needless to say he thinks she is the cutest, prettiest, and
smartest baby in the world. He plays grand with her, so
much better than I ever could.

It is time for lunch now. I have written such a long letter
and still I haven't told nearly all I wanted to. Give my love
to everybody. I am very, very happy. Mr. Liu is all I thought
he was and more.

Lots of love,

Grace

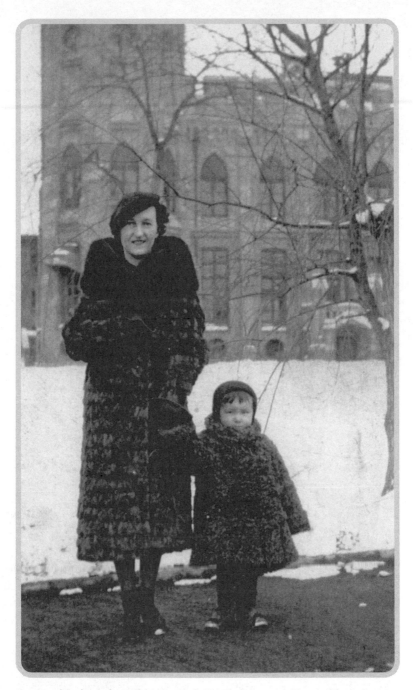

Grace and Ju-lan in front of Gordon Hall, British Concession, Tianjin (Tientsin), 1935.

點水萍綠亂牽風行帶長萍

吹不定幽趣在濠梁

紅

Fu-chi, Ju-lan and amah Wang Nai-nai, at Victoria Park pavillion, Tianjin, 1935.
Grace and Ju-lan alongside Water Works car, Tianjin, 1934.

THREE

GRACE'S FIRST THREE years in China were the end time of a disappearing world. Unaware of what was passing and what was coming, life in semicolonial China was for her an extraordinary interlude of untroubled happiness. She saw and heard much that was shocking and troublesome, but none of it adversely affected her life. Like having a box seat at an opera, she could be shocked, saddened, and even frightened and still feel safely beyond the play going on. She lived in a small, confined world inside a larger, unpredictable one. Grace wrote home after three months that she had "really not seen anything of China"—that was the feeling of one living in the foreign-controlled territories inside China in the 1930s.

Since the end of the British Opium war in 1842, foreign countries had claimed rights to areas of China, called "concessions." When Grace arrived, Tientsin was divided into the British, French, Japanese, Russian, Italian, and Belgian concessions; the former German and Austrian concessions were called the "Special Areas." Each of these foreign-controlled territories had their own businesses, parks, police, schools, languages, architecture, banks, restaurants, and laws. The combined effect made Tientsin a busy cosmopolitan and commercial city. It served as the port for Peking [Beijing] and the center of foreign trade, commerce, banking, and military operations in Northern China—smaller but similar to Shanghai in the south.

Life inside the foreign concessions was like a country club. Servants were abundant and cheap. Whatever one's activity during the day, it ceased at five o'clock when the drinking began. The social life was extraordinary. Horse races, costume balls, movie theaters, and private clubs both brought together and kept separate the lines of class, race, and national origin. Most of the Lius' associates were foreign-born or foreign-educated, in mixed marriages or of mixed blood. Grace did not like most of the foreigners she met, calling them "tacky," meaning they lacked values like her own. And she, in turn, was snubbed by the Westerners who looked down on the Chinese and those who married them. This prejudice permeated all aspects of colonial society, even the church that Grace attended.

Fascinated by her newly acquired status and privilege, Grace wrote glorious details of her new life, intending to impress and reassure her family that she had not "married down" and was not suffering with the masses in China, as they may have assumed. Her letters provide intimate, immediate images of her first impressions, untroubled by the significance of events. But in her reflections, written forty years later, she knew what she did not know at the time, that China and her life were about to change dramatically. The distance of time allows her not only to laugh at herself as a blundering, innocent newcomer but also to see the irony of her innocence within a world unconscious of its own demise. The relationship between Grace and Fu-chi is central. The roles are reversed now. Grace is no longer in her cultural milieu, but in one that operates in ways unknown and unknowable to her. Her husband, whom she calls Mr. Liu when writing to her mother and Fu-chi in her later writings, is her support and interpreter—of language, customs, and current events. He, in turn, includes her in all he does. She listens in on his conversations with co-workers in the afternoons at their house; she reads his reports and edits his English; she learns from him what is happening around them and the news of the world beyond. At first her assumptions of Chinese politics are based on current news reports, but over time she becomes aware of the difference between what was in the newspapers and what was really happening. Ultimately, because she identifies with her husband, she identifies with China.

The following descriptions of the first six months in China alternate between her letters (which are dated) and her memoir (which is titled).

August 9, 1934

Dear Mama,

I got your first letter yesterday afternoon. I read it aloud to Mr. Liu and Fuchina. Fuchina hung around my neck and tried to get in the letter. When we said it was Juie's letter she took it and looked all over it and hugged it all up under her chin.

THE FOREIGN CONCESSIONS
Our small flat was on the French side of the road that was the boundary between the French and British concessions. Therefore we did not really live in China, but in French territory in China, under the jurisdiction of the French Municipal Council. It was the same with the British, Japanese, and Italian concessions, all managed by their respective municipal councils under their respective home governments.

These "concessions," as the foreign-controlled territories were called, became the foreigner's paradise that gave even the most insignificant little clerk sent out from home a luxurious lifestyle he could never know in his own country. Ordinary Westerners, including missionaries, enjoyed a higher standard of living and had more status than they would have had at home. Here the British were the elite, all other nationalities were inferior to them, either slightly or greatly. Chinese, or "natives," were on the bottom. All the rest of Tientsin was called the Chinese or Native City, and to most foreigners was considered uncivilized territory.

Our snug little flat of three rooms and a tiny balcony overlooking the courtyard was in a racially and internationally conglomerate compound—a Russian Jewess with a German husband, a British newspaper man and his Russian wife, a large Chinese family, a Greek couple, some Italians, and a number of mixed Chinese and Western families.

October 5, 1934

You asked about the foreign element here. Where I am there's nothing much but foreign element for we live in a foreign concession. Our apartment building is in the French concession but the British concession is across the street. Our street has two names. The French side is called Rue St. Louis and the British side is Bristow Road. Just a block away is Victoria Road which is the Wall Street of Tientsin with all the big banks and British stores. The same road runs into the French concession on one end and becomes the Rue de France, on the other end. It goes into the Chinese Special Area and becomes Woodrow Wilson Street.

The people around here are mostly French, British, and Russian. I don't like the foreigners here. They are mostly business people and tacky.

Most of the Americans live in the Special Area, which is under Chinese control. It is really the prettiest and nicest part of the city. There are some beautiful houses there. But the trouble is that Mr. Liu can't live out of the district that's furnished water by his company or he will forfeit his house allowance. That means that we have to live in either the French, British, or Italian concessions.

We went to see Wallace Beery in "The Bowery" the other night. The picture was so typically American I don't see how most of the audience understood it. We have been to several picture shows and the audiences are very interesting to me. I never realized how different from each other the various nationalities, much less races, looked.

They always have a ten-minute intermission here in the middle of each picture and I love to watch the audience. There are always quite a lot of Chinese, in foreign dress and Chinese dress, Chinese flappers with permanent waves and long earrings, old fat Chinese gentlemen in long gowns and modern young Chinese men in foreign clothes. But I haven't seen a Chinese girl in foreign clothes. There are some Japanese in kimonos and wooden shoes. There are about an equal number of French, Russian, and British and some Italians and not very many Americans. The British are nearly always dressed in evening clothes.

The other night we were picking out the different nationalities and we couldn't find any Americans. Suddenly I said, "Oh, look, here come the Stones. They are going to sit in front of us." Mr. Liu had to laugh out loud, for here came a family dressed in tailored sport clothes with long sharp faces and slightly dried-up looking and so unmistakably American.

Mr. Liu doesn't like Tientsin nearly as well as he did Nanking. This is just like any city—streets, sidewalks, buildings, and crowds. Nanking was more in the country with fields and farms and water buffalo. He said there were lovely places to walk in the woods and up the mountains. Here there are only the sidewalks and city parks. There's no place to go with a baby. The park is too far to walk to and the streets are so crowded it's not very pleasant walking with a baby. Nanking is much more typically Chinese, not as many foreigners. There he was working in the government and could hear all the political gossip daily that he loves so much. Here you have to depend on just what you read in the papers.

November 23, 1934

I do want to write something about China but I have
been here only a little over three months and I really have
not seen anything of China. Tientsin is just a big
commercial city. Nothing pretty, nothing artistic, and
nothing typically Chinese. It is much more foreign than
Chinese. In a foreign concession you would forget you
were in China if it weren't for the rickshaws and Chinese
people.

One thing that really is Chinese is the little food stand
on nearly every street. Some of them look like small hot dog
stands and they sell the most delicious smelling concoctions
of vegetables, meat, onions, garlic, and red peppers in pretty
Chinese bowls. There is one right in front of our house. And
you can't imagine how tempting the food smells on a cold
frosty morning. The rickshaw coolies and people going to
work stop there and eat a hot smoking dish or two.

Another kind is just two big trays a man carries around
on a bamboo pole across his shoulders. It always looks
tempting, too. There are piles of fresh scraped raw carrots,
long white turnips, red turnips, long white radishes, and
other Chinese vegetables that are eaten raw. Then there are
big bins of wonderful fat chestnuts roasting in hot charcoal.

You know how the Chinese love tea. On nearly every
corner there is a little contrivance that looks like a China
cupboard. It has pots of boiling water, tea bowls, and tea.
They are for the outdoor workers, rickshaw men,
policemen, watchmen, etc. The other day I saw a
policeman during a traffic lull standing in the middle of the
street drinking his cup of hot tea as nonchalantly as if he
had been sitting at his own table.

In the Chinese native city of course it's very different
from the concessions. I have only been thru it once. The
streets are very narrow and crowded and swarming with
children. I was surprised to see how very fat and healthy
most of them look. I suppose the sickly ones simply don't
last long. Mr. Liu's office is in the native city and he says it's
very interesting. The other day he was walking along the
street and a man in front of him was carrying a rather long
bundle wrapped in bamboo matting. When he passed the

man he saw that the bundle was a little dead baby that the
poor man was taking away to bury somewhere. Mr. Liu said
it gave him such a shock that he felt bad all the way home.

A CAREFREE EXISTENCE

Charles Ruas, the French engineer at the Water
Works, lived in the same compound. He had been
divorced for a year and had no wife at that time. His
cook found a cook for us, a nineteen-year-old boy named
Sun Pao-san who had been a "small cook" [apprentice] at
the famous Astor Hotel in the British Concession, and
Sun, in his turn, found me an amah [Chinese female
nurse]. That's the way things were done. If you didn't
have a cook, you asked a friend's cook to get you one,
and then if you needed an amah or houseboy, you asked
your own servant to find you one. The cooks, amahs,
and houseboys of the concessions made up a close
community of friends and relatives, a convenient and
readily available supply of domestic help.

As young as he was, Sun Pao-san was an excellent
cook, but, in my arrogance, I considered him still better
after I taught him how to cook vegetables Southern
style and how to make American pies.

Wang Nai-nai, the amah, was a middle-aged woman
who had been a nurse for British and American families
and, therefore, spoke some English. She was
experienced and capable and took the baby over
without any trouble. A daily routine was soon
established that left me time to explore and investigate
my new world. Sun Pao-san and Wang Nai-nai were
with us altogether for twenty years, until Ju-lan was a
grown woman.

I had never known such a carefree existence before
and never knew quite the same again. I had no
housework to do, no cooking, no marketing, and no
baby tending. I could sit down in the middle of the
morning with a new book and not feel guilty.

I was happy and pleased with my new life and so
hypnotized and intrigued by the life around me that

happenings outside the tight little world of the
concessions seemed unreal to me.

October 5, 1934

I have just finished reading yours and Julianne's weekly
letters. Mr. Liu hasn't come home yet. I usually read them
aloud to him. He is always so interested in everything you
all say. He gets quite homesick for N.Y. and you and
Julianne.

The weather has turned much colder in the last week.
One day it was downright cold. We have no heat on yet.
There is a fireplace in the living room, but Sun will not build
a fire in it unless I insist. He considers it very foolish and
extravagant. He is the most "saving" soul I've ever seen. He
says oranges and lemons cost too much money and when I
insist that he buy oranges every day he shakes his head and
looks as if he thought the foreign "missy" were completely
crazy. He is an awfully good faithful boy and he is grand to
the baby and she likes him fine and calls him "Dun."

It is after five o'clock now and Mr. Liu has just come in.
He is reading your letter now. Ju-lan is playing out in the
court with amah and the other children. She has been out
there since 2:30. She stays out nearly all day long. I can
hear the children yelling and screaming and Ju-lan's voice is
the loudest of all. She is a little roughneck. You would die if
you could hear her imitating amah's Chinese. She wrinkles
up her nose and squints her eyes and says "Mei Yo" just
exactly like amah. That means "have not."

October 19, 1934

I am studying Chinese at the Y.W. now. We have two
lessons a week. Then nearly every night I have another
lesson with Mr. Liu. Sometimes he has too many things to
study to help me. In the meantime I practice on Sun and
amah. They beam with pride on me when I can make them
understand something I say in Chinese.

November 11, 1934

Chinese is as hard as the dickens. The writing and reading aren't so hard but speaking!—Each sound has four different tones and each tone means something else. For instance one tone of a certain sound means chair, another tone of the same thing means soap. Yesterday when the rickshaw man took me to the park I told him to come back and get me at 11:30 in Chinese and he understood me. I talked to the amahs in the park, too, and they can understand me. I am always so proud when they know what I say.

Ju-lan talks the funniest language you ever heard now. She tries so hard to talk Chinese. When her father talks to Sun or amah, she will imitate him. And when she tries to sing Chinese like Sun it's the funniest thing you could imagine.

November 22, 1934

I know it sounds like I would have nothing to do when I have two servants. But I find plenty to occupy my time and I don't read as much as I did in N.Y. When I first came I was so exhausted that I didn't even tell Sun what to get to eat. I just let him do it all. But in two or three weeks I got tired of fancy heavy cooking and it was bad for me, too. So now I plan all the meals and help cook a lot too. I have been teaching Sun real physical culture cooking. I am sure we have the best food in Tientsin. Then I take most of the care of the baby. Amah keeps her clothes clean and mended and plays with her but I do the most important things. My Chinese lessons take up nearly three whole mornings a week and I have to study in the meantime.

OMINOUS CLOUDS GATHERING

But, indeed, my conventional ideas of life and the world were about to be considerably shaken.

I knew that dark and ominous clouds were gathering and spreading, that the Japanese, already in Manchuria, were coming down into Hopei [Hebei], the province we were in, and were establishing a Japanese-controlled demilitarized zone between Peking and Tientsin and were smuggling drugs and Japanese goods into the Chinese cities.

The Japanese concession in Tientsin was full of opium and heroin dens. Dead bodies were nightly picked up around the low-class heroin dives and thrown into the river. I was horrified, of course, when floating bodies were pointed out to me a time or two. But it all seemed to have nothing to do with my life.

At the time of my arrival in Tientsin, the Japanese were encroaching farther and farther into North China, but the Nationalist Kuomintang [Guomindang] Government in Nanking was making no efforts to resist them. Instead, we heard that Chiang Kai-shek, the supreme leader in the Republic of China, was beginning his fifth extermination campaign against the Communists.

But what we didn't hear about was the Red Army's breaking out of Chiang's encirclement in October 1934, two months after I reached Tientsin, and starting on what became known as the "Long March" to Shensi Province. No word of this penetrated the confines of the concessions.

October 5, 1934

The National Government is much stronger than it ever was and fast progress in every line is being made all over China. Chiang Kai-shek is much more popular than he used to be and even those who never liked him say he has changed.

The Chinese government is desperately fighting the opium and drug traffic. There is a death penalty for being caught dealing in drugs and every day the paper tells of some drug dealer being executed. But the Japanese are trying just as hard to force the drugs on the Chinese. Everywhere in N. China where they are in control they protect the drug dealers. Right here in the Japanese concession there are hundreds of shops where drugs are sold openly to Chinese but no Japanese are allowed to buy any. It is the same in Manchuria. Everywhere there are shops selling drugs to Chinese but not to Japanese. Japan is trying to flood China with drugs and make wrecks of as many Chinese as possible.

But China today is stronger and more united than any time since the Revolution [overthrow of emperor in 1911]. The foreigners have been pushed back and are taking a decidedly back seat. The Chinese themselves are in control of the big business, banks, railroads, etc. And the men who are doing the real work and getting things done are the Chinese students who studied in America.

America and Russia are probably the only two countries who would welcome a strong China. England certainly does not want a strong China on account of India, and neither does France. Next to the Japanese, the British are the most disliked people in China.

CULTURAL BLUNDERS

The foreign country club life in that "never-never land" of the concessions—with its horse racing, entertaining and being entertained, the rivalry of hostesses, the British club where members got respectably drunk at five o'clock, and the constant struggle of the lower ranks to climb into the society of the higher—went on unconcerned in the path of a coming hurricane that would sweep it away forever.

So ignorant was I of the life and conditions that I had come into that I was apt to commit stupidities and make blunders. Fu-chi, also a greenhorn about life in the concessions, couldn't brief me beforehand. He hadn't lived in a Chinese family since he was thirteen and was more used to Western ways than to Chinese. He never realized that I knew very little of Chinese social customs. I had only my own foreign manners and ideas of courtesy to go by.

There were a number of Fu-chi's former Tsing Hua classmates living in or near Tientsin when I arrived in

1934. Several were teaching at the two nearby universities, two doctors and a businessman. I was soon getting some practice in how to behave properly in a Chinese social setting.

August 9, 1934

We have had an awful lot of company since I have been here. All of Mr. Liu's friends in Tientsin have been to see us and we have had two dinner parties here. The dinners were absolutely no trouble to me. I didn't even know what we were going to have until it was put on the table. Our cook, Sun Pao-san, took care of everything.

Wednesday night we had the Police Commissioner Mr. Yang, his wife, and his secretary Mr. Chen. Mrs. Yang couldn't stay for dinner as she was going to a party given by Madame Chang, the young Marshal's wife, at the Villa Westlake. [Chang Hsueh liang is referred to as "the Young Marshal"; see page 73.]

We first had consommé, then baked fish with potato salad, then squash with red cabbage cooked with apple, then stuffed tomatoes, apple pie and coffee, and lastly fruit. Sun makes wonderful coffee. I just tasted a drop but I never drink it. Chinese men are crazy about pie. Sun's pie isn't quite like our pie. It's more like apple shortcake. Please tell me how to make pie crust and I can tell Sun. He is very smart and I know he could make it right if I told him what to do.

THE HONORED GUEST

One of the first lessons I got was at a dinner party of these classmates and their wives. It was an elaborate banquet with about fifteen guests seated around a big round table. I did not know that the seating of guests went according to a prescribed ritual in which hostess and guests played their accustomed parts. When the hostess told me to sit in a certain seat I did so and was amazed to see every other guest refuse to take the assigned seat with much waving of hands and loud protests of "No, no, let someone else take this seat."

After much persuasion and more protests everyone was at last seated and the feast began.

As we walked home I said to Fu-chi, "How terribly rude not to sit where the hostess tells you to."

He burst out laughing. "It was you who were rude. You promptly took the most honorable seat without a word of protest."

"But," I said, "the hostess told me to sit there."

"Of course she did, but you should have protested loudly your unworthiness of such an honor until you were practically pushed into the seat."

"That's silly," I said indignantly. "Anyway, why didn't you tell me beforehand?"

"I never thought of it. Besides, it is just a piece of old Chinese etiquette that would not suit you at all. Nobody expected it of you. Don't worry, you behaved very properly."

November 11, 1934

I am sending some pictures we took last Sunday at Nankai University right outside of Tientsin. We were invited to spend the day with Dr. Chang, head of one of the departments. It is a lovely place. So much nicer than inside the city. All the faculty live in cute little bungalows on the grounds. They have tennis courts and a playground for children. Big iron pots were full of beautiful and unusual fish. There are at least a hundred rabbits of all kinds and sizes, including the giant Siberian rabbits with beautiful fluffy white fur, six and seven inches long. Ju-lan had a grand time. She screamed and yelled when it was time to go home.

We invited Dr. and Mrs. Chang here for dinner today. We ate about two o'clock and had a real American dinner. Dr. Chang liked it fine, but I think Mrs. Chang thought it was very flat and tasteless. She tried her best to eat but she couldn't make much of it. We had soup, roast chicken, mashed potatoes with peas and carrots, asparagus with white sauce over it, slaw, and apple pie. I made the pie. It was my second attempt and was not quite as successful as my first. It broke all to pieces when I tried to cut it. My first pie fell to pieces too but not quite as bad as the second.

I had forgotten to buy a pie pan and Sun borrowed one. The system of borrowing that the Chinese servants have is very funny. For instance, if we don't have enough plates or cups or glasses, at the last minute, Sun will go out and borrow some from some other cook, a friend of his, and we will be eating out of somebody's dishes that we don't know at all. Or sometimes I miss a certain bowl or pan and Sun has lent it to somebody's cook.

POT OF RICE

The next lesson I took more seriously and felt very embarrassed when Fu-chi told me what I'd done. This time we were having a family dinner with an old classmate, his wife and two children, and another close friend.

At a medium-sized round table there was a bowl of rice at each place and three rather small plates of vegetables stir-fried with silvers of meat. A huge pot of rice stood on a side table. This was the kind of Chinese food I loved. I piled the vegetables and meat on top of my rice, putting more on as I ate it off with a little rice at a time. My one bowl of rice was quite sufficient to last the whole meal, but everyone else got up and refilled their bowls several times. I noticed that by the time my rice was almost gone, so were the vegetable and meat dishes.

Again on the way home I commented. "I loved that food, but there wasn't enough of the vegetable dishes."

"You think that because you eat like an American. Chinese consider rice the main food. They fill up on that with just enough vegetables and meat to help the rice along," he explained. "But you," laughing as if it were a huge joke, "you do just the opposite. You ate up all the vegetables and meat with only a half a bowl of rice."

"Stop laughing. You're mean," I said. "Why didn't you tell me? Why did you let me make such a spectacle of myself?"

"Don't worry. Mrs. Tuan was very pleased that you liked her food so well."

I had to laugh, but I felt terribly embarrassed and determined never to make that blunder again. Naturally in making my way in an alien culture I was bound to get myself laughed at occasionally.

October 27, 1934

We went to a wedding this afternoon of one of Mr. Liu's schoolmates. As they are both Christians they were married in the Chinese Christian church. It was not a Chinese wedding but just like an American one. The bride wore a beautiful white satin wedding gown with a long train and lace veil. The maid of honor was extremely pretty and wore a pink satin foreign style dress. Their hair looked beautiful—they both had permanents.

The church was crowded. There were lots of foreigners, the British Consul General being one of them, and nearly all the prominent Chinese of the city. A famous general sat right in front of us. I can't remember his name. All the Chinese men had on long heavy silk gowns and silk trousers tied around the ankles with bows and velvet slippers. Of course the younger men wore foreign clothes. Most of the women had on Chinese dresses. One of the prettiest women there had on a foreign dress, a black velvet afternoon dress with pearls. She looked stunning. The groom and best man wore tails and high silk hats.

The best man was Mr. Ding, one of the schoolmates that visited us in New York. The groom and Mr. Ding stood beside the pulpit while the maid of honor, the little flower girl, and the bride and her father crept down the aisle—and were they painful to see! The groom looked as if he might drop dead any minute and Mr. Ding looked as if he wished he were dead and buried. Mr. Liu just suffered for them. He wouldn't even look at them. And when the procession started down the aisle he said, "Why don't they come faster?"

The preacher was an American and he used the ring service. After he got through, a Chinese preacher said a long prayer in Chinese and then the audience sang a hymn

in Chinese. An American doctor with his wife and daughter
sat opposite us and they sang loud and lustily in Chinese.

Sunday October 28

We went to church this morning in the Anglo-Chinese
college run by the London Mission. Most of the audience
were Chinese students but there were about a dozen
English people, at least they looked English. The man who
spoke was very good—nothing particularly spiritual, but all
right. As we were walking home afterward, Mr. Liu was
picking the preaching to pieces. He said, "Oh, the man was
just rambling," when a donkey pulling a big load of coal
right beside us on the street suddenly gave a loud
"ouk-a-ouk-a-ouk"—or whatever it is they do—right in Mr.
Liu's ear. And the poor man almost jumped out of his skin.
He laughed and said, "Well, I certainly did get a good horse
laugh for saying the preacher was rambling."

THE KITCHEN GOD INCIDENT

One of my favorite pastimes during my first months
in Tientsin was wandering around in the curio shops,
looking at and often buying fascinating little objects of
porcelain, ivory, lacquer, etc.

One morning I bought what I thought was a real
find—a scroll picture of a beautiful white-bearded old
man in a rose-colored long gown, gesturing with
graceful hands to the birds flitting through the flowers
and trees. Oh, it was a lovely picture!

I hurried home with it, pleased and excited. I wanted
to hang it on our dining-living room wall. It was
lunchtime and Fu-chi had just come in. I proudly
unwrapped my picture and held it up.

"Isn't this lovely? Won't it look wonderful against this
wall?"

He stared, shocked, as if he couldn't believe his eyes.

"Oh, no," he said seriously, "not on this wall. You'd better give it to Sun."

I was astonished and hurt. "But, but," I stammered. "What's the matter with it?"

"It's the kitchen god. Here, Sun," he said as the cook came in. "You take this. Tai tai wants to hang him up on the wall in here."

I knew Sun wanted to laugh out loud, but was too polite to do it.

I later saw my picture in the coal bucket and learned about the kitchen god and the reason for the horrified look when I wanted to hang him up in the living room.

He was a sort of New Year's joke and it was part of the New Year's celebration to put a plate of sticky candy in front of his picture to stick his teeth together so he wouldn't be able to tell tales on people when he made his annual report to heaven at New Year's.

The kitchen god incident didn't cure me of visiting the curio shops, but I was no longer such a gullible greenhorn.

August 9, 1934

It's terribly hard to shop here. Of course I can't go by myself except to one or two English stores and they are so much more expensive. Any time he wants it, Mr. Liu can have a marvelous-looking big car and a chauffeur in uniform. You should see me going shopping in a big car with a chauffeur, having the clerks take all the packages out to the car instead of carrying anything.

He is quite a "big dog" you know. Every morning the chauffeur comes after him and takes him to work. He usually goes about 8:30. Then he comes home at twelve and goes back to work at two and stays until five.

We have ridden several times in rickshaws, too. Fuchina sits in one rickshaw with her daddy and I sit in another. That's lots of fun.

THE WATER WORKS COMPANY

One day I heard a car stop in the courtyard and then
another one.

"Sun," I called. "Have you got the beer on ice?"

"Long time on ice, Tai-tai."

Men's voices, loud, coming up the stairs . . . and a
minute later, Fu-chi came in with two of his fellow
engineers, Charles Ruas, the Frenchman in his thirties,
and Mr. Cudzilo, a middle-aged Pole. I was greeted in
three accents and my hand kissed in both French and
Polish style.

An after-work discussion of the affairs of the Water
Works and of the world, enjoyably helped along with
glasses of ice cold Tsing-tao beer, became an almost
daily custom. I enjoyed listening in on these discussions.
They were both amusing and educational for a rather
provincial-minded American.

The fight to wrest control of the Water Works from
British to Chinese hands was not finished. It swayed
back and forth keeping everything but maintenance
work at a standstill. The three engineers were vehement
in their criticism of the way the Chinese directors were
dilly-dallying—so much needed to be done. The whole
company was just wasting time. Charlie Ruas denounced
Mr. B—; the Danish chief engineer. "He's no engineer.
He was just a ship's mechanic and got that job because
he married the daughter of the British manager of Hall
and Haltz [a British department store]."

October 5, 1934

No wonder the Chinese have boiled with fury against
the foreigners. Ignorant, incompetent men who probably
couldn't get any kind of a job at home have come over here
and because they were foreigners have gotten enormous
salaries and been put over Chinese who knew ten times
as much.

The present chief engineer of the Water Works
company is an ignorant Danish mechanic, in no way
qualified to be an engineer. He got his job thru pull with

the British directors because he married an English girl. Mr.
Liu says he is a complete joke. He does nothing at all. They
despise him. Mr. Liu does not work under him nor have to
take any orders from him.

Mr. Liu is more or less his own boss and is put there by
the Chinese directors to gradually take control of
everything. When the company becomes Chinese they are
going to keep some of the best foreign engineers and
mechanics—Mr. Ruas and Mr. Cudzilo and some others. It
will be the first time they have had a Chinese boss. But they
all like Mr. Liu very much and treat him so respectfully it
tickles me.

October 20, 1934

Last night Mr. Liu went to a banquet for the Yellow
River Commission. When he came home at 9:30, he read
me the report he had written on the condition of the
company for the board of directors so I could correct
the English. You would be surprised at what good English
he can write when he really tries. It was sixteen pages
long, though, so it was after twelve when we finished. He
is typing it tonight and having an awful time as he is not
used to the typewriter. He has already spoiled about a
dozen pages and is swearing in both English and Chinese.

November 22, 1934

I had dinner by myself tonight. Mr. Liu was invited to
eat with some official of the company. They are going
through the red tape of changing the company from a
British one to a Chinese one now. It will all be over some
time in December. Of course there is an awful lot of feeling,
gossip, and crookedness going on. But the Chinese will win
out this time, thanks to Mr. Liu. Without him they would
be pretty helpless.

November 24, 1934

This is Saturday afternoon and Mr. Liu has just come in.
He had been having lunch at Homer Lu's home. Mr. Lu is
the richest man here and probably one of the richest in
China. He is the chief Chinese director of the Water Co.
besides owning the biggest cement company in North
China. He is going to Nanking today to arrange with the
government about changing the company to a Chinese
one. His plan is to get all the private-owned water
companies in China in Chinese hands. He has control
of a water company in Peking and he is planning to get
the water company in the British concession. Mr. Liu will
be the chief engineer of them, too. Dr. Li, the head of the
Yellow River commission, told Mr. Homer Lu that there
was no other engineer in China who knew what
Mr. Liu did.

Mr. Liu said Mr. Homer Lu's house was beautiful and his
radio must have cost thousands of dollars. He can get any
place in the world on it. He gets all the music from
America, Paris, Berlin, anywhere—It was especially made
for him.

Fu-Chi's Colleagues

Charles Ruas had lived most of his life in Tientsin, as
had his father. He had been educated in France, but
most of his life had been lived in this port city of old
China, which was a bad place for young men like
Charlie, where the social life centered on drinking.
When he was cold sober he was glum and moody,
when really drunk he was dreadful, but when he'd
had just enough he was a delightful, witty, and charming personality.

Mr. Cudzilo ("sky" had been discarded on the end to
make the name easier for Chinese to pronounce) was a
relative newcomer to Tientsin, a Polish man of profound
education and culture. During the First World War, he
was in the Russian army, had been captured by the
Germans, escaped, and in the chaos of the Russian

Revolution had walked through Siberia down into
Manchuria. There, starved and exhausted, he had been
jailed as a vagrant. He told me that the Chinese jail
seemed to him like heaven—to sleep warm and safe, to
eat three delectable meals a day, to be treated with
kindness after the horrors and miseries of war, and his
long ordeal through Siberia. For this he said he would
be eternally grateful to his kind Chinese jailers.

Released when he was able to travel, he came down
to Tientsin where there were other Polish refugees. The
Danish manager of the Water Works had hired him as
an engineer at a salary several times that of a Chinese
doing the same work, making him, in the refugee world,
a very wealthy man with servants and a big house.

Charlie Ruas declared that on payday, most of the
Polish refugees in Tientsin were waiting in the Water
Works compound to divide up Cudzilo's salary.
Generous-hearted and unselfish, he did, in fact, support
many of them. He could not see suffering without
trying to relieve it.

In the eight years we knew him, we went many times
to Polish gatherings at his house, where we ate Polish
food, danced Polish dances, and met all manner of
refugees, who fled from Poland for diverse reasons.
They all flocked around kind, credulous, unsuspicious
Cudzilo—once, at least, dealing him a shocking disillusionment.

One night we met at his house a handsome, well-
dressed doctor and his strikingly beautiful wife. The
tragic look on her face startled me. I thought she must
have gone though some unforgettable and terrible
experience. Not long afterward Mr. Cudzilo told us she
was dead. Her husband was a blackmailer and had used
her to extort money from wealthy men, treating her
with the utmost cruelty. She had refused to help her
husband blackmail Cudzilo and had shot herself. I don't
know what happened to the husband. Of course, we
never saw him again.

November 11, 1934

The Armistice was celebrated here in all the concessions
and there were French parades, British parades, and American
parades. Last night Mr. Cudzilo had another party. There
were a Polish doctor and his wife, an English newspaperman
and his wife, M. Ruas, another Polish man, and several kinds
of wine, beer, whiskey, and vodka. Everybody drank
something but me. Mr. Liu drank a little beer but I drank
plain water. M. Ruas got drunk and sang at the top of his
voice. The Englishman drank vodka until he was terribly
drunk. He said I had remarkable self-control not to drink or
smoke. I assured him that self-control had nothing to do with
it as I had not the slightest temptation in either direction.

THE DAILY CIRCLE EXPANDS

For five or six months, we had been settling down
into a pleasant domestic routine, livened by occasional
dinner parties and movies, when we unexpectedly
acquired an addition to our daily circle.

"Pao-san," Fu-chi said to Sun one morning. "Go down
to Ruas' place and tell him I want to see him." Ruas lived
three doors away in the same courtyard.

When Sun came back a little later, I heard him talking
to Fu-chi in the dining room and they both sounded
amused and at one point I could tell that Fu-chi was
astonished. When I went in, Sun had gone to the kitchen.

"What's the matter with Ruas?" I asked.

"Sun says he brought a girl home with him
yesterday."

"Oh," I asked. "Is that his custom?"

"Perhaps. He's been divorced about a year. But the
funny thing is, this girl brought a child with her, a little
boy about Ju-lan's age."

"Well," I exclaimed. "That is something new!"

That afternoon Fu-chi told me that Ruas had talked
to him about the girl. She was from Bonn, Germany, and
was an actress in German movies. She was part-Chinese
and part-German. Ruas said he was very serious about

her. He wanted us to meet her and would bring her over that evening.

They arrived promptly after supper.

"This is Erika, Madame Liu. I hope you will be kind to her."

With this simple introduction Charlie ushered in a young woman who, though pleasingly shy and modest, was not at all timid. Fu-chi and I greeted her with matter-of-fact friendliness and she behaved with considerable poise and dignity in a situation that would have been painfully embarrassing to me.

Her voice was clear and well-modulated. She spoke English with a charming accent, undefinable since she spoke German, French, and Chinese fluently. I saw she would be very good-looking made up and dressed properly. She wore no makeup at all and her dress bespoke German, not French influence.

Sun brought in tea and we had a pleasant visit. The conversation was limited and general, of course, I don't remember now what we talked about. But I asked her to come see me the next day and bring the little boy.

And then what a fantastic story I heard! She told me that her father was a Manchu prince who became the ambassador to Germany before the 1911 revolution. He met the daughter of a German manufacturer at a party in Bonn and fell madly in love with her and she with him. When the Dowager Empress called him back to Peking in a time of emergency, he delayed leaving for almost a year. Erika was born at the end of 1910 and when he learned she was a daughter, not a son, he left immediately for China. Erika never saw him. Her mother married her former German boyfriend who adopted her. Erika loved her German stepfather who, she said, always treated her as if she were his own child.

Erika grew up in Germany under considerable restrictions. She was educated in a Catholic girls' school to protect her. She grew increasingly rebellious and strikingly beautiful. Someone who saw her at age nineteen offered her a role in a German film. After making three films, she was quite well known and loved the attention. A "flashy" character on the staff of a Chinese general traveling around Europe for his "health" enticed her to follow him to Paris, married her, and brought her back to China with him.

"It's not an uncommon story," she said, "but when I arrived, I found out that he already had a wife and children. He took me to his parents' home in the Chinese city where his first wife and children lived."

She went on to tell me that the first wife, of course, hated what she considered the foreign interloper. The wife succeeded in turning the husband against her because she was already pregnant and was losing her looks. Her baby turned out to be a boy which increased the first wife's jealousy and fury. The husband, an utter weakling, was completely under the first wife's thumb. She ordered him to turn Erika and her child out of the house and he had done it, first giving her fifty dollars.

"How outrageous!" I exclaimed. "Couldn't you have him arrested?"

Erika laughed. "A woman in China has no protection from a husband."

"What did you do? Where could you go?"

"I tried to find my father, only to discover that he was dead and his family would have nothing to do with me. I knew the German Consulate and his wife and they helped me get a divorce and custody of my child. Mr. Ruas has been very kind to me. And I appreciate your kindness as well."

They were married soon after, and Erika Ruas became my good friend and almost daily companion through those early years in China.

January 15, 1935

We are quite a settled old married couple now, boring everybody with tales of our "extraordinary" child. And I'm even calling Mr. Liu "daddy" myself. You would think we had been married for ten years. But my heart still jumps as it always did when I hear him coming up the steps and he still looks beautiful to me when he comes in.

I think it is so remarkable that two people who are born and brought up at the opposite ends of the earth almost, in different countries, different races, and different civilizations, and yet have customs that could be so very congenial. We like the same books, the same kind of people. We enjoy the same shows, and the same music. We have the same outlook on life, more or less the same philosophy, and the same ideals.

Ju-lan speaks a funny mixture of Chinese and English now. She says lots of Chinese words. Mr. Liu says she will beat me in a few more months. Just now she is standing in front of me showing me her hands and saying "Tsang-a, tsang-a" meaning "dirty-dirty." Whenever she doesn't want anything she always says "bu-yow, bu-yow." That means "don't want it." And she calls "Daddy-lai, Amah-lai" or "Gracie-lai" when she wants any of us to come—"Lai" means come. The amah's name is Wang and Ju-lan calls her "Wang-ma." You always call amahs by putting *ma* onto their last names.

Amah comes a little before seven o'clock and Ju-lan always wakes up a little before she comes. She immediately sits up and begins calling "Wang-ma" at the top of her voice. Amah takes her up, puts her on the "potty," dresses her, and gives her her orange juice and bottle. Then I can sleep till eight.

Mr. Liu and I both get up at eight o'clock and then Ju-lan has some oatmeal with her daddy at nine. Amah takes her to the park at 10:30 and brings her in at 12:30. She eats her lunch, tomato juice, vegetables, and milk, sits on the "potty" again, eats an orange, and then goes to the park again. She comes in at five o'clock, has her supper at 5:30, and goes to bed at 7:30.

She is wild and "woolly" and into everything. Right now she is worrying me to death. She says she wants to "write Juie." So I have given her a pencil and piece of paper and I will send you what she wrote.

All the whole Water Company now is sitting holding its breath waiting for Mr. Homer Lu to come back from

Hangchow. Everything is all ready for the final meeting now. I will be glad when it is all settled. It's been an awful strain on Mr. Liu, just sitting . . .

Please send me some sheet music. There is no duty on anything under $10.

Just continue to address me in care of Mr. Liu, Tientsin Native City Water Works Co., Tientsin, China. It certainly takes an awfully long time to get letters back and forth.

I wish you and Julianne were here.

With lots of love,

Grace

Grace Liu, Mrs. Holmberg, Erika Ruas at a costume party at the French Club, Tianjin, 1936.
(See letter, page 68.)

點水萍綠亂牽風荇帶長蘩

紅吹不定幽趣在濠梁

Charles Ruas, perched on statue.

Nini, Lewis Ware, and Franklin Ruas, on the beach at Peitaiho (Beidaihe), 1937.

FOUR

AFTER 1936 NONE of Grace's letters are addressed to her mother. From this point on, Grace sends her letters to her brothers, Tom or Sam, with whom her mother stayed most often. Tom and his wife Mary Hills Divine became Grace's link with the family. Her desire to communicate her experience to her family reveals the characteristics which make her a reliable observer and guide—her straightforwardness, curiosity, and ultimately, her willingness to change.

But at this point, none of the imminent changes in China were evident to Grace. She was absorbed in a world that was not only alien to her family but also alien to the nation in which it thrived. The bizarre nature of this colonial subculture within China is reflected in the picture she sent home in a 1936 letter. She wore to a costume ball, not a costume at all, but a Chinese dress. For her, she was almost as far from China as she had been in Chattanooga when she dressed up as Princess Ting Ling in an operetta about ancient China.

In her letter of January 31, 1936, Grace refers to her daughter as "Nini" and to her husband as "F. C." Ju-lan has nicknamed herself "Nini," using the last sounds of "Fuchina." While Grace is struggling with Mandarin, Nini is absorbing two dialects in both Chinese and English:

> . . . It is snowing this morning and Nini has gone out with her rubber boots on with amah to play. She is getting so tall. I think you would have a fit laughing if you you could hear her talk now. Her Chinese is better than her daddy's. He speaks still with Shensi dialect but Nini speaks perfect Mandarin. But her English is so funny! It's not American English at all. It's British. She talks about the motor cars, tram cars, and she has tiffin instead of lunch. She takes a "bahth" and says "cahn't." The other day F. C. asked amah to hand him the paper and he used the Shensi dialect word for paper. Nini said, "Daddy that's not proper, you should say "chih" not "shih."
>
> I can understand almost any ordinary communication and I can talk, too, when I have to but I am very timid about it because I am afraid of saying something ridiculous. It's so easy to make a mistake. If you use just a slightly different tone, a difference so slight as to be imperceptible to an unaccustomed ear, you have changed the meaning entirely.
>
> I am sending you a funny picture taken at a masquerade party at the French Club at about 3:30 in the morning. In the picture of three, the woman in the middle is Mrs. Holmberg. She is Korean and her husband is Danish. He is a director of the Water Co. and was the Danish Minister in Peking a few years ago. The picture does not do her justice as she is really quite beautiful. She has on an Arabian costume she got in Egypt. The other woman is Mrs. Ruas. She is part-Chinese and part-German. Her father was a Manchu prince who married the daughter of a German manufacturer during the time of the Empress-Dowager and

was cut off from his family. So she lived all her life in
Germany until she married and came to China. Her husband
is a Frenchman and is an engineer in the Water Co.
We have all been very well this winter and I am almost
fat, though I haven't got a double chin like the picture. The
Chinese high tight collar makes it look like that.

Business went on as usual in the foreign concessions of Tientsin,
like the other treaty ports of China in the mid-thirties. Industries
prospered, transportation and communication lines were greatly
improved, and the standard of living in the foreign areas was relatively high. In these protected zones, business could go on almost
undisturbed by the ripples of civil conflicts. Even wealthy Chinese
found that having a "safe house" in one of the concessions was like
having money in a Swiss bank. The native city, already dirty and
disorderly, became increasingly demoralized. The narrow, dusty
roads became more deeply rutted by rickshaws, and only gourd
vines covered the gray mud or brick walls of the one and two-story
buildings that predominated. The smug foreign community had little to do with the shabby, dilapidated Chinese city, where beggars
and prostitutes caused a visitor discomfort. Drug addicts, especially
near the Japanese concession where heroin injections were sold to
Chinese for a few coppers, were found dead in increasing numbers
on the streets or in the river.

Seldom did the two worlds meet. For Grace and most foreigners in the concessions or missionary compounds, life in China was
quite satisfactory, but for a majority of the 500 million Chinese, life
was a constant struggle. Grace was shocked one time when a starving man wandered into her courtyard and dropped dead under her
kitchen window.

The 1936 letter describes a rare adventure for Grace outside the
safe world of the concessions. Grace goes with Erika Ruas, who has
now become her constant companion, into the Chinese part of
Tientsin. Erika's verve and ability to speak Chinese embolden Grace
to try what she dares not do alone:

Yesterday afternoon Erika Ruas and I went to the
Chinese city to see the preparations for Chinese New Year.
I have never been in the Chinese City except in a car and
you can't see very much that way. We went in rickshaws
and then got out and walked thru the narrow crowded little
streets. They were lined on each side with little markets,
bazaars, and shops selling all sorts of New Years'
decorations—gorgeous paper boats, fish, flowers, lanterns,
and everything imaginable. Every few minutes a big
firecracker would go off and make me jump almost out of
my skin. Very, very few foreigners ever go there so everywhere we stopped, such a crowd gathered around we had a
hard time getting out. Incredibly old-looking hags ran after
us and wanted to tell our fortunes.

We went into an old temple. They were having a bazaar or
market in the courtyard. Inside, people were burning joss
sticks and kowtowing to a big image of Buddha. It was
terribly, terribly cold and our noses got stiff and our feet
turned to blocks, but the cold air was delicious with the odor
of baked sweet potatoes and roasted chestnuts. Every few
steps there was a big round stove with something cooking.
We bought a bag of hot, hot chestnuts. My! but they are
delicious. They are roasted in hot charcoal and sugar and taste
marvelous. I bought several things for Nini and Erika bought
some things for her little boy. We had a hard time getting
through the crowd without getting our things smashed.

There are no beggars in the Chinese city now. The
Chinese Municipality has taken them all up. Those that are
able-bodied are given work to do and those not able to
work are fed and housed.

Nini and amah have come in and Nini is eating her
lunch of raw carrots, celery, spinach, and goat's milk, and
she talks to me so much I can't write.

Between January and June of 1936, change was in the air. The
weather went from cold to very hot, and the political climate was
heating up as well. Grace heard only "rumors of trouble" and hoped
the "hostilities" would not disrupt her trip to Peking. Six months

earlier, students in Peking had protested violently against Japan's encroachment in North China. This letter contains Grace's first mention of Japanese involvement. Although she described it as too "complicated," her mention of it is an indication of how involved they already were in the city's government.

Even Grace's style of writing and vocabulary are beginning to change, but for the most part, she still lives in a world of dress-up. She drops into the envelope a sapphire ring and says she regrets the loss of the silver bracelet she placed in the last letter, wrapped in a handkerchief.

June 5, 1936

Dear Mary Hills,

This spring has been very cold and disagreeable, windy and dusty. But summer has come at last. Last week has been so terribly hot I haven't had the energy to make the least effort, either physical or mental, that wasn't absolutely necessary. Yesterday it was 105 degrees in the shade and 118 in the sun. Of course, if this were not a dry climate it would be utterly unbearable. But it's bad enough. Our apartment is very hot. It's small and right under the roof and the sun beats in on both sides, and the building is between two bigger buildings so most of the breeze is cut off. The other afternoon when I was out at six o'clock, the sun was still hot enough to burn.

We are planning to go to Tsing Hua the first of July. F. C. is going to meet some of his classmates there for a reunion. The rumors of trouble we heard two weeks ago have died down. If there are any hostilities, Tsing Hua is liable to be a rather dangerous place, otherwise it's lovely. It's almost right in the Western Hills, little mountains that rise right out of the plain a few miles from Peking. It is cooler there and will be a good place to pass the hot days. There is a wonderful dairy and library and swimming pool. I've lived in China two and a half years and have not been to Peking yet.

On Saturday I got Mr. Liu to take me to see Shirley
Temple in "Captain January." I am not a Shirley Temple fan
but I used to love the book when I was a little girl. Mr. Liu
went under protest and when we got there and found the
theater just overrunning with children and their amahs, he
was so annoyed. I had to laugh! It's very funny to hear all
the little English and American children talking Chinese
with their amahs. Nini talks Chinese altogether to Amah
and some to her daddy but she always talks English to me.
She knows quite a lot of Russian, too, as so many of her
playmates are Russian.

Sunday afternoon we went to see an English picture
(very slow and tiresome) and we met Mr. and Mrs. Lin in
the theatre. We hadn't seen them for about two months
because they live at Nankai University, which is some
distance outside the city. Mrs. Lin's name is Adeline—she is
an American girl from Washington state. She is a graduate
of the University of California. She met Mr. Lin there while
he was teaching Oriental literature. She is a tall pretty girl
very much like Julianne except she has black hair. Mr. Lin is
a classmate of Mr. Liu's, a very brilliant man but small and
quite insignificant-looking. She is teaching at Nankai, too.

We invited them to join us later at our favorite Chinese
restaurant for dinner. Mr. Liu and I got to the place quite a
while before the Lins did (guests are always late to Chinese
dinners) and I had eaten up nearly all the watermelon and
sunflower seeds before they came. The seeds are dried and
salted and you crack them with your teeth and eat the
kernel and throw the shell on the floor. They are delicious!

We had a very good dinner. First, cold chicken liver and
duck with cucumber slices covered with Chinese sauce.
Then the hot dishes—fried frog legs with bamboo shoots,
shrimp with sliced chicken, chicken fried and glazed with
sweet and sour sauce, meat balls wrapped in lotus leaves, a
Chinese green vegetable called "tsin tsai" with bamboo
shoots and onions, another Chinese vegetable "bo tsai" with
celery and green peppers, mushroom soup, chow mein
(noodles) with shredded ham, fish, rice, tea of course, and
last the dessert—delicious almond soup. It looks like thick
cream slightly beaten and tastes marvelous.

I wore my new Chinese dress, white silk with a tiny red stripe going crosswise. It is made in the latest style, very long, just escaping the floor, very short sleeves, the right side split up an inch below the knee and a group of pleats inserted on the left side that open up like a fan when I walk. With it I wore red satin sandals, red earrings, and a red lacquer bracelet. I love to wear Chinese dresses. They are very comfortable.

There is going to be a shift in mayors soon. The present mayor failed to please either the Japanese or the Chinese. The Chinese said he was too pro-Japanese and the Japanese said he wasn't pro-Japanese enough. It's all very complicated.

The bell in the French church next door just rang for twelve o'clock and it's time for Nini to come from the park and Mr. Liu to come from work. I hear Nini and Amah coming up the steps now so I will have to stop.

Give my love to Mama
and everyone,

Grace

GRACE DIDN'T EXPECT the rumors of trouble to break out into war when her cousin Mary came to visit. Mary arrived in China in 1936 with her husband Robert (Bob) Ware, a lieutenant in the Medical Corps of the U.S. Navy. While Bob was assigned to the *U.S.N. Tutuila*, a gun boat on the Yangtse River, Mary and their baby son Lewis stayed in Hankow (Hankou). Mary wrote to Grace that she would come to Tientsin the next summer when Bob had leave.

Meanwhile, Grace heard on the radio on December 12, 1936, that General Chiang Kai-shek, head of the Nationalist government, had been kidnapped in Sian (Xian). The incident immediately spurred an international crisis. One of Chiang's own generals, Chang Hsueh liang (Zhang Xueliang), known as "the Young Marshal," spearheaded the kidnapping. His father Chang Tso Lin (Zhang Zuolin) had been assassinated by the Japanese in Manchuria in 1928, after which Japan had occupied Manchuria. His intent was to force the Generalissimo into resistance against the Japanese. Chiang had been too preoccupied with fighting the Chinese Communists to oppose Japan in any significant way. Chiang hoped that Japan would squeeze the Red Army from the North while he pushed from the South. The Communists, on the other hand, had gained popular favor by supporting a resistance movement against the Japanese. If Chiang agreed to fight the Japanese, it meant not only abatement of his determination to exterminate the Communists but actual cooperation with them in a "united front" against Japan.

The explosive situation was resolved on December 25, 1936, with a verbal agreement, at least temporarily, for a united national resistance against Japan. Chiang Kai-shek's wife, Madame Chiang, educated in America and well-known through her frequent coverage in *Life* magazine, interceded on her husband's behalf; Chou En-lai (Zhou En-lai) negotiated diplomatically for the Communists, and the Young Marshal willingly gave himself up.

The spring of 1937 was one of relative calm. A change of government in Japan reaffirmed a commitment to the status quo and the tension between the two nations seemed to be easing. But Japan's military presence in Tientsin was already evident. The Japanese concession, adjacent to the French and British concessions, was constructing a fortress-like "police substation" at its entrance. The reinforced concrete barriers covered with brick gave a formidable appearance to the already impenetrable compound on Asahi Road. If the police station wasn't warning enough, the presence of armed sentries in drab olive green dress should have been. But Japan had secured a truce in 1933 which allowed it to maneuver troops in North China without Chinese opposition.

When F. C. first came to Tientsin, the Water Works company provided water only to a few concessions and parts of the Chinese city. After a year on the job, F. C. designed a plan to extend the water system throughout the city, but the company's board of directors, made up of six foreigners and three Chinese, did not want to invest the money. F. C. convinced the board, however, to let him build a modern filtration system, the first in North China. After the filtration system was in operation in 1935, the daily supply of water increased to 6 million gallons a day. The company became so profitable that its stock soared from $100 to $180 per share. These profits accrued primarily to foreign shareholders and those board members who controlled the company.

For several years, the Nationalist government, headquartered in Nanking, had been trying to counter these colonial practices. Homer Lu, one of the wealthy Chinese on the board of the Water Works, had made several trips to Nanking since F. C.'s hiring, to negotiate the transfer of the Tientsin Water Works to a Chinese-held company. At the end of 1936, the government ruled that a joint venture of Chinese and foreign capital must be registered in Nanking and have a 51-percent Chinese majority of shareholders and board members, as well as chief positions held by Chinese.

By spring of 1937, the negotiations were complete. The company received a license to operate under the new structure. F. C. was designated Chief Engineer and Homer Lu the General Manager. Mr. Ruas was the Deputy Chief Engineer, and Mr. Holmberg, who supported F. C.'s hiring, remained a board member. F. C. had worked with Mr. Holmberg, Mr. Ruas, and Homer Lu since coming to Tientsin and his relationship with them extended beyond the workplace. They socialized frequently, and their wives and children were close.

The apartment on top of the Water Works was designated for the Chief Engineer. In March 1937, the Lius moved into what Grace described as "one of the fanciest flats in the whole city." Grace was not quite settled by the time her cousin Mary Ware came. The spacious rooms were only partly furnished with a mixture of Western and Chinese furniture, some supplied by the previous Chief Engineer. There was plenty of room for Mary to stay, along with her two-year-old son Lewis, called "Lolo," and his amah, whom Mary had hired in Hankow.

The apartment was located on Rue Fontanier in the French concession. To Mary, the street where Grace lived looked very

European. There were wide paved boulevards, tree-lined sidewalks with street lamps and large Western-style buildings. A courtyard garden provided a good place for the children to play and the perfect setting for the two cousins to visit—if it had not been for the heat. Many of the foreigners in Tientsin and Peking got away from the heat by spending all or part of their summers in Peitaiho (Beidaihe). Grace described this seaside resort in North China as "the loveliest place on earth," between the sea and the mountains, only thirty miles from the end of the Great Wall known as the gate to Manchuria.

When Mrs. Holmberg heard that Grace's cousin was coming, she offered her beach house in Peitaiho. It had an orchard with cherries that grew as large as apricots and servants to tend to the house and garden year round. Grace invited Mrs. Ruas and her son to join them. When the three women, Grace, Mary, and Erika; their three young children, Nini, Lolo, and Franklin; and three amahs set off for the beach at Peitaiho in late June 1937 it did not cross Grace's mind that they might be in the path of troops invading from the North.

The three women waded with the children ankle-deep in the surf, stirring up shoals of silver minnows and blue crabs. Squeals of delight were the only sounds they heard above the rhythm of the waves and the salty breezes. Nothing seemed more threatening than a huge jellyfish with tentacles almost three feet long they found one morning in the sand. Mary left her son and amah with Grace and took a train to Peking to spend a few sightseeing days with her husband, Bob, before bringing him to Peitaiho.

On the morning of July 7, 1937, Mary and Bob Ware departed from the Peking station at 6 A.M., not knowing that only two hours earlier serious fighting had broken out at the Marco Polo Bridge on the Yongding River, just ten miles west of Peking. When news reached them in Peitaiho of a Japanese attack, they gathered up Lewis and left for Tientsin. F. C. met them at the East station and said he had sent a man to Peking to find out the situation. Not waiting for the news, the Wares embarked on a boat for Shanghai, transferred to a Navy vessel, and within two days, departed for Manila.

It was two weeks before F. C. learned that the fighting in Peking had grown fierce and threatened to control the rail lines into Tientsin. Mr. Ruas left immediately for Peitaiho to accompany the women, children, and amahs on the journey back home. Japanese troops were evident at every station along the way. Grace was relieved to be safely back in the French concession when she learned they were on the last train to Tientsin before the Japanese took over the lines.

The concessions responded with emergency measures and forbade entry of all troops bearing arms. The concessions were considered foreign territory, and attacking them would have been tantamount to attacking France or Britain. Japan did not wish to invite the hostility of the European nations at this time and used the opportunity of their preoccupation in Europe to make its move on China unchallenged. The Nationalist army offered only minimal resistance. Peking surrendered without a fight, and Tientsin was left virtually undefended except for a paramilitary police force.

When the bombing started on July 27, Grace and the other foreigners in Tientsin watched from the rooftops. Several friends and family members found refuge in the Liu home. Mrs. Holmberg and her daughter Dorothy were there, along with Adeline Lin, the American woman married to the Chinese professor at Nankai University, and F. C.'s niece who was a student in Peking. All of them were on the roof the afternoon that the Japanese air force rained bombs continuously on the Chinese city.

The planes flew from bases only a few miles away, carefully hitting some targets and avoiding others. At first the bombing was sporadic, with simultaneous strikes at different points throughout Tientsin. Great columns of smoke with bursts of flame shot up as incendiary bombs hit government buildings and Nankai University. Adeline Lin fell on Grace's shoulder and wept bitterly as she watched the destruction of her once-sheltered college. The pleasant campus, a few miles from the city, with its lotus lakes and tree-covered pathways had gained international acclaim for its impressive library, large academic buildings, and research facilities. Mrs. Lin protested that the attack was a ruthless retaliation for the recent anti-Japanese demonstrations led by students at Nankai.

The fight for Tientsin lasted five days. Truckloads of dead bodies were hauled through the Chinese part of the city. By the end, the Japanese controlled not only Tientsin and Peking, but the whole region surrounding them. Hearing news of the attack, Mary wrote Grace to leave China and join her in Manila. When the fighting died down, with its aftermath still unsettled, Grace wrote back.

September 15, 1937

Dear Mary and Bob,

I certainly appreciate your invitation to come to Manila, but it's quiet here now and so far reasonably safe. Of course there is still fighting going on all around Tientsin. Especially at night we can hear sounds of firing, sometimes quite near, but the city itself is very quiet. The concessions have within the last week completely resumed their normal appearance but the Chinese city is like a dead place. Most of the shops are closed and the streets that were swarming with people just a few months ago are almost completely deserted except for Japanese soldiers.

The future is very uncertain. We don't know what will happen from day to day but we will hang on here until we are sure the Japanese are going to really *take over and settle* and then we will *certainly* try to get out, perhaps to Western China.

Mrs. Lin is staying here now. [She was] afraid the Japanese would occupy Nankai, but nobody dreamed they would actually destroy it. Mrs. Lin had gone back to her house to get some of her furniture and books out and left there only a few hours before the bombing and shelling started. Her cook barely escaped with his life.

We left Peitaiho two weeks after you did . . . Everything was quiet for four days after we got back but on Wednesday morning at two o'clock we were awakened by the telephone. F. C. went to answer it and when I sat up in bed I heard loud machine gun and rifle firing very close. It was

Homer Lu at the phone saying fighting had broken out at the central station (the one not far from us). We partially dressed and rushed up on the roof. The firing sounded uncomfortably close. It kept up steadily all the rest of the night and as far as I can remember for several days.

To tell you the truth that week was such a nightmare I have very little remembrance of what happened. One afternoon does stand out. We all stood on the roof in the broiling sunshine and watched, dazed and speechless, two dozen Japanese airplanes dropping bombs all over the Chinese city. Every time one dropped there would be a deafening explosion and fires would immediately spring up. And of course the shelling and bombing of Nankai was terrible and terrifying. For three days and nights they poured shells from big guns and bombs from airplanes into the university buildings. We watched one night from the roof. It was a beautiful and awful sight. The sky was red with flames and the noise was terrific.

The concessions put up barricades and nobody could go from one to another without a pass. British and French and Italian soldiers were stationed along the border of every concession. Martial law was declared and no one was allowed out on the street after seven-thirty. It didn't seem like the same city anymore.

The heat continued to be terrific and Nini broke out with prickly heat and boils on her legs. F. C. has lost his appetite and is quite thin, but strangely enough I have felt just fine thru everything. I have felt bewildered and dazed as if I were in a bad dream but I haven't been nervous or frightened or sick in any way.

F. C. was in really terrible danger only one time. Fortunately I didn't know anything about it until it was all over. On one afternoon of the fiercest fighting and bombing, a bomb hitting the ground broke a very important [water main] connection that had to be fixed regardless of danger or the city would suffer from a lack of a very definite necessity of life. So F. C., Mr. R., and one of the directors, an Englishman, and a Chinese workman went to the place, which was in the street in front of the governor's *yamen*. The Japanese airplanes [were] bombing it

at that moment and there was firing from both sides. F. C.,
Mr. R, and the Chinese workman had to go to the middle
of the street completely exposed to the firing from both
sides and the airplanes. While they were there the
governor's yamen was completely destroyed and the bank
building opposite collapsed when a bomb went thru it.

F. C.'s cousin, who was in school in Peking, has come to
live with us as her school is closed there and it's very
dangerous for girls in Peking. Lots and lots of girls have
been taken from the trains by the Japanese soldiers.

Oh, I almost forgot to tell you. You remember the
rickshaw man who always took you and Lolo around? Well,
he begged so hard to come home with us, saying that with
everybody leaving, business was so bad he couldn't support
his wife and mother and father, that I finally brought him with
us and his rickshaw too. So now he is my private rickshaw
man and I don't see how we ever got along without him.

When fighting started Sun brought his family of nine
and amah brought her daughter and granddaughter and a
couple of friends from the Chinese city and they are all still
living here. Their houses were destroyed.

Please write and send me pictures of Lolo so we can see
how he is growing. Lots of love,

Grace

As the Japanese advanced Southward, Chiang Kai-shek made a
new resolve for the united front. His nationalist forces intended to
bomb Japanese warships off the coast of Shanghai but missed and
hit civilians instead. The Japanese used his response as cause to
retaliate with "all-out measures," and by December 1937, Japan had
taken control of Shanghai and Nanking. The brutal Japanese attack
is recorded in history as the "Rape of Nanking." The Nationalists
were forced to retreat further inland to Chungking (Chongqing).
By October 1938, the most fertile farmlands, the most productive
industries, and the cultural heartland of China had surrendered.

The Communists, beleaguered by fighting both the Nationalists
and the Japanese, were forced into a remote, poor district of north-
central China in Yenan (Yanan). The Japanese campaign to "kill all,

burn all, destroy all" actually aided the Communists in attracting more people to the resistance movement. The Communists moderated their land reform practices in order to allow both landlords and peasants to fight the Japanese. "Chinese do not fight Chinese" was the slogan which was used to pull the Chinese people together against the Japanese.

Even the foreign residents were stunned as Japan's undeclared war on China went unchallenged by the Western powers. In fact, American forces pulled out of Tientsin in 1938. British troops remained until 1940 but yielded to most Japanese demands. Soon all businesses, ports, industries, transportation, and communication were under Japanese control. Japan consolidated its control of China by creating a puppet government and placing Chinese collaborators in positions of power.

Life in the concessions went on despite the fact that the sea around their island haven was completely altered. Grace gave birth to a baby girl on October 21, 1937. The baby was named Ai-lien, or Ellen, after Grace's grandmother. For the birth, Grace went to Dr. Ding's private hospital on London Road. Dr. Ding was an older Chinese woman, a Christian, who had two entrances to her hospital, one in the concessions for foreigners and one for the poor in the city. There was no anesthesia but the labor was short.

At this time Nini started kindergarten at the Tientsin American School. Most of the students were foreign and Nini later recalled experiencing discrimination for the first time: "At first I didn't feel any different. I didn't know until later that this school was any different from the Chinese schools in the city. All the classes were in English; there was no Chinese at all. When it got cold, I wore Chinese padded clothing to school, and the foreign students snickered at me. But it didn't bother me; I was warm."

Without actually attacking, the Japanese found ways to exert pressure on the foreign settlements in Tientsin. First they curtailed foreign trade by eliminating all non-Japanese goods, retaining receipts from foreign customs, and replacing the *fabi* (Nationalist currency) with a Japanese printed currency. The value of all currency fell rapidly. Next the Japanese controlled rail and river traffic, including the mail delivery—foreigners' vital contact with the outside world—which was sent by river tug to Tangku.

Then one day in mid-June 1939, Grace woke to find that what had once been a refuge for her had become a prison. In the night, the Japanese had erected barbed wire barricades at every entrance to the concessions throughout the city. At checkpoints, steel-helmeted and bayoneted Japanese guards forced residents to fill out forms and subjected them to interminable delays to exit or re-enter. Likewise Chinese entering the areas, especially those bringing food and supplies—whether on foot, rickshaw, truck, car, or horse—were held up and sometimes turned back. Chinese farmers or delivery-men waited patiently, sometimes two or three days, in sweltering heat. Soon the concessions were suffering from lack of supplies and labor.

F. C. had to cross the barriers several times a day to supervise maintenance or attend to duties outside the French concession. Every time he crossed the barriers in either direction he was delayed, questioned, and subjected to humiliations. Every time he returned, however, he brought a vital resource to Grace and the family—information about what was happening outside the concession.

To get home from school, Nini had to pass through the barricades and bow to the Japanese guards. To avoid bowing she would slip through a hole in the wall and end up back in the concession.

Despite the invasion, the bombing, and even the blockade, Grace remained neatly sequestered behind safe lines. The sweep of the Japanese army across China barely penetrated the political barriers of the foreign concessions. The forces of nature, however, were no respecter of the imaginary boundaries of national territories.

The flood of 1939 was the worst in North China that anyone could remember, eclipsing that of 1917 and covering more than two thousand square miles. Five rivers flow into the Hai Ho River that passes through Tientsin. When the summer rains did not let up for days, the rivers swelled and swelled, moving massive amounts of water toward the city. Mud houses in the countryside simply disintegrated under its force. Food, trains, and electricity were cut off. Millions died or were made refugees as the city prepared for the approaching waters, but no one was expecting the onslaught that occurred.

On Sunday, August 20, the flood waters broke through the sand-bagged barriers into the concessions. People in the lower levels worked through the night to remove furniture or personal belongings of worth. A parade of men, women, and children of all ages slogged past their compound in knee-deep, then shoulder-deep waters, carrying everything they could in bundles. Ponies from the Race Club were brought with cattle, pigs, and goats to higher ground. Nearly everyone in the British concession had to be removed to hotels. The French concession was on higher ground, especially at the point where it rose to meet the International Bridge. The city streets turned into a Venetian-style network of canals. The foul, black waters soon became intolerable with the stench of gases from dead and decayed material.

Grace wrote to her brother Sam during the flood. Everything about her letter shows distress—the paper is irregular and torn, the handwriting disorganized, words omitted, and pages stained or missing.

August 26, 1939

Dear Sam,

I enjoyed your letter very much. You and Mama are certainly marvelous. I got a letter from her at the same time I got yours, the first in ages, and I answered it immediately. But before I had a chance to answer yours, this last horror had descended on poor old Tientsin. I don't know why any one place should have to take such punishment. But compared to this flood everything proceeding has been a delightful picnic.

I hate to think that we complained one breath of the inconveniences before. This is death and destruction staring us right in the face.

A rather serious flood was expected, but not that the concessions and the city itself would be so devastated. There is not a dry spot in the British and Japanese

concessions. Water from four to ten feet everywhere. And
in the French concession there are about four or five dry
blocks. That is, comparatively dry—the middle of the street
and sidewalk. But our place is far from the dry area. There is
more than six feet of water surrounding us. Of course the
basement and the furnace room and coal room are
completely submerged. All the first floor is flooded and the
water comes up to the first landing on our front stairs and
higher in the back.

Our court and garden is one big lake. Only the tops of
the trees and grape arbor stick out. The garage is full and
the car covered. And from the roof as far as we can see the
streets are like canals full of people on every kind of thing
that will float—tubs, oil drums, big bamboo baskets, rafts,
doors, beds, overturned tables, pieces of the pavement,
boats of every kind from little homemade ones to big river
junks. And whole families from old grandmothers to
newborn babies together with the few household things
they had managed to save—

This is the fifth day of the flood and I think the water
has stopped rising. The smell is indescribable. For the first
two or three days there was no bad odor beyond a slight
fishiness. But the last two or three days has been like living
over the most awful sewer on earth.

The magnitude of the flood was so unexpected that
everything has been completely disorganized. Of course
everyone knew there would be a flood and preparations
were made and what the authorities thought were the
proper precautions were taken. Barriers of sand—

August 31

This is the eleventh day of the flood. The water rose
about four inches after I last wrote. Then for two days it
stayed at the same point and day before yesterday started
going down. It has now gone down about a foot and we all
feel very encouraged and not so hopeless. Of course they
say there are bound to be epidemics of some sort as the
water recedes and everybody is trying to get cholera and
typhoid injections.

I think I had better go back and tell you all about it from the beginning—fifteen days ago on Saturday the water started coming into the low spots of the concession. Everywhere at strategic points were three-foot barriers of sandbags and dirt. People who lived on low streets had bricked up their basement windows and doors. In the 1917 flood that everyone thought was so terrible the street that we live on had about two feet of water on it. So to make everything safe the windows facing on the sidewalk were bricked up and a two-foot wall was built on our top doorstep in [*page torn*] of the front door. A three-or-little-more-foot wall was built across the entrance to the court. All the yard and court is surround[ed] by a high wall, but about four feet up there are moon windows.

On Saturday night the south dike broke and the water started flooding the first special area (ex-German concession). We had been invited to have lunch on Sunday with the Ruases in . . .

On that Sunday, the 20th of August, the Lius had gone to lunch with the Ruases and then to a movie matinee of *Jesse James* starring Tyrone Power at the Empire Theatre in the British concession. Halfway through the film, the lights went out and the film came to a sudden, faltering stop. F. C. knew immediately what it meant— the floodwaters had reached the power station in the British concession, which was on lower ground. The water had caused a shutdown of all electrical machinery of the British pumps. The two men left immediately to rescue the failing system by connecting the British pipes to the main water system. In the sweltering heat, they sloshed through the putrid waters until after dark, locating and turning on valves that were already underwater, until the connections were complete.

Grace and Erika quickly returned home to the French concession and found the amahs still in the park playing with the four children, Nini, Ellen, and the Ruas boys, Franklin and Charles. As they walked home, Nini saw for the first time the water gurgling up into the drainage grids, sputtering and spewing, as if the system were regurgitating, before the dark waters emerged and began to flow rapidly into the streets.

During the ensuing days, the two men were gone for long hours and did all they could to protect the water system from contamination. In waist-deep waters, foul and smelly, they found ways to keep the putrid liquid from seeping into the drinking water. They knew how things were connected, but they had no control over the rising waters, and they did not know what would happen when the power failed.

As head of the water system, F. C.'s every action was closely watched by the Japanese who controlled the city at this time. The Japanese commander of Tientsin had cause to suspect foul play. In 1937 Chiang Kai-shek had intentionally blown up the dikes on the Yellow River causing a flood that held off the Japanese advance for weeks. This time, the Japanese were determined to prevent possibilities of sabotage from those in charge of the system. One day the Japanese commander threatened F. C. at gunpoint, "If there is any interruption in services . . . or if the flood waters leak into the city's water . . . the first one shot will be you."

During this time, Grace often went to the tap to check the water. If the tap water ran clear, she was relieved. But her nerves were wrecked as she and the children waited, helplessly, and the waters continued to rise. F. C. returned home to find his family stranded on the second floor of a flooded house.

August 31, to Sam, *continued*

All the ground was covered even the concrete court between the front office which our apartment is on top of and the back offices. The men were still piling earth around the wall. The roaring from the front hall had gotten so loud we ran out to look again. It was horrifying. The water was apparently rushing thru the door in a torrent and was covering the first step of the staircase. We ran to the telephone and called downstairs that water was rushing into the front hall and up the stairs. Just then my rickshaw man

came running in, saying, "Tai-tai, tai-tai, the water has come in the back door and is going in the cellar." We ran to the windows again. The water was pouring over the wall and thru the moon windows. All that work for nothing.
Mr. Ruas had come in the meantime. He was forced to leave his car in front of the French Club about a half a mile away and wade thru the water the rest of the way—

When they saw it was hopeless and that the flood was so much higher than anyone had dreamed of, the men all left the court, which was now covered with about two feet.
F. C. and Mr. Ruas came upstairs by a ladder put on the roof of the office porch to the cook's window. Before they came up, they turned off the electricity to avoid fires or short circuits. Fortunately we had a few candles in the house. But before the light went off we looked down the stairs and the water was coming up to the first landing.

When F. C. and Mr. Ruas got upstairs the water was rushing into the court and basement with such a roaring that we had to scream over it to be heard. I don't think I've ever been so frightened. The house was all dark but for a few puny candles and that awful noise of rushing water.

Then the streetlights went out and we knew that the French power plant was under water. And they had taken such precautions to protect their engines. We sat around the dining room table with a piece of candle in the middle and another piece on the sideboard—

We were stunned; it had happened so quickly. Then I said, "We'll have to use the coal stove now." And F. C. said nobody had thought to bring the coal out of the basement and now it would be impossible to get it out. And then I realized that we would never be able to go to the French market and we had no vegetables and no eggs and no bread. All we had were twenty-five cans of evaporated milk, two cans of Quaker Oats, seven cans tuna fish, two cans corn beef, two cans sauerkraut, one can tomatoes, and some cans of Del Monte juice, tomato, pineapple, grapefruit, orange, etc. Anyway we thought the children could get along awhile if we could make a fire.

By and by the water had stopped rushing in with so much noise and we went to bed in what seemed a very

different world. I was afraid to sleep for fear the water
would come all the way up while we slept. I got out of bed
again and again to look out the window. It was a clear night
with stars. The court and garden was a lake and the streets
were rivers. I felt like Aladdin and his wonderful lamp—our
house seemed to have been in the twinkling of an eye
transported to some far place.

The next morning only the top of the car, which had
been standing in front of the garage, was visible. The
telephone house was full of water and the switchboard
covered. Men were walking in the street with water up to
their necks.

Well, here we were, no coal, no wood, no electricity,
no boat.

The workmen who lived out in the lower places of the
concession had brought their families in on the day before
and now there were about ninety people—women, men,
and children crowded into the back office rooms. The
chauffeur's house which is in the garden was almost covered
so he had to move into the office building with his wife,
mother, and eight children. The first floor of the building is
about four feet from the pavement of the cou— [*torn page*]
and about three hundred dollars worth of rice and flour
were stored there. It was partly submerged. They saved
what they could of it.

That next morning was terrible. Our children were
hungry and all the children in the back, I don't know how
many, were hungry and frightened and crying. F. C. had the
men tear down the matting that covered the roof and court
to protect it from the sun. There was not a stick of dry
wood so we just kept on stuffing . . .

The rest of the letter is lost.

Refugees of the flood, Tianjin, August 1939.

Empire Theatre under water, British concession, 1939.

紅吹不定幽趣在豪梁鼉鼉長落

Grace with Nini and Ellen, pregnant, 1941.

FIVE

O N SEPTEMBER 1, 1939, Germany attacked
Poland and soon afterward Britain and France declared war on Germany. As the waters which bound them to the fate of the Chinese
subsided, the foreigners in Tientsin now found themselves enemies
at home with those who had once been their compatriots abroad.

These transforming events happened at a frightening pace, leaving everyone shaken. Before the floodwaters had dried, the Japanese intensified the blockade. Barbed-wire defenses were added to
every barricade and to garrison posts along the railways, control-
ling movement to and from the city as well as within. Loudspeakers were installed at the barricades and turned on all the time,
blaming the foreigners for the troubles in China. For the residents
of the concessions, the shock of the outbreak of World War II was

tinged with the deadening realization that their world was disappearing forever. The Japanese were doing what the Chinese had been unable to do for a hundred years—dissolve the grip of Western imperialism in China.

The prevailing concern the winter of 1940 was food. The flood had caused a famine that drove thousands of peasants into the city. The harbor was thick with sampans, long boats, junks and rafts, tightly packed with refugees of all ages in starving conditions. Many of them came directly from the river into the concessions. The food crisis reached catastrophic levels. Imports stopped, grain was hoarded, supplies were turned away, and currency was invalid. The Japanese blamed foreign control. The Nationalist government blamed the communist-controlled countryside. And the Communists blamed the Nationalists for the spiraling inflation, doubling and redoubling monthly. Hunger fueled the fury of a world out of control.

When shiploads of flour arrived in Tientsin in March 1940, the flour became an object of speculation. Those who were wealthy enough to acquire large amounts stockpiled it, waiting for the price to go up.

With disgust for the new breed of "hoarders and speculators," Grace began to realize that the Chinese leaders did not really care about the conditions of the people. Her disillusionment was centered on the directors of the Water Works as she recounted in a taped interview:

> At this time when the poor were being forced into the city, some of the directors of the Water Works were hoarding flour and waiting until the price would go just high enough, then they would sell it. That's the way they did everything. They didn't care at all how many people died. There were too many Chinese anyway, was their thinking.
>
> The scoundrels made money off these conditions and then they bought wives. One director told the board he must have a raise in his director's fee because he wanted

to buy a new concubine, as he had seen a new girl and
she was very fascinating. One would think that that
would be nonsensical for a man to say how he might
want to buy another woman—he might think it and do
it surreptitiously—but then this was the thing to do. He
didn't mind saying it out loud; he didn't mind that
everybody knew it.

Grace felt overwhelmed by the distressing conditions on such a
large scale. But when she came face to face with one poor woman,
begging for help, she responded instinctively:

There were so many poor people pouring into the
city at that time. Of course, I wanted to give the
beggars something—but if you dared, you would have a
mob around you—you couldn't get out. But one time I
was walking home near where we lived, and there were
not so many people around. A beggar woman came up—
just a country woman, holding a baby in her arms, about
the age of Ellen and another child was holding on to her
jacket, just about Nini's age. She was so gaunt and
looked so starved, and the baby was just a little bundle
of bones. She wanted something. I opened my purse and
got out a bill—I suppose it was a dollar bill. It might
have been a five-dollar bill. I didn't even look. But
nobody ever gave a beggar a bill! You gave a beggar a
copper. Well, I handed her the bill. And she looked like
she thought I was crazy. Maybe she'd never seen one. I
saw a car pass me just at that time. So I hurried off. That
car was a Water Works car and it had Water Works
directors in it.
    The next day my husband said, "Well, you have
certainly created a scandal. Those directors saw you
give the beggar woman a bill."
    "I told you about it. I couldn't stand it. Those
children were the same age as my children. So I just had
to give her something," I said.
    "But the directors said that they saw you give this
woman a bill and that they were so angry. They said,
'We cannot afford to have a chief engineer with such an

extravagant foreign wife who actually gives beggars
a . . . a bill!' " He was laughing. "Well, this won't hurt
them," he said.

But it did hurt . . . not the directors, of course, but Grace, and
indirectly her whole family. The accusation of "extravagance" was
an easy one to acquire since many of the customs that sustained her
ordinary existence, such as eating oranges or drinking milk daily,
were items of indulgence for Chinese. But the label was indelible
and would hurt her even more in later years. While the directors
were outraged by her extravagance, Grace was repulsed by the sor-
did lifestyles of the wealthy, both foreign and Chinese. Nini
recalled Grace describing a visit to a Chinese woman's home during this period:

> She was the daughter of a warlord, who owned land in
> Tientsin. He had a house like a palace in the British conces-
> sion. When he died, the huge garden surrounding the house
> became his burial ground and an enormous marble tortoise
> was built as his gravestone. His daughter wanted to meet
> Grace because she was looking for a husband who was an
> intellectual, not a rich man's son nor a businessman, and she
> knew Grace and F. C. were connected to different circles.
> When Grace came, there was chaos in the house. She was
> told that the concubine had just run off with a lover and a lot
> of jewelry. The servants sat in the corridors on hard old
> antique chairs smoking opium. Grace was fascinated and hor-
> rified by the lifestyle. The young woman pleaded with Grace
> to find her a husband; F. C. later introduced her to an engi-
> neer, but he objected because she smoked opium. He said he
> wouldn't marry her unless she stopped smoking.

At a time when foreigners were both envied and despised by the
privileged classes in China, Grace's presence muddied the waters
for F. C. Being married to a foreigner and not treating her in the
way a rich Chinese would treat his wife (and concubines) made
F. C. incomprehensible to the other Chinese men who were directors of the Water Works. He was not considered one of them: he

was not to be trusted. And yet F. C. was not easy to cast aside. F. C.'s forceful personality and strong temperament made him formidable. Most important, the directors needed his skills to keep the company in their control. According to Grace, their way of getting at him was a traditional Chinese one, not entirely unique to China. Again, she recounts:

> He would have to go to these directors' meetings sometimes. They would have them in restaurants or tea houses. They would deliberately try their best to get my husband to take a few girls. At one party they offered some money to any of those girls to get F. C., "because he thinks he is a one-woman man so we will give you so much to get this man." That was supposed to be a huge joke.
>
> F. C. would come home and tell me about these parties. One time he came home looking sad and said, "They had a new girl there, and she was only fourteen. They had just gotten her in some town. She must have been less afraid of me than the other old men, so she came and asked me if she could please sit by me. She said she was so frightened that I told her, 'All right. As long as I'm here, nobody is going to even look at you.'" And so she sat with him and told him her story, that she came from a poor family in a small village, that her father had had to sell her . . .

As early as 1937 the Japanese appointed one of their own engineers, Mr. Yasemoto, to work at the Water Works. Mr. Yasemoto was friendly at first and seemed to cause no harm. He offered to help F. C. carry out his duties. But while Homer Lu was absent, the other directors replaced him as managing director with another of the Chinese directors, one more cooperative with the Japanese. Then after two unexpected and sudden deaths, the management's support for F. C. began to dissolve dramatically.

For Grace and F. C., the aftermath of the flood was even more devastating than the flood itself, as told in a letter six months later:

March 14, 1940

Dear Mary Hills,

I was *absolutely delighted* to get your letter. Nobody has written to me for ages. Of course I can't complain as I haven't written to any of the family since the flood. I don't know why it is so hard for me to get a letter down on paper. I can write the most marvelous ones in my head.

We have had many upheavals, trouble, worries, and so forth. But I am thankful our family have all stayed well, that is, all but me. Since I have been in China I have been in better health than I ever was in my life. Up until last June when the blockade began and I began to get thin and lost my resistance to colds (but more about that later).

These past nine months since the beginning of the blockade last June have been a very bad time for Tientsin and especially the Water Works. First the blockade with all the terrible inconvenience and scarcity of food, then the dreadful heat of July and August, and then the flood! After that was over we all were as limp as rags. The children were quite pale and thin but not sick and they soon recovered when they were able to get outdoors. F. C. was exhausted but all right. But I hadn't been able to get any milk after the blockade started. The children drank canned evaporated milk but it was so terribly expensive that I did without any milk at all. And as I am very dependent on milk I lost more pounds than I could afford. The reason we couldn't get milk after the blockade is because all the dairies are outside the concessions. And the milk men weren't allowed to bring the milk in. And for a long time it was very difficult to get vegetables. And for a while no meat at all.

In November the Water Works got its first blow. Mr. Holmberg, one of the founders of the company and the first chief engineer, a former minister from Denmark and just then one of the directors of the company, had taken his seventeen-year-old daughter Dorothy to Denmark to put her in a university. He died there very suddenly of heart failure. It was a great shock to everybody. His wife is one of my best friends and he was one of F. C.'s best friends and a great help and support to the company.

After his death things began to go wrong. The other directors were demoralized, and treachery and intrigue started. Homer Lu, the managing director, a very smart and able man and the one who brought F. C. here, was then on a six-month leave in the States on a very important mission, the purpose of which would be very unwise to speak of in these parts. He left in his place a man supposed to be very honorable and honest and his very good friend but he was really very weak and easily led and persuaded. So a very stupid and corrupt bunch of directors and shareholders got a hold of him and they accused Homer Lu in his absence of all sorts of things and at a directors' meeting voted him out and put another man in his place, a former schoolmate of F. C.'s, a lying, treacherous Chinese politician of the worst sort. Then they tried to get F. C. on their side. If they could win him, they were fixed, then Homer Lu could do nothing.

But of course F. C. told them he did not choose to play their game and told them to their faces exactly what sort of swine they were. In the meantime they had turned the Japanese man who worked for the company against F. C. F. C. had always gotten along very well with this man (who was really a sort of spy for the Japanese army) and had been very wise in his conversations with him. This man now turned rabidly against F. C., accused him of being anti-Japanese (as of course he is) and demanded his pass (permit to pass barriers). So F. C. gave back his pass and resigned. But the directors were afraid for him to resign—it might mean a strike of workmen and technical staff and there was no one else who could do the job. So they refused to accept his resignation and gave him a four-months leave.

F. C. appointed Mr. Ruas, the French engineer, to take his place outside. F. C. stayed at home and Mr. Ruas reported to him. So things went along until January when Mr. Ruas suddenly got a mysterious and violent pain in his leg.

He went to the hospital one Wednesday afternoon, they operated on his leg Thursday morning at eleven, discovered a deep abscess, and he died of blood poisoning at three o'clock Friday afternoon, January 12. It was a terrific shock to us, as F. C. and I and Mr. and Mrs. Ruas had been together almost constantly for the last four years. We lived together in Petaiho, they stayed with us during the flood, and I don't think that there was ever a day that we weren't in their house or they in ours.

The day he died I had planned to stay in bed all day as I had caught a bad cold. But Erika (Mrs. R.) called me at eight o'clock from the hospital (a German-American hospital in the ex-German concession). She said Charlie was dying and she wanted me to come so I threw on my clothes and flew out as fast as possible. F. C. couldn't go as he couldn't pass the barriers without his pass. I have my American passport. I can't remember the details of that hectic morning. Only I know I went back and forth thru the barriers over six times and one time is no fun. I never get used to those dreadful faces and naked bayonets. It was very cold and windy and my teeth chattered. I knew my cold was getting worse but I couldn't help it.

Erika was seven months pregnant and almost out of her head—she began to vomit terribly and at twelve o'clock I made her come home with me. The doctor said they would telephone if there was any change. We got her two little boys and came home. At two o'clock the hospital called and told her to come. I went back with her. They said he wouldn't last long and we stayed with him until about ten minutes before he died. He died very, very hard and it was dreadful to watch. I never saw anybody die before. I finally called the doctor and told him he must take Erika out of the room. She couldn't stand anymore. So they took her downstairs. And he was dead in about ten more minutes.

He was only thirty-five and looked as strong and healthy as a bull. The doctors were very puzzled and said they did not know what it was he had. Probably something he got during the flood when he had to walk in the filthy water. Erika and her children have been with us ever since. Last Sunday morning her baby was born, another boy. He weighs 8¾ lbs. and is marvelous. After Mr. Ruas's funeral my cold got me down and I went to bed for three weeks.

Homer Lu came back and now there is a fierce silent fight going on. Silent because nothing can be done above board on account of the Japanese, who would like nothing

better than an excuse to take over the company. Now it all
depends on which side wins. If the other side, then F. C.
will go South and into the interior. If our side, then he stays
here and goes on with his work. The other side wants to
keep him but he would not work for them. In either case I
stay in Tientsin . . .

The contrast in the remainder of Grace's letter is remarkable.
Despite the flood, the blockade, the birth of a child, the death of
two friends, and all the political intrigue, social activities continued
with an amazing sense of normalcy. At the same time that their
world is crumbling around them, clubs continue to meet, people
go to church, children go to school, and Grace even begins to
sing again:

> Tientsin is a very hard place to get well in once you get
> down. It's the most social place I ever saw. Either we are
> always going someplace or somebody is coming here.
> Everybody has to keep engagement books. So just as soon
> as I was better I started running again.
>   Did I tell you all in another letter that I had started
> singing again, not like I used to, of course, but people here
> think it's marvelous. I'm quite famous as a "prima donna" in
> Tientsin and another thing (I'm sure you will laugh or Tom
> will), I also have the reputation of being very "smart."
> People are always asking me if my clothes are imported.
> When I sang for the Women's Club, I wore a thin blue
> (powder blue) wool dress with a black velvet bolero and
> turban and white jade earrings and necklace. I sang
> Michaela's aria from *Carmen*, Shubert's serenade, "Ave Maria"
> from *Cavallier Rusticana*, and four smaller songs.
>   Last month on my birthday I sang at the big Rotary
> anniversary banquet and dance. I wore a black satin skirt
> and light red velvet basque with leg of mutton sleeves and a
> three-row crystal necklace and crystal earrings and a huge
> red flower on top of my head. I sang "The Kerry Dance"
> and "My Laddie," "Will You Remember" from *Maytime*,
> Shubert's serenade, and a Rotary song to the tune of "A
> Perfect Day."

Mrs. Walker, the wife of a very popular American lawyer, plays my accompaniments. Mr. Walker used to sing a lot when he was younger. And he still can sing. F. C. and I go there a lot and we have an awfully good time. Mr. Walker and I sing duets (they have all the opera scores nearly). Mrs. Walker plays the piano and sometimes Mrs. Hinke (wife of one of the American consuls) comes with her cello.

We have just lost two of our most congenial friends, Mr. and Mrs. Bakker, an American girl and her Dutch husband. They have just gone to Italy on leave and will be stationed in Shanghai when they come back. Of all the foreigners we know, F. C. liked them the best. How he and Andries (Mr. B.) loved their political discussions!

I forgot to say that at the Rotary banquet F. C. was there and when I went back to the table after singing my first group, everybody was laughing at him. They said he was so nervous he almost had a fit. I remember one time when I sang at the University of Tennessee and Tom was so nervous he wanted to crawl under the bench.

Nini is in the second grade at the Tientsin American school and is doing well. Her teacher says she is exceptionally bright and the best behaved child in the class. Nini is quite pretty and piquant-looking. But my little Ellen (Ai-lien) is a real beauty, the kind people gasp over. F. C. and I look at her and wonder how on earth she happened. F. C. adores Nini, but he can be quite stern with her if necessary. But Ellen just turns him to jelly. He almost tiptoes around her in awe. And her amah! She would take off her skin for Ellen. Consequently she is very spoiled. I have to give her all the discipline she gets and her amah and daddy think I'm very cruel.

One time when I had shut her up in a room till she got tired of screaming for something I wouldn't let her have, her own amah and Nini's amah both came to me to kowtow and knock their heads on the floor and beg to be allowed to take her out. They were wringing their hands and bowing and bowing and saying "Che che, Tai tai, che che, tai tai." "Please, please," (Tai tai means the "lady of the house"). I told them if they didn't go away and stay in the kitchen until Ellen behaved herself I would fire them both. F. C. was pacing the floor and wringing his hands, too, but I glared at him and said only over my dead body would anyone take her out until she stopped yelling. She finally did stop yelling and got as sweet as pie, but she didn't get what she was yelling for!

You see, Mary Hills, I have been carrying on about myself! I'm sorry Tom had to quit engineering but his insurance job sounds good. The main thing, I suppose, is to have a job!

When I showed Tom's picture to one of the amahs and asked her if he looked like me, she said, "All same long face." I wish Mama would write to me. I never know her address. I wrote a long letter and mailed it during the flood but she never got it. I suppose it got "drowned."

Nini is standing over me talking and asking what I'm writing and if I'm telling you anything about her. So I'm afraid I'm becoming incoherent and jumping around from one subject to another. I have just been out of bed two days after having the flu for nearly a week. The doctor said the flu wasn't serious but that I was very run down and must stop absolutely all my activities for the time being and do nothing but eat and sleep. And we were just in the midst of preparations for the Easter music at All Saints Church! It's Church of England and the rector is an Englishman whose wife was born in Macon, Georgia.

Have you read Lin Yutang's novel *Moment in Peking?* It's wonderful. Please write to me again, Mary Hills, and tell me about everybody. It's my fond hope that we can all come to see you one of these days. But I'm afraid I'd talk myself literally to death.

With much love to everybody,

Grace

On June 21, 1940, the blockade was lifted. Immediately the roads were full of people on bicycles, cars, trucks, and rickshaws passing from one side to the other, reuniting families and resuming business. With the blockades down, F. C. was able to cross through the barriers and return to his position at the Water Works. But now everything had changed. Mr. Holmberg and Mr. Ruas were dead, Homer Lu had been replaced, and those cooperating with the Japanese were in control not only of his workplace but of all the city.

Grace's third child was born on May 16, 1941. Nini described her brother's birth:

> Willy was born in Dr. Ding's hospital, too. He came so fast, he almost dropped on the floor. Dr. Ding caught him and announced, "It's a little William!" The name stuck, and we called him Willy from the start. His Chinese name was Wei-han. I remember when Willy came home, he was in a blue blanket and he stared at me and I stared at him. He became the favorite of the amah. She always liked the babies best but this one was a boy. Grace and F. C. did not show the Chinese preference for a boy—they were pleased to have a son, but not overly so.

Early one morning when William was about six months old, Grace was nursing him in the back room. She heard F. C. anxiously hollering to her. She handed William to the amah and went forward to see what was upsetting him. Before she reached him, she heard a strange noise and looked out the window. Long rows of olive green trucks were moving down the street. Their engines groaned in low gear. Marching alongside, in helmets and rubber boots, were long lines of the dreaded Japanese soldiers. Even throughout the blockade and all the time the Japanese were in Tientsin, they had not dared cross the barriers into the concession. She did not have time to ask why they were pouring into the concession now.

F. C. was at the fireplace, feeding a roaring flame. "Quick, empty that drawer," he said. "Get rid of anything they could use against us." Grace grabbed letters and papers, without looking at them very carefully, and threw them into the fire.

It was December 8, 1941, in Tientsin, December 7 in the United States. As bombs fell on Pearl Harbor in the Pacific, Japanese troops occupied the foreign concessions.

Japanese soldiers unloading at East Station, Tianjin, 1937.

Japanese troops marching, Tianjin, July, 1937.

Liu family after World War II, seated on U.S. Marine jeep, September, 1945.
Photo Credit: Giles Brooks, USMC.

點水萍綠亂拂風行帶長落

紅吹不定幽趣在濠梁

Six

OR THE FOUR years of the U.S. involvement in World War II, Grace did not hear from her American family, nor they from her. As an American trapped inside Japanese-controlled China, she escaped internment in a concentration camp by sheer luck. She wrote later that even though she had no way of knowing how the war was going, she never gave up her faith that the Allies would ultimately win. Finally, in the summer of 1945, the sight of U.S. B-29s lifted her hopes that the war was nearing an end.

Following the atomic bombings of Hiroshima and Nagasaki, Japan surrendered on August 14, 1945. U.S. forces in the Pacific were sent immediately to China to keep order until the National-ist government, then in retreat in Chungking, could return and accept the surrender of the Japanese. The first marines in Tientsin found a forlorn city and a downtrodden population.

When the Third Amphibious Corps of the U.S. Marines steamed up the Hai Ho River to Tientsin in September 1945, a large throng was waiting. As Private Giles Brooks stepped off the dock, he was greeted by an American woman in the crowd who asked where he was from. When he replied, "Chattanooga, Tennessee," she responded, "I know a woman from Chattanooga and I will tell you how to find her."

He took the address of a Mrs. Liu but did not look her up until a week later. When he knocked on the door of the given address, a Chinese woman answered. Seeing an American G.I. at the door, she ran back inside calling out in Chinese. A moment later a young Chinese-looking girl, her hair in braids and wearing a dress too small for her, appeared at the door. She spoke in casual English, "Oh, hi, soldier, come on in. We've been expecting you."

The girl, Nini, called to her father. When F. C. came into the room, Giles started to introduce himself. F. C. interrupted. "I know. You are the marine from Chattanooga. Our friend told us. We were hoping you'd come."

Grace was ill and unable to meet Giles Brooks the day he knocked on the Lius' door. But F. C. invited him back for dinner later in the week and told him to bring some other G.I.s. The Lius had little food or money so F. C. invited other Chinese who could help entertain the G.Is. Soon Giles and his buddies were frequent guests and there were many celebrations.

Before Giles Brooks's news of Grace's survival reached Chattanooga, another American also found Grace. Lloyd Hindman, chaplain for the U.S. squadrons entering China, had received a letter from Mary McCallie Ware, Grace's cousin who had fled China when the Japanese attacked in 1937. Mary asked her friend from the Navy to find out if her cousin survived. He asked at the YMCA if anyone knew her. According to Grace, the first person he asked was a friend of hers. Chaplain Hindman soon tracked down Grace's family and sent the following description to Mary on October 24, 1945:

Mrs. Liu has lost a great deal of weight, but other than that is in good health. She weighs only eighty-six pounds. She escaped being interned in a concentration camp by some miracle and was able to be with her family during all these years of Japanese occupation. Mr. Liu was fired from his job in 1941 due to the pro-Japanese interests at the head of the local water works. However, they have been able to live in a small apartment in the ex-British concession.

Their children are precious. Ju-lan, the eldest, is twelve years of age; Ellen is eight years of age; and the baby, Wei-han (William) is four years of age. The girls bear a strong family resemblance to Mary's people and the little boy looks more like his father.

Hindman wrote that the Lius were thrilled to have contact with someone who knew the family. Then he suggested to Mary "that the women in your family get together and send some clothes over, as the Lius are wearing the same clothes they had four years ago."

Before either of these chance meetings occurred, Grace had tried to contact her family but failed. In early September, when the first rescue team parachuted into Peking and came down to Tientsin by train, Grace received a notice that letters could go by air via the Swiss Embassy in Peking. She sat down immediately to write, and her letter was in the Swiss Consulate that afternoon. She waited but never heard anything back.

When Giles arrived, Grace wrote again. Giles sent her letter by the Marine Corps post. He addressed it to his mother in Chattanooga and asked her to deliver it to Grace's brother Tom. But Tom no longer lived in Chattanooga. Mrs. Giles found another "Divine" in the phone book and called him. Grace's brother, Sam, was so excited to hear that his sister was alive that he called the local newspaper before contacting Tom. The *Chattanooga News-Free Press* carried the headline: MARINE FINDS EX-LOCAL WOMAN GIVEN UP AS DEAD BY FAMILY.

Grace's letter was the first word the family had from her since Pearl Harbor Day.

November 20, 1945

Dear Tom,

Four years is a long time and if I tried to tell only a part
of what we've been through since I last wrote I would fill a
book. I will say right away that we suffered none of the
horrors that went on in other places. Tientsin was lucky and
was, to the last, one of the best places to live. In '42 we still
had some of our own money and the cost of living hadn't
yet become so impossibly high. But 1943–44 were the
worst years for us. We didn't have any money and with eggs
$140 apiece, milk $100 a glass, and butter $6000 a lb., you
can see we had to do without many things. For a large part
of the time there was no fruit at all or it was too expensive
to think of. For instance, one apple cost $100. The two
years '43–44 are like a nightmare in my mind, of cold, never
quite enough to eat, sickness, and such weariness that I
didn't know a person could be so tired and keep on living.

In January '45, I applied through the Swiss Consulate for
relief for myself and the three children, and from January
through September that practically saved our lives.

During the first month of the war, I lost twenty pounds,
and not only never gained it back but kept on losing. In '44 I
weighed seventy-nine. Now I weigh eighty-six, and for the
last nine or ten months I have felt much better and stronger
but I look awful! F. C. is well but he looks much older.

In a later letter, Grace explained what happened after the Japanese came into the concession.

In 1941 just before Pearl Harbor, F. C. was fired from the
Water Co. by the pro-Japanese management for refusing to
cooperate with them, and also because he had an American
wife. They said it didn't look good to the Japanese to have a
chief engineer with an American wife. Homer Lu, the
former managing director, had been replaced by two
managers who collaborated with the Japanese, Ray Chang
and Franklyn Koo. They came with a group of Japanese up
into our apartment in January 1942, and ordered us out of
the place. Mr. Chang and Mr. Koo led the Japanese into my

bedroom where I was putting Wei-han (then eight months old) to bed. The Japanese advisor wanted to see what of our furniture to take. We had to let go whatever he wanted. Mr. Koo told him that my beautiful Mongolian rug was company property. Those two men, Chang and Koo, sold or gave company shares to the puppet government [so that they could] live in luxury during these last five years.

They starved the workmen and held them down with the Japanese gendarmeries. Ray Chang informed the Japanese on Homer Lu, who had been his best friend, but when the gendarmerie went to take Homer they went at first to his concubine's house by mistake. She cried and carried on, allowing him to escape by a scant half hour. He has fled to the interior.

In 1941 they [had] tried every inducement to get F. C. to throw in his lot with them. When he refused and told them in a very plainspoken way what he thought of them in a letter to the Board of Directors, they fired him, with all the humiliating trimmings they could think up. They put up huge signs in every company office, trying to blacken his character and humiliate him.

A delegation of workmen came to F. C. and wanted to strike. Some wanted to assassinate Chang and Koo. F. C. calmed them down and reminded them that we were completely in the power of the Japanese and to fight and protest was worse than useless. They actually cried and one huge foreman, about six feet three and a few hundred pounds, just wept out loud. All the workmen and all the staff were intensely loyal to F. C. When we left the company, Chang and Koo refused to give us F. C.'s savings. Finally the Japanese advisor made them give him about one-half the amount. It was the Chinese traitors who fired him, not the Japanese.

In early 1942, all foreigners in Tientsin had been told to move into the British concession. By the end of February, they were required to register and wear armbands identifying the nationality of the wearer. Whenever Grace went out, she wore the red armband with a black circle around the bold, black Chinese character for "America."

On March 28, 1942, during a sweeping dust storm, the British concession was handed back to China. In a formal ceremony in which the howling wind drowned out any words spoken, the Chinese collaborators, under the supervision of their Japanese leaders, formally accepted the territory for China. By mid-August the remaining foreign diplomats and other professionals were loaded onto trains and sent to Nanking, and from there shipped out of the country. A short time later, all foreign residents still remaining were rounded up and sent to an internment camp in Wei Hsien, Shandong province. In the course of a year, Japan had successfully orchestrated the ouster of all foreign residents from China—that is, all but the Japanese.

Grace's letter of November 20, 1945, continues:

It just happened by a lucky chance that I was not sent to "Wei Hsien," the concentration camp for allied civilians. In 1942 all "enemy nationals" registered with the Swiss and Swedish consulates. As we did not need relief at that time, I did not register with them. And that saved me, for it was from those consulate lists that the Japanese Consulate took the names of the people to be sent to the camp. I registered four times with the military, but they did not have charge of sending civilians to camp. I knew that I had been really "miraculously" overlooked, because with all their spies they usually knew everything.

I was so scared that they would see that I was there and that I hadn't been sent to a concentration camp that they would gather me up and send me. I was afraid to be seen on the street. So I just went into hiding. For one year and a half I never went outside our door except at night, disguised as a Chinese. I would cover my head with a black scarf and dress in Chinese clothes. Nini went with me. She would stop at each corner and check to see if it was safe. We went to see my friend who had T.B. and her daughter who was Nini's best friend.

. . . 1942 was one of the coldest winters I remember. We had to move out of our comfortable and warm apartment over the Water Works into a huge barn of a place. It was so huge we rattled around in it and when the wind blew, everything rattled. It was impossible to heat and we all nearly froze. It was the only place we could get because it belonged to Homer Lu. His concubine rented it to us and to my friend Mrs. Holmberg. Her daughter, Dorothy, came back from Denmark after her father died there in 1939. Mrs. Holmberg was just recovering from T.B., but her husband's death, the war, and troubles in Denmark, brought it all back. She coughed all the time and her voice was hoarse.

The children and I had flu and bronchitis for the rest of the winter. Willy was so sick that I carried him all the time. I tried to sing him to sleep in my arms, but I developed rheumatism such that I couldn't lift my arms. It lasted all winter.

In the summer we were lucky enough to find a very nice little apartment on Colombo Road. We live there still. It is divided into two flats; we live on the bottom and Mrs. Holmberg and Dorothy live above us. It is very easy to heat when there's any coal. Coal became so scarce that during last winter ('44–45) it practically disappeared, except a very little for cooking, at $100,000 a ton. Living through a North China winter in a house with no heating is something I don't like to remember. We wore padded Chinese clothes—long pants, gowns, shoes—everything padded. I wore a fur coat on top of that even in the house. And we never had any hot water. Our stove never got hot enough to heat the tank. Soap, even the worst, and it was all bad, cost around $200 a cake. So you can imagine how clean we were. Just about like the Mongols.

Our own money was gone by the end of 1942. It was impossible for F. C. to get any work unless he worked for the Japanese which, of course, we never considered for a moment. Later on, near the end of the war, he was able to get work with a conservation bureau, but up till then there was nothing to do but borrow where and what we could. We had some awfully good friends. Most of our friends though had gone to the interior. Of course, F. C. couldn't go and leave me and the children, not knowing what the Japanese might do to us. If my face were not so long and

my nose so big, I might have gotten by, but there was no
disguising my face!

There was no such thing as being careful with our diet.
We had to eat whatever we could get. The cook had left
because we could not pay him and there was no food.
Sometimes I tried to cook but I wasn't strong enough. If I
tired to do any kind of work that made me too tired
I started running a temperature and had to go to bed. I was
so afraid of getting T.B., because there was much of it here.
We ground whole wheat and boiled it into porridge. We ate
a lot of that. The flour was rancid but we ate it anyway,
even with bugs in it. The children discovered that wild
wheat grew in the field behind the house and Ellen got sick
from eating too much.

F. C. and the children stood it all physically much better
than I did. I just held on by the skin of my teeth. I began
losing my hair. Last year in the spring my eyes just went to
pieces, I think from lack of proper nourishment and
vitamins. I couldn't read a word for three months and had
to keep my eyes bandaged for several hours a day. I
steamed liver in a jar and drank the juice with ginseng. It
tasted like something the donkey made, but when I began
taking that liver tonic and liver pills, my eyes got all right
and I felt better in every way.

There were many epidemics of cholera, typhoid, and
typhus. The children came through it all surprisingly well.
They all had whooping cough at the same time. It
developed into serious asthma for Nini. Last spring Nini had
jaundice and an operation for chronic appendicitis. Willy
had measles. Last year Ellen had typhoid for seven weeks.
One day she went with amah to get the rationed grain. It
was hot and they had to wait in the heat for a long time
while numbers were called out. Ellen complained of a
headache and wanted to go back home but amah would not
let her leave. When she came back, she went straight to bed.
I knew something was wrong then. She had a fever and was
delirious. I was so weak during that time, I usually slept with
her. We had no particular medicine. When I tried to brush
her hair, her hair began to fall out and I had to cut it short.

A letter, written in Nini's own hand (errors are included), provides a rarely seen view of the war and Japanese occupation in China from a child's perspective. Nini's letter was sent to her American cousin, Elinor Divine (Tom's daughter) and is dated May 1946.

I am 13 year old, but I don't know what grade I am in, because I went to the Tientsin American school till the 3rd grade. Then in 1940 there was no more American school. Then I went to a French convent school. Then in 1942 the Japs made us move to the British concession. Then I went to a chinese school. I had never been to a chinese school before, so I went to the 2 grade. Now I am in the 6 grade. I am not in school now. I stoped in June 1945. I will go back next term. At that time all the schools were so dirty and full of flies and in the winter there was no heat besides 90 percent of the children had T.B. 5 of my classmates have already died of it.

All we learned was Japanese propaganda. They told us that the Americans were trying to invade china and make all the chinese into slaves. So Japan had sent her Army and Navy to help china because Japan like the chinese so much; and the Americans were so bad, oh dear, the Americans loved to cut off children's heads off and some of the Americans had two horns and oh yes the Japanese were our brothers. Oh they told such funny stories most of the stories sounded like fairy tales. We had to lea[r]n Japanese we all dint like it, so we all flunked in it, and the teacher dint care if we passed or not.

⌁

THE ONLY OFFICIAL news the Lius had during the occupation was the *Peking Chronicle*, a Japanese-controlled newspaper. It reported the Japanese victories which came in rapid succession—Guam, Wake, Hong Kong, and then Singapore. A large sign posted on the Empire Theatre read: SINGAPORE HAS SURRENDERED! The devastating news of Allied defeats was blasted from loudspeakers with strident militaristic music. Grace threw the newspaper down and stomped on it, yelling that it was lying. She never lost hope of the eventual Allied victory, but the wait seemed so endlessly long. The only scraps of hopeful news she could get were over somebody's hidden radio. News of the victory at Midway spread rapidly from person to person.

Likewise, the "grapevine" was the usual means of hearing what was happening inside China. News of anti-Japanese activities in the countryside was smuggled like contraband into the city. Occasional fire between Japanese and the Communist Eighth Route Army could be heard just outside the city. Friends came by and brought word or F. C. took walks and spoke with others. In this way, the Lius were never completely cut off.

In 1944 Grace began teaching English in her home for income. Students were plentiful because the Japanese did not allow English to be taught in the schools. Most of her students were school-age but some were professionals or housewives who wanted to keep up their skills. She taught seven or eight hours a day when her strength permitted. Several of Grace's pupils, high school and college boys, escaped to the interior and joined the resistance.

Another young man of whom Grace was particularly fond came to the Lius frequently. When he discovered that Grace had been an opera singer, he asked her to teach him. Using the techniques that Franz Proschowsky had taught her, she had some success at coaching the hopeful tenor. Even during the occupation, music could transform her life. With a record of *La Bohème* playing on the Victrola, they sang together in their own cold garret, of Mimi, a sick girl, and her Bohemian lover Rudolfo. William's earliest memory is hearing his mother sing with her student: "I remember him singing 'Your tiny hand's so cold' while the Victrola played. I was three or four years old and I danced while they sang."

Dancing and singing were revived after the G.I.s came. Grace's letter of November 20, 1945 concludes:

//

Since the marines came we have been having a
marvelous time. They all looked positively beautiful to us
after the occupation. How happy we were to see Giles
Brooks from home! We have enjoyed him and his friends
more than we could tell, and they have kept us supplied
with candy, chewing gum, cheese, Woodbury Soap, tomato
and grapefruit juice, and things we haven't seen for years.
And how F. C. has enjoyed Camels, Chesterfields, cigars,
and Edgeworth pipe tobacco, after years of smoking what
smelled like burnt peanut shells and incense. There are
about six boys that we know best and they have met and
been entertained in the homes of several of our Chinese
friends. They are making a pleasing impression on the
Chinese. I am very proud of these nice American boys.
Giles is very popular and gets along with everyone—men,
women, and children—and the way he is picking up
Chinese is amazing.

   I must stop before this letter gets too big. There are so
many, many things I could write! I am trying to give you
just a very general idea of what our situation was like, but
you can be sure that we did not see the horrors of the
occupation other people did. Remember I have heard
nothing from any of you since 1941. Please make
everybody write and tell me all that's happened.

   With all my love to all of you,

                          Grace

   Sam was the first to write back. When Grace received his letter,
she was just sitting down to lunch: "I was so excited and my heart
beat so fast I could hardly open it. But when I had finished reading
it aloud to F.C., all appetite for lunch had vanished." After four
years of silence, the news from home was both thrilling and dis-
turbing. One brother had died, another had become a war hero,
and a third had moved away. Grace had addressed her first letter
after the war to Tom because she thought he was the most likely of
her brothers to still be in the same place. But during the war, Tom
had been transferred by his employer to Oak Ridge, Tennessee,
about twenty miles from Knoxville. It was not known until after the

war that Oak Ridge was part of the Manhattan Project, a top-secret operation to build the atomic bomb.

The scope of the surrender was enormous. There were three million military and civilian Japanese in China. The Nationalist government was unprepared for reoccupying the vast country and had no means of moving personnel rapidly to fill positions vacated by the Japanese. The U.S. army flew Chinese commanders to sites to receive the surrender of the Japanese officers, but it took much longer for civilians to return. The management of utilities, banks, trains, and other essential organizations had to wait. Those assigned to leadership positions were chosen politically whether or not they had the necessary skills or knowledge. Often the same manager who had collaborated with the Japanese was retained. As the populace waited, shortages increased and inflation spiraled with two currencies in use.

By the time Grace wrote Sam back, her situation had improved. Both she and F. C. had jobs; her cook and amah had returned, and food was available again, especially with supplies from Giles. Grace described the conditions in post-war China when she wrote to Sam on December 11, 1945:

Everything is in an awful mess. The new Mayor sent from Chungking is incompetent and stupid and too much like the old-time Chinese official. There are millions of necessary things to be done quickly and nothing is done but the silliest things such as turning some old temple into a memorial. And they have conference after conference and nothing is done but talk, talk, talk. F. C. simply can't stand that sort of thing. He is so practical and direct. He is a doer rather than a talker. I don't know how long he will stand it before he blows up. He is working for the Municipal Bureau of Sanitary Engineering now. In the Water Co. he was more or less his own boss so he is not used to waiting until some impractical official decides every little matter.

We are now waiting for Homer Lu, the legitimate managing director, to come back from the interior and take the Water Co. over from the traitors who still have control of it. Then F. C. will be managing director and chief engineer.

I have a job, too. I have been working for about two weeks at the Tientsin Transportation and Warehousing Bureau of the Chinese National Relief and Rehabilitation Administration (CNRRA). You know UNRRA, of course, the United Nations Relief and Rehabilitation Administration. The foods, medicines, and materials given China by UNRRA are distributed by CNRRA. I am English secretary to the directors and English advisor to the rest of the bureau. All the English communications go through my hands, and none leave until they have been okayed by me. I write all the important letters myself; those written by someone else I look over and correct. All of the corrected drafts of letters must have my signature before the Director will sign the typewritten copy to be sent out. Besides the letters I write a summary of letters, cables, telegrams, and reports to be translated into Chinese.

Dorothy Holmberg, the daughter of Mrs. Holmberg, who is very ill with T.B., is working with me. She is the stenographer and typist. Our boss, the director of the bureau, is a Tsing Hua (F. C.'s school) graduate of 1923. His English is not so very bad, neither is it at all good. So when he dictates to Dorothy in his Chinese-English I have to rewrite the letter in correct English. Then Dorothy types it. It's quite interesting and not hard, and I certainly like it a great deal better than teaching. It gives me a feeling of independence and importance that I really enjoy. But I don't feel good about leaving the children all day. With the cook and both amahs back, the children aren't neglected. I go home by "san-leur" (three-wheeled rickshaw) and see them at lunchtime. But sometimes I feel guilty about leaving them.

Nini is quite a big girl now. She lacks about an inch of being as tall as I and is a great deal fatter. She looks very much like F. C. but she also has a McCallie look. Ellen is eight now. She looks more like me. But she is a hundred times better-looking than I ever was. She is really beautiful. F. C. says she looks like Mama. To my mind William looks like you [her brother Sam], although he looks distinctly Chinese with very black hair and almost black eyes. When he is well and plump he is a very good-looking little boy, but when he is thin, his ears look too big. The marines call him "Mickey Mouse."

Prices are so high now (higher than during the war) that although F. C. and I are both working we can no more than make ends meet. I will get $50,000 C.N.C.—that's $250,000 F.R.B. F. C. will get a little more maybe from the municipal job. Together we will have around a half million F.R.B. With that we can pay servants, house rent, food, milk, butter ($7,000 per lb.), but no clothes and no coal. Coal is nearly $100,000 a ton.

Nini's clothes have been handed down to Ellen and Wei-han. Mine has gone to Nini and she has long ago worn out and outgrown my things. Nini has grown so fast I had to get her something the other day. The material for a Chinese padded gown and three yards of cotton coolie cloth to make a gown to wear over it cost me $50,000. The tailor would have been another $10,000, but one amah sews very well so she made them. She also has made padded shoes for the three children.

All these years during the winter I wore Chinese clothes, but now in the office I wear a knitted suit from 1940. It is absolutely the only thing I have left. I will be very, very pleased to get anybody's used clothes whether they fit or not. The Chinese tailors are very clever about making over old things. Everything we have has been made over out of something else.

The conflict between the Nationalists and Communists, despite the temporary wartime united front, had not abated. From August to October 1945, the United States tried to mediate a settlement between the two sides, even bringing Mao Tse-tung and Chiang Kai-shek face to face, but with no success. In December 1945, President Truman sent his top negotiator, General George C. Marshall. In response to his leadership, both sides agreed to a cease-fire. A political consultative conference was convened in January 1946 in Nanking. Both sides sent high-level representatives. In addition to the Kuomintang and the Communist Party, other parties present included the Youth League, which had demonstrated for peaceful reconstruction, and the Democratic League, which advocated a centrist position of democratic reforms. The conference met January 11–31 and was widely reported in the national and inter national press. Basic terms were agreed upon: constitutional government, unified military, national assembly, and reduction of troops. Momentarily there was a glimmer of hope for China's future without civil war.

During this time, food prices rose daily with no central government to hold them at a reasonable rate. Prices increased fivefold between September 1945 and February 1946. The government response was to print more money, causing prices to skyrocket by May.

Grace was referring to the political conference when she wrote to Mary Hills, on March 8, 1946:

> We're all glad they've come to some agreement. That is China's only hope. I am not a Communist and never could be, but the Kuomintang party is so corrupt that there would be no hope for China if it stayed in complete control of the present government.
>
> The food is not so bad now. We are getting plenty of very good eggs for two hundred dollars apiece. Meat, beef and pork, is plentiful at $2,600 F.R.B. a pound. Carrots, spinach, beets, Chinese cabbage, and onions are about the only vegetables. There's UNRRA flour on the market, so the bread is quite good again. Fruit is scarce and terribly expensive. The other day I paid $11,000 for four small Japanese oranges. $11,000 F.R.B. is somewhere around $1.25 U.S. Lately I have been buying black market grapefruit juice, pineapple juice, and tomato juice. It is only $5,000 or $6,000 a can and is much cheaper than buying the fruit I think our diet has been greatly deficient in vitamin C. Not long ago Ellen and Wei-han had a fever with swollen glands and red and bleeding gums. They got well when I gave them grapefruit, pineapple, and tomato juice.
>
> Nearly every day some boys would drop in for lunch or supper. We spent every cent we could get hold of on food. Maybe it wasn't exactly sensible, but F. C. felt the same way

I did. He never cared how many came or what it cost. He always said, "Never mind, I'll get some money somewhere." And he did. We have some very good friends who have a great deal of money. I think F. C. used to tell them that it was their duty to help entertain China's allies!

Those boys had been in the Islands so long eating out of tins that anything fresh tasted wonderful. And I always had lots of vegetables and salad. You should see those boys eat carrots and spinach! They kept me pretty well supplied with coffee and sugar, and canned milk and cocoa, and they would bring the cokes along. That was just too expensive for me.

With the United States troops present, not only was there food, drink, and parties, but Grace was singing again:

> Besides my own parties we were invited to many others. The last one we went to was a dinner dance given by the American University Club. It was held in the Astor House ballroom. General Rockey, General Worton, General Woods, and many other Marine officers were guests of honor. I sang "Carry Me Back to Old Virginny" impromptu! Paul Young, the UNRRA Director, was Master of Ceremonies and practically forced me to do it. I hadn't sung a note for several years, but he insisted so that it would have been embarrassing for me to continue refusing. There was a microphone and loudspeaker so it wasn't too bad.
>
> We entertained nearly as many officers as we did boys, and quite often had them together. One night we came home from a dinner at the Banker's Club and brought a major and a lieutenant home with us. When we went into the living room there was one of the boys stretched out in a big chair sound asleep. He got up rubbing his eyes but not the least embarrassed over the "brass." A few minutes later a Private First Class came "busting" into the room with "Hi folks." They were soon all good pals.
>
> Our apartment is small but very convenient for entertaining. The living room and dining room are together in one long room, and between the dining end and living end is quite a good-sized space for dancing. In 1941 we had

a lot of beautiful things, nice carved Chinese furniture, bowls, vases, tapestries, etc., but what the Japanese didn't take the children have broken up, especially Wei-han. He is terribly hard on furniture.

Mrs. Holmberg and Dorothy live in the apartment above us. We moved here in 1942 and she has been in bed with T.B. for the last three years. She is not expected to live out the winter. A friend of mine died of it last spring. Two of F. C.'s friends died the year before. When people get T.B. here, they very rarely recover. Dorothy is twenty-three now and is getting married next week to a very nice young man in the Danish Consulate. Dorothy is exceedingly attractive. A Marine chaplain is going to marry them.

I simply must go back to visit all of you before much more time rolls on. The intention is firmly fixed in my mind, and I have hopes!

With love to everybody,

Grace

But Grace's intention to go home for a visit was not soon to be realized.

Passport photo, 1946, taken in anticipation of a visit home that was delayed for nearly thirty years.

點水萍綠福牽風荇帶長落

紅吹不定幽趣在豪梁

SEVEN

THE FIRST MONTHS after the war were exhilarating. Letters and packages poured from Tennessee to Tientsin. But it was also a difficult time. Grace's eyes had been opened. The protected boundaries of her former life, which had once kept her separate from China's fate, had eroded during the occupation. She now saw China in a way that most foreigners did not. The story she had to tell was not one that the folks at home or the rest of the Western world, for that matter, wanted to hear.

"People then didn't want to hear what they didn't want to hear," was Grace's comment about the news correspondents that came to China to report on the conditions of the Far East.

One of those reporters, the young Seymour Topping, later became managing editor of the *New York Times*. When the young reporter arrived in Tientsin in 1946, he was invited to her home with a group of marines and other guests. "Oh, he made me so mad," Grace recalled in an interview. "He came to dinner and was asking everybody all sorts of questions. After he asked me a few questions, I could tell he didn't like the answers. He didn't say he didn't like them, but I saw that he didn't listen to what I said. I tried to tell him about the goings-on, what it had been like and what it was still like. He would turn and talk to someone else. He simply wouldn't listen, so I just shut up."

Years later Grace read Topping's book, *Journey Between Two Chinas*: "I didn't agree with everything he said, but he said it in such a way that I could accept his point of view. I wrote to him all the things I liked about it. I reminded him of our earlier encounter in China in '46. I said that I thought he was very arrogant and pigheaded because he wouldn't listen to me. But I read his book twice and think he did a wonderful job, and he wrote me back a very nice letter."

Beginning on April 9, 1946, Grace wrote three letters in a row over a ten-day period to her brother Sam. She was unable to mail the first two before some upsetting things began to happen to F. C., which she described in the third letter and mailed them all together. She typed the letters at work on CNRRA stationery. When she started the first letter, the dinner parties were still in full swing. One hilarious episode was described to her brother, whom she knew would enjoy the humor of it. She was planning a dinner party for Major Snell, a Sanitary Engineer sent by the Army through UNRRA to work with F. C. on the sanitation problems of the city. She didn't get off work until six o'clock so she and Sun, the cook, had planned a simple buffet supper that could be prepared ahead.

> But everything refused to go according to schedule—the stove wouldn't work, and the coal wouldn't burn. Sun's bicycle broke and he had to market on foot. So I left the office early and hurried home to help. We were having potato salad with celery, carrots, and beets, salmon salad (the salmon was a gift of a Marine), meat loaf sandwiches,

bacon and lettuce sandwiches, cottage cheese and peanut sandwiches. I had ordered from the Victoria Cafe a lovely big cream cake, half-chocolate and half-white—It was beautifully decorated and tasted delicious. It cost $9,000 C.N.C., but that's cheaper than I could have made one, and what a lot of trouble it saved. We had American coffee and American sugar (also from the Marines).

When I got home I rushed like mad making the salmon salad, and oh yes, I forgot, the deviled eggs. Then I was going to mix some cocktails (very, very mild). I had some grapefruit juice, crushed pineapple, and about one-third of a bottle of gin (also presents).

But a little after six, a British couple came to call. They had been in the concentration camp at Wei Hsien and I hadn't seen them for several years, so of course, I had to drop everything and sit down and visit with them.

I prayed for F. C. to come quickly so I could dress and get all the last-minute things ready. He's very rarely later than six-thirty, but at seven he still hadn't come and the people wouldn't go and my supper guests were supposed to come between seven and seven-thirty. Finally when I was desperate I asked them to stay for supper. They had another engagement for the evening, so they gave up waiting for F. C. and left. But their staying so long had made me so nervous. I could do nothing right.

I mixed cocktails and dressed at the same time all over the house, one amah carrying my blouse, and the other putting on my shoes, while I poured the things together and mixed and stirred and tasted! I was already in a dither, and tasting the cocktails didn't make me any steadier. I am not used to drinking anything alcoholic, so I am easily influenced. Fortunately, all of the guests were late as well as F. C.

The party was quite a success and everybody had a good time, even the children and the dog and cat. Our flat is so small there's no place to stick the children away, so they are always underfoot.

Not only packages, but people from home made life constantly interesting.

Wednesday evening F. C. came home bringing a big six-foot, barn-door-shouldered boy. He said, "Here's another Marine from Chattanooga and he's graduated from McCallie School!" His name is Jimmie Lail, and he's only eighteen, although he weighs 192 lbs. He's a very nice, sweet boy. Sunday night F. C., Ju-lan, and I took him out to a Chinese restaurant to eat Chinese food for the first time.

Ju-lan and I had a very exciting time trying on the clothes. All the skirts and sweaters fit Nini perfectly. But I can wear the green-and-white-checked dress. It's a very good style for a very skinny person. It needs to be made tighter around the waist and the sleeves need to be shortened, but I couldn't wait to wear it so I just pinned it. How marvelous to have on something I haven't worn every day for the last five years! In fact, I have it on in the office now. I make all sorts of excuses to walk around the office to show it off. And I'm wearing it to a party tonight.

The party that night was at Homer Lu's mansion. Among his guests were high-ups in the Kuomintang government who were involved in resettling Tientsin. With one exception—a foreboding reference to F. C.'s health—Grace's letter, continued the next day, showed how much things had improved:

I went to a lovely party in the green-checked dress last night. Among the guests were the head of the Chinese Secret Service, who tends to the traitors, and Lieut. Gen. Yen of the 94th Army stationed in Tientsin. He brought a beautiful movie actress. After dinner she sang and I sang, and then there was dancing. I have danced so much since the Marines came that I am quite expert. I can tango, waltz, rumba, and most everything.

Last week I received a package containing a bottle of capsules. I don't know who sent it. The capsules are filled with a yellow powder which I think must contain vitamins. The bottle doesn't say what it is, just to take two after each meal. I have taken not half a bottle yet and I feel very much stronger and more energetic. Please tell whoever sent it to kindly send me some more. It's doing me so much good. I

was happy to get the wonderful Pet milk. It's been many a
year since I've seen that.

The children are getting along much better now. Ju-lan
is getting fat, and Ellen and Wei-han look brown and rosy.
But F. C. who all during that last four years never got sick,
now has developed some peculiar trouble. His left arm has
gotten weak and slightly numb and causes him a great deal
of annoyance.

My salary has been raised. I now get—at least, I got for
March—$97,000 CNC. That's around $50 U.S. For April I
will get $122,000 because the cost of living keeps going
steadily up. F. C. is still at the Sanitation Bureau. The Water
Works has not been taken over yet [with Kuomintang
management]. Our crooked mayor is holding everything
up. But it can't be very long now or there'll be no hot water
this summer.

About my coming home—of course you must know how
crazy I am to come, and as soon as possible. But F. C. must
get firmly established in the Water Works first, get a strong
hold on it, and the management firmly in his hands.
Anyway, I am determined not to wait too long to come. I
have my passport ready.

Please tell Mama or whoever to send me some more of
those capsules.

Homer Lu finally returned from the interior and resumed his
position at the Water Works. F. C. rejoined him there and negotiations began with the intent of merging the Tientsin Water Works
with the former British water company. However, the Tientsin government delayed in removing those who had collaborated with the
Japanese. This inaction outraged the local citizens who had suffered under these puppets. The reoccupation of the country was
taking place in a way that denied the suffering that had been
endured at their hands.

F. C. hoped that Homer Lu would set the situation straight, but
instead, Homer Lu delayed taking any action to clean house and
turned his back on F. C. Nini described Homer Lu's betrayal of F. C.
and Grace's outrage:

"When Homer Lu came back from Chungking, he sided with those who had collaborated with the Japanese against F. C. When my father became ill, Homer Lu did not come to see my father or show any concern. We had no savings and no money coming in so my father asked to borrow some from Homer Lu. Then, while my father was down, Homer Lu asked for the money back. My mother was so angry that she got the money from someone else, took it over to his house during a party and threw it in his face and called him a skunk."

Grace's third letter to Sam in April 1946 explained why the first two were not mailed earlier. Her husband's sudden failing health reflected the stress that the family and, indeed, the nation were undergoing.

April 19, 1946

Dear Sam,

I haven't had a chance to get this letter mailed yet. I've been so worried and busy for the last week I haven't had time to tend to it.

Earlier I mentioned F. C.'s arm. It has turned out to be more serious than we thought. Not only his arm, but his shoulder and neck muscles on the left side start jumping when he gets the least bit excited or upset. Fortunately his blood pressure is normal (110) otherwise it would be exceedingly dangerous. We have fine doctors. Three of them are very intimate friends and know our circumstances. One is a nerve specialist. They all agreed that he smokes entirely too much. And they all said no tobacco, no alcohol, no coffee, no tea, no irritating spices, hot peppers, etc. He has to have injections of Thiamine chloride (B_1) and other vitamins. The doctors say he must have a complete rest. He has been in bed a week now and his general condition is better. He looks more rested and his color is better. But he is very difficult to manage. He's so impatient. He's never been sick before and he doesn't know how to take it calmly and philosophically.

For the last two months he's been under a terrific nervous strain over this maddening, crooked Water Company business. If the mayor had been an honest official, and if Homer Lu hadn't been stupid and cowardly, one week could have seen the whole business finished. That's what everybody expected. But instead, this incomprehensible delay until a perfectly clear-cut, straightforward situation has become so muddied and ambiguous that the accuser has become the accused and the innocent has become guilty, so that finally a compromise must be effected.

Homer Lu is the former managing director appointed by the Government to take the Water Company from Ray Chang and Franklyn Koo, the two managers who collaborated with the Japanese and kicked F. C. out. They are the two who came personally with a group of Japanese up into our apartment in January '42, and ordered us out of the place. Naturally, everybody expected that when the Chinese National Government officials returned to Tientsin, people like that would be made very short work of. And they themselves expected it, too; but week after week passed by and nothing was done, giving the traitors time to take heart and get to the corrupt Kuomintang Government officials with their money and lavish entertainment.

Homer Lu has been back in Tientsin nearly two months. If he were a man of some character and courage, the situation would have been quickly settled. But he is too much the rich playboy with plenty of physical courage but no moral courage. By playing around and dilly-dallying because he hates to face a disagreeable task, he has given his enemies time to accuse him of corruption and using company funds. Fortunately, F. C. had saved at considerable risk a secret government document that proves Homer innocent of any misappropriation of company money.

However, Homer has had to compromise. The same corrupt directors are to stay on the Board, and Franklyn Koo is to keep his position of deputy managing director. The traitors are not only not being punished but are having their faces saved. And the mayor and director of public utilities will get a rake-off from both sides.

After four years of humiliation and poverty and suffering for the sake of a principle, to be still further humiliated by

being compelled to go back to work under Franklyn Koo
was more than F. C. could take calmly.

Sam, you can't imagine how corrupt the officials of the
National (Kuomintang) Government are—from the bottom
to the top, especially the top. The good men have no
chance.

A capable, honest, straightforward man is something to
be feared by the powers that be. Honesty is not the best
policy. Dishonesty definitely pays much better. Efficiency
gets you nowhere. In fact, to do things efficiently and with
expedition is bad form. It is much better to delay and beat
around the bush, to give everybody time to line his
pockets—that is everybody who is high up enough to have
access to the Government pocketbook.

And then there's the red tape! I know all Governments
are more or less bound up in red tape, but for really
expertly hampering all progress and completely
discouraging any initiative and ability, Chinese red tape
could make that of the Western governments commit
hari-kari for shame. I work in a Government office and I
know. Corruption, stupidity, inefficiency, and red tape
strangle every effort for the good of the people and the
country.

Lately I have read articles in the *Reader's Digest* and *Life* by
Congressman Judd, Henry Luce, and others whose names
I have forgotten. And when they praise what the
Kuomintang (Nationalist) government has done for China I
could laugh. The present government will never be
democratic. The Kuomintang officials who've been in
power so long do not believe in democracy. Chiang's "Blue
Shirts" are just like Hitler's "Brown Shirts," his secret police
just like the Gestapo.

The Kuomintang propaganda that is pouring from the
newspapers, movies, and radio now is sickeningly like the
Japanese and German propaganda we listened to for eight
years. The U.S. newspaper correspondents who come out
here and travel from place to place and stay a few days or a
few weeks or even a few years, never really see the true
picture. They are always on the outside and see only what
they are allowed to see. I am on the inside and know what I
am talking about.

I know of so many of F. C.'s friends—Tsing Hua
schoolmates, graduates of American universities—as well-
trained, capable, efficient a group of men as you could find
in any country in the world, that are held down in
mediocre positions because they would be a threat to those
in authority. The present government would prefer to
engage expensive foreign technicians than use the skills of
educated Chinese.

I saw it happen right here in our office [CNRRA]. Our
director was a capable and honest man with plenty of
common sense, who could have run this Bureau with some
degree of efficiency if he had been allowed to. But after two
weeks, he was demoted to deputy director from director.
No one knows why. And a stupid stickler for form and red
tape was put over him as director! He is probably some
government "big-shot's" nephew or cousin.

Consequently, our whole outfit is a joke. There are a
hundred people and five departments in the Bureau, and I
don't think anybody knows what's going on. In the
beginning, all English correspondence was kept together in
one file. But the director decided it would be better for each
department to keep whatever English letters concerned the
affairs of each; and as some letters refer to several
departments, nobody can decide where they belong.
Consequently, when a certain letter is wanted, the whole
office has to be turned upside down.

Personally I don't mind in the least running around all
over the place to track down a letter I have to answer. But it
certainly isn't efficient or the way an office should be run.
Not long ago, after hunting for a letter for two days, I went
to the director's office and told him he had better hire a
detective to run the letter down, that I had done my best
and I couldn't find it—he's such a stupid, pompous fool! I
have talked to him very straight several times about the
stupid time-wasting way the letters were handled, but it
doesn't do any good. He is very nice and polite to me, but
it just goes over his head and makes no impression. The
deputy director could run the place with half the people
and a hundred times the efficiency. So I don't bother about
it anymore. When a letter finally comes to me, I write it or
correct it and if it's three weeks late it's not my fault.

I think the United States will make a great mistake if they give too much money to help China without insisting upon and seeing to a complete revolution in the present National Government set-up. It is not democratic, doesn't want to be, and doesn't intend to be! It is completely in the grip of the Kuomintang party and the Kuomintang party is made up of and ruled by a certain class and type of Chinese, irrevocably hostile to any kind of true democracy. That type includes the big landowners, the big merchants, the militarists, and the old official type that ruled under the Manchus.

To them, a man's being capable, honest, and straightforward, and believing in methods that are not devious, circuitous, and obscure mark him as an enemy. There is no place in Chinese officialdom for the qualities one usually thinks of as admirable.

A smooth, charming social manner, a glib tongue, the knack of suavely turning one's coat, absolute unscrupulousness about pocketing high sums of other peoples' money, and above all, the ability to out-crook the other crooks—these are attributes that make for success. Sometimes an honest man, if he is stupid enough, can get by very well, as the cleverer crooks can use him.

These people who control the present Chinese National Government will fight for the old order, whereby they can continue to amass their great fortunes, with every means in their power.

That is the reason they are in such deadly fear of the Chinese Communists. That is why they hated the Communists worse than they did the Japanese, and kept 80,000 troops, that might have been fighting the Japs, blockading the Communist territory.

I am not a Communist. I don't want to see China become Communist. At least I haven't hitherto. But all during those years when we were so completely under the Japanese fist and so cut off from all communication with the outside world, the Pa Lu (Eighth Route Army) was our only comfort. We knew they were not far away. We often heard fighting, and many young high school and university boys threatened with conscription by the Japanese disappeared into the country and were helped to escape into Free China by the Pa Lu. Several of my own pupils escaped in that way.

All during the last four years we have have taken comfort in the thought that somebody was nearby fighting for us. The Communists held the countryside so that the Japanese could never get the firm hold on North China they had on Manchuria. And they had practically nothing to fight with. Their best and most modern equipment was what they had captured from the Japanese. They got none of the American supplies sent to China. They lived so poor, not only the soldiers but the officers, even their highest officials.

When you compare the way the high Kuomintang officials live with their huge fortunes safely locked up in foreign banks, their palaces and motor cars, their selfishness, corruption, and hypocrisy, with the simple hardworking life of the Communists, you can see how we think they have been very badly treated since the end of the war. They were given no face, allowed no credit for their eight years of fighting the Japanese. They were given no share in the victory. Their efforts and sacrifices were ignored. And Generalissimo Chiang asked for the Marines to come in and hold North China for the Kuomintang Government. They not only get no credit for all their years of fighting and no acknowledgement of their part in the war, but the Marines and the Nationalist Army actually used the Japanese to fight them and guard the railroads against them.

That is a disgrace to the Chinese government. I hope General Marshall will not be fooled by the Chinese charming manners and delicious food and lavish entertainment that is dished out to him.

I just now looked at the clock. It's time to go home. I certainly did not intend to write a whole letter on Chinese politics; but I had nothing to do in the office this afternoon and as I was rather steamed up over this question I just took it out on you. I could write pages and pages more. I wish I were an American newspaper woman for a while and knew all I know.

The presence of the Americans, which should have helped the situation, was actually making it worse. In order not to bolster the Communists, the U.S. forces often backed up the Chinese who had collaborated with the Japanese. Grace read in the newspaper that one of the collaborators who had taken over the Water Works and kicked F. C. out was being placed in a position of leadership over the whole city. She could tolerate it no longer. In an interview years later, she recalled:

> I got so mad I didn't know what to do. So I went to the American Consulate and told the American Consul that I knew that man, that I had known him a long time, and knew he was a Japanese puppet, and I did not think it right that the Chinese people should be placed under such a person.
>
> He replied apologetically, "Well, those things happen. Even in Europe, they had to use puppets . . . and well, what can we do? This is a matter of the internal affairs of the Chinese. As Americans we have no right simply to say what they should do."
>
> I said, "Well, you know quite well, Mr. _____ that whatever you say goes. That if you tell this minister, they have to do it. You cannot fool me if you say, 'Oh, now it's the Chinese and they have to do as they please; we have nothing to say.' I know that's not so!"
>
> "Well, we . . ." he hemmed and hawed. He said he didn't want to interfere in the city; it would get him in trouble.
>
> And I said, "All right. I don't want to get anyone into trouble. But I'm not going to put up with this. I'm an American citizen and I know some people in Washington and I will write to them. I will write to Washington and I will complain. I will say what's going on here!"
>
> "No, no, no, no. Don't do that. Don't do that. No, no. That's . . . that's . . . we'll think it over, and we'll work it out somehow or other," he stammered.
>
> I replied, "Well, I don't mind writing at all!" and I left.
>
> Then I saw a few days later in the paper that Mr. Chang had been replaced by someone, maybe just as bad—but I had won my point.
>
> One of the young men working in the consulate later told me, "I remember so well you laying down the law to the Consul General . . . We could hear you all over

the place. The rooms had only temporary partitions so
the whole office could hear. Everyone stopped and
listened and were just about to die laughing."
    I was stunned for I had no idea anyone had heard me.

By August 1946, the agreements reached in the consultative conference earlier in the year had come to naught. General Marshall
succeeded in getting both sides to agree to another cease-fire, but
Chiang Kai-shek prepared to attack Communist troops in Manchuria while the Communists reorganized their forces. Both sides
were preparing to fight, not talk.

At the same time, popular Chinese sentiment turned against the
American presence. In Tientsin, student demonstrators protested
against the American armed forces after an American G.I. raped a
young girl. Grace observed a difference in the G.I.s being sent to
China in 1947:

    The first combat troops that came into Tientsin knew
what they were fighting for. They just came from the
islands where they had been fighting the Japanese. But
they were taken out in December [1945] and sent home
and a new batch was sent in. They did that two or three
times. As new ones came in, they changed. They weren't
combat troops; they hadn't fought. They didn't know
really what the World War was about. They treated
China like a conquered country. They treated the
Chinese like the old colonialists had. So they got to be
very unpopular. At first, they were greeted like
liberators and welcomed, everybody entertained them.
They were more concerned about the condition of the
people. On the whole they were older men. But when
the later batch arrived, they were no longer liberating us
from the Japanese, instead they were holding off the
PLA [People's Liberation Army] so that the KMT could
come and take control. They were younger, new
recruits, and they didn't have a mutual rapport with the
people. They acted like conquerors.

There was a party given by one of F. C.'s classmates
after the KMT had come back. There were some
American officers there and some other Chinese. One of
these American officers began to talk about how the
Red Army hadn't done anything to help the KMT
during the war. I was so angry. I said, "That's not true at
all. The KMT ran away."

"They did not run away," he said. I told him that no
KMT army helped us in the Japanese occupation. The
Communists were the only ones who fought the
Japanese and he shouldn't be fighting them now. He
started saying that wasn't true. I replied, "You weren't
here, we were." It started getting very hot. We almost
had a fight, right there at the party. My husband was
getting angry, too. He turned absolutely white and I
thought we had better quit.

Grace let out her pent up rage in a letter home dated August 1,
1946:

Even for people with American money the cost of living
is exceedingly high. We are spending over one million
dollars C.N.C. a month. Apples are $13,000 a pound.
Prices are out of all reason, and there's no end in sight.
Politically and economically, China is in a hopeless mess.
Under the present government and its blind and selfish
leaders there is no hope.

And why should the American government back up with
military and financial help a political party and a system
that is crushing the Chinese people almost beyond
endurance? The corruption and selfish stupidity of this
present government are making it so impossible for anyone
not a clever crook to earn an adequate living—many are
being driven to suicide and Communism. If the government
were thoroughly cleaned out and the people given a chance
to live there would be no need to maintain huge armies to
fight the Communists, or to keep the American marines in
North China.

The government leaders are not fighting the
Communists patriotically, for the good of the country, or

for the sake of the poor people, but to save their power and colossal fortunes. . . . There I go! Rambling off into politics.

By August, school was approaching. Ellen was nine and had been to school only one year, due to the Japanese occupation, the disorganization of the schools, and the fact that she had typhoid the previous fall and was unable to start. She and William were only one grade apart and both started in Chinese schools. Grace wrote home about the worries of a parent:

> I am just now trying to find schools for the children to go to in September. It's not an easy matter. Ellen and Wei-han have never been to school and Ju-lan was out the last two years because the schools were so very bad during the war. About eighty percent of the pupils had T.B. Ju-lan will be ready for middle school this fall. That's about the same as high school. All the middle schools in the concessions are crowded and dirty, so we are thinking of sending her to the Keen School far in the Chinese City. It is a Chinese girls' school run by American missionaries. I know the principal and several of the other women. Most of the teachers are Chinese and even the American teachers teach in Chinese. It is a good place to get a Chinese education in an orderly clean environment. Many prominent Chinese send their daughters there. It is so far, though, that she will have to live in the school during the week and come home over weekends. At first, I didn't like the idea of her staying away from home at all. But F. C. is very much for it. He said he left home when he was twelve and it was good for him. Ju-lan herself is anxious to go. She is not the "mama's baby" I was. In fact, she is only like me in loving to read and being lazy and messy. She is independent, saucy, and somewhat belligerent. She loves mathematics and works arithmetic problems just for fun as one would work a crossword puzzle. And I still use my fingers to add!

After the war, F. C. resumed contact with his former classmates. In Grace's letter, she describes a surprise visit from one who had

served in Burma during the war and was now a general in the
Nationalist Army.

Last night we had a famous guest for dinner—Major
General Chia Yu Hui, the Vice-Commander of the Chinese
New First Army [KMT], that fought in Burma and India
and is now in Manchuria. General Chia is on furlough in
Peking, but he came down to Tientsin for two days to see
F. C. and me and the children. He is F. C.'s oldest and best
friend. They were together in the same class in school from
the time they were seven until they were twenty-two.
When they went to the States and General Chia went to
the University of California and F. C. went to Cornell they
were separated for the first time in over fourteen years.
General Chia later went to Harvard. I knew him in New
York. He is here very quietly. If the papers find out then he
must be entertained by the mayor and the commanders of
the 94th Army stationed here. So last night there was only
another Tsing Hua classmate and his wife for dinner besides
General Chia and my family.

But my boss, the director of our bureau who was
appointed by the government, heard he was here and
before we had settled ourselves at the table he came in with
his wife and concubines and five children. Fortunately they
had had their dinner, and some Chinese wine and coffee
kept them occupied until we finished. But with eight
children and four schoolmates who were together again for
the first time in ten years, and two Chinese women whose
tongues clacked like typewriters, it was not a very dignified
and orderly meal.

We had plum pudding for dessert—an American-canned
one procured by my cook from some mysterious place
where he occasionally gets other things that I don't inquire
too closely about. There was enough of the pudding for
everybody, even the unexpected guests. But I didn't have
enough cups and saucers and spoons. The neighbors were
called upon for help and the dinner came to a very
successful and satisfying end.

I don't suppose it is necessary to tell you that I am
just learning to type. I am using a U.S. Armed Forces

self-teaching manual. It's my ambition to become a good
typist in due time.

Meanwhile, the "hopeless mess" continued to deteriorate. On
August 10, 1946, President Truman wrote a letter to Chiang Kai-
shek informing him that his confidence was shaken: "A China dis-
united and torn by civil strife could not be considered realistically
as a proper place for American assistance." For the next six months
letters passed between Chiang, Chou, General Marshall, and President Truman but were followed with little action on either side for
conciliation.

By January 1947, General Marshall was forced to declare his
mission in China a failure. American troops were withdrawn. The
Chinese would have to fight it out themselves.

The Liu family, 1948. The last photo taken before the advent of the Communist era.

EIGHT

BY 1948 THE exodus had begun. Before the year was over, Grace, like many others in China, had to decide whether to leave or stay.

The conflict between the Nationalists and the Communists had been brewing for over twenty years, but after the removal of the Japanese and General Marshall's failure to create a coalition government, civil war broke out in earnest. On January 4, 1948, the writer of the "Week in Review" for the *New York Times* described the conditions that prevailed in China: "The military position of the Central Government has worsened to the point where the Nationalist Army appears to have lost the initiative on all major war fronts . . ."

Although numerically superior and better armed, the Nationalist forces became overextended as they pushed the Communists further into Manchuria. The Communists had primarily a pre-modern army, with no air force or navy of any kind, and equipped largely by weapons seized from the Japanese or retreating Nationalists. But they were mobile, highly committed, and suffered few losses. By 1948, the Nationalists forces had dwindled not only from defeats but also from massive defections. Gradually the Nationalist army lost support not only from its own ranks but from many civilians who once supported it—the intellectuals, professionals, students, and workers of the urban centers.

The conditions that Grace had described in her earlier letters grew worse. Inflation flared into fantastic proportions. One U.S. dollar brought $200,000 Chinese and the rate changed again in the course of an hour. In early January, after Grace completed a twelve-day stay in the hospital for a hemorrhoid operation, she was handed a bill for $15,000,000 C.N.C. She wrote her sister-in-law: "Sounds a lot doesn't it? But in C.N.C. it doesn't mean anything."

America threatened to withdraw aid if the national budget of $9 trillion in 1947 could not be contained. In January 1948 the Nationalist government projected a $90 trillion budget for only the first six months. One price control program after another was scuttled, until in November the government announced a new series of economic regulations based on "accepting inflation as a recognized fact."

The Chinese economy was collapsing while corruption, speculation, and profiteering were commonplace. Taking advantage of the general collapse of the Nationalist government, the Communist forces reorganized as the People's Liberation Army (PLA) and moved forward rapidly, attacking transportation and communication lines. They first established control in the rural areas, then gradually surrounded cities in North China.

Life for the Lius grew more difficult as the civil war intensified. Frustrated by the bureaucratic mismanagement of CNRRA, Grace had stopped working. When the Water Works managers posted accusations against F. C., he quit, and then was called back because so many other managerial personnel had left.

Likewise, school conditions deteriorated. With inflation changing the value of money daily, the schools required students to pay tuition with sacks of flour. On the first day of school, Ellen and William had to take a rickshaw in order to carry the sacks of flour. Facilities were inadequate and resources dwindled as the year progressed. Grace wrote in February 1948:

> Their school has practically no heating and in December and January the poor children had to sit in rooms of almost Arctic temperature. Their hands were so stiff they couldn't write. The teachers would take them out occasionally and run them around the block to limber them up a little. But they, the children, didn't seem to think anything of it. They've never known a nice warm comfortable schoolroom so they don't miss it. I am the one who suffers for them.

Mail was sporadic. Letters were lost, and boxes of relief sent from home never arrived. Instability in the postal service caused Christmas to be delayed until February.

February 19, 1948

Dear Mary Hills,

The box has finally arrived! We got the post office notice day before yesterday, and yesterday morning F. C. sent a man to get it. They, the post office, had broken the box almost entirely to pieces and opened every package. They wanted to confiscate the nylons but Mr. Wu, the man F. C. sent, had some influence and argued with them. They said if we could prove they were a gift and not for sale we could have them. Isn't that idiotic? I gave your letter in which you described the contents of the box to Mr. Wu and he let them read it. So F. C. brought home the spoils yesterday afternoon.

The children were terribly excited and when F. C. came in the door with the box they nearly knocked him down. I'm afraid I was almost as bad. Nini and I nearly had a fight over the nylons. We've decided to share them. They're a lovely color—all the stockings you can buy here are still the old light shades. The soap smells heavenly. I've seen it advertised in the magazines but I've never seen or smelled it in the "flesh" before—I washed my hair with the shampoo this morning and it's wonderful even in our hard, hard water. I have my hair rolled up now. We're going out to dinner tonight. I'm going to take a bath with the "heavenly" soap and I'll certainly feel like a glamour girl smelling so good!

F. C. and Wei-han and Ellen are running the little train round and round the coffee table. Wei-han is jumping up and down and they're all three screaming and yelling. The little thing really goes fast. Nini and Ellen were making dresses for the doll last night and Ellen has already put the puzzles together. They've chewed up all the chewing gum and are just now finishing the Life Savers.

As Grace thanked her American family for the Christmas presents, President Truman requested $570 million in aid for China. He stipulated that it was restricted to economic purposes, not military. The president's proposal was intended to mediate between the conflicting voices in American politics over the China problem. Previously, Secretary of State George C. Marshall had withheld support from the Nationalist Government until they "put their house in order" (report to House Foreign Affairs Committee). His stand had been opposed by the pro-Chiang Republicans in Congress. Marshall himself was seen as the chief stumbling block to all-out aid for China. But on February 21, 1948, Secretary Marshall reversed his stand and urged passage of Truman's request: "The rapid deterioration of China must be checked promptly for the world's good."

Former missionary-turned-ambassador to China, Leighton Stuart, had not given up hope for a unified approach. In a last desperate plea, he declared on February 22, 1948, that the "best possible solution is still a coalition government of the Kuomintang and Communists."

Two outspoken advocates for increased aid were Bullitt and Judd. William C. Bullitt was a former American ambassador to Russia. He saw China as the key to resisting Communist world conquest. On March 3, he accused the U.S. State Department of "blindness and apathy" and urged Congress to grant outright military aid to Chiang Kai-shek. Republican Congressman Judd, a former medical missionary in China, urged not only military aid but deployment of U.S. armed forces.

As the debate over aid to China was thrown into bitter partisan wrangling, Henry A. Wallace, a third-party candidate for president, running in 1948 against Democratic Truman (for restricted aid) and Republican Dewey (for all-out aid), announced that he opposed *any* U.S. aid to China: "U.S. intervention has already cost the American people four billion in dollars and the friendship of several hundred million Chinese people, victims of a civil war we prolong by our support of the dictator Chiang. . . . Sending money and military supplies to bolster reactionary governments against the will of their people serves the cause of reaction and war, not democracy and peace."

These political debates were well known to Grace from U.S. newspapers and magazines available in China. She wrote the following observations to her sister-in-law in her February 19th letter:

> I don't wonder that the average American is completely
> puzzled about the situation in China. When I read the
> things printed in American newspaper and magazines
> supposed to inform the American people of the truth of
> conditions, I wonder if the reports about different parts of
> Europe are as wrong or are interpreted as wrongly as those
> on China. Any investigator or fact finder who comes to
> China and is wined and dined and lavishly entertained by a
> certain party or clique naturally sees everything through
> the eyes of that party, unless they are very wise.
> I think General Marshall saw a lot of truth and that's
> why he is apparently holding off the aid to China. He
> knows too well where the aid would go and that no amount
> of foreign help can stop this civil war!
> Bullitt and Judd talk like crazy idiots. Maybe Judd is
> sincere and believes what he says, but Bullitt is just making
> a big noise to call attention to himself. All Chinese but the

one group are hoping and praying that not a cent of
American money will be forthcoming to help prolong the
war. A decent government is the only thing that would stop
it and that means the present government would have to be
completely wiped out from top to bottom, especially top.
The Chinese people have been sold down the river by the
worst bunch of big-time gangsters in the world. But they
are nearing their end.

What's coming after nobody knows, but the majority of
Chinese, and there's an awful lot of them, are on neither
side of this conflict so something may be worked out.

On March 30, 1948 the U.S. Senate approved $463 million in
aid for the Chinese Nationalist government.

Despite U.S. aid, by spring it was clear to those in China which
way the tide was turning. People associated with Chiang Kai-shek's
government made plans to exit. Others with wealth or property cal-
culated their risks. For the professional Chinese—those who had
committed themselves to China's future, those educated abroad, or
those married to foreigners—the decision was particularly poignant.
Nini summarized her father's quandary:

> F. C. was very patriotic. He believed in China. During the
> Japanese occupation when the Kuomintang collaborated with
> the Japanese and the Eighth Route Army [Communists] were
> the only ones actually fighting against the Japanese, he began
> to be disillusioned with the Kuomintang. The Kuomintang
> returned to power in late 1945 or early 1946. All those who
> had fled, like Homer Lu, returned and they took over every-
> thing. Those few years were just a mess, lots of inflation,
> money lost its value. Students began to strike.
>
> By the late 1940s F. C. was thoroughly disillusioned with
> them [KMT] and began to have sympathy with the Commu-
> nists. But nobody knew for sure what they would be like.
> There were underground rumors and occasional reports from
> occupied areas, but nothing was certain. American observers
> in the liberated areas often came to stay at our house and told
> us about the other side. They said things were very different,
> there was no corruption, people were working, there was land

reform—but of course, they always ended by saying, "but they're Communists . . ."

It got to a point where people like my father had to decide. They were professionals or intellectuals, unaffiliated, but it came to a choice and the only choice for patriotic Chinese was the Communists, even though people had many misgivings, doubts, and miseducation about them.

By the end of October 1948, the U.S. consulate sent letters to all Americans in the Tientsin and Peking areas stating, "As a result . . . of Chinese Government troops crushing defeat, the U.S. consulates in Peking and Tientsin advise all American residents with unessential duties leave while transportation facilities still are available." After receiving the letter, Grace went to see Sam Yeats, the U.S. Consul in Tientsin. William recalled his mother's conversation with F. C. when she returned, and a subsequent exchange with their longtime friend, Dorothy Holmberg:

> One day I had just finished my homework and was about to ask if I could go out to play when Nini suddenly shushed me and stopped me from speaking. I then noticed that Grace was talking to F. C. She had just come home from the American Consulate.
>
> "They told me it was time to leave, that everything would be arranged for our passage and that you would be guaranteed resettlement. But I said I had to discuss it with you. I know I don't want to be a refugee without you." Grace said.
>
> "It is impossible. If I leave now, no one is left to protect the Water Works. I have worked so hard to build it. I can't just leave it to ruin," F. C. said.
>
> I knew that my father had fought for the Water Works. But, now, the Kuomintang were fleeing, and he feared they would blow it up if he were not there.
>
> "But what will happen to the children?" Grace glanced over at us and we pretended not to notice.
>
> "We don't know what is in store for them, but this is their home. I don't believe that what is coming will be worse than what they've already been through."
>
> "Well, we survived the Japanese occupation . . ." Mother

didn't say any more but I knew she was not just thinking about the war but also the years after the war.

By the fall of '48, the exodus was in full swing. Many of my friends were leaving and there was a general feeling of uneasiness. Erika Ruas and her three sons left for France. Dorothy Holmberg, her husband, and their new baby came to say good-bye. Dorothy was in tears. The last time she had gone to Europe, her father had died. Her husband's company had agreed to transfer them to Japan instead. Dorothy was holding her baby tightly and cried as she said goodbye, "At least Japan is close. I will be so homesick."

"I know," Grace said sympathetically. So many of her longtime friends were leaving—in fact, almost all the people she had known since coming to China.

"Aren't you leaving, Grace?" Dorothy asked.

"F. C. and I have been talking about what to do. He feels he cannot leave, not now. We will stick it out."

"But, Grace, haven't you heard of the atrocities under the Communists!" Dorothy exclaimed. She had recently seen their former boss from the CNRRA, where they both had worked after the war. He had told Dorothy, and she repeated it to Grace that he was leaving with his wives and concubines because he had heard that the Communists would take all his property and divvy up his wives.

"Dorothy," Grace laughed. "The press has been saying such things for years. But think who is behind all that. And besides, unlike our previous boss, I don't have any property and F. C. has only one wife!"

For Grace the decision was not as simple as she made it seem to Dorothy. The air was electrified with anticipation. She, too, was gripped by fear and anxiety, intertwined with many layers of complex emotions. Her husband's decision to stay was clear. Her first commitment was to him, second to her children. If he felt he must stay, then she and the children would take the risk with him. But safety was not the only issue. For herself, she dreaded the thought of being a refugee more than anything else. While working for the CNRRA, she had seen the incredible desperation of families left homeless as a result of the displacement of war. She did not want to be one of them. Furthermore, returning to Tennessee as a refugee did not seem an option to her. What would happen to them there? She was determined not to be dependent on her American family for relief. She had survived a great deal and could survive even more.

Further, Grace had seen China suffer for so long. She hoped for China to rebuild itself, a dream she shared with her husband. It was a dream whose fulfillment had been thwarted many times and was still unfulfilled. If her husband must stay, then she wanted to see for herself what was going to happen.

BY LATE 1948 THE Communists controlled the North China countryside surrounding Tientsin and Peking. The Nationalist army withdrew hurriedly and in its retreat, destroyed property rather than leave it in Communist hands. The approaching Communist army distributed circulars to local citizens in advance of its arrival in Tientsin in order to allay fears of the remaining citizens. F. C. received the following notice at the Water Works:

November 1, 1948

TO EXECUTIVES, TECHNICIANS, AND LABORERS:

After the liberation of Manchuria, our armies will proceed to capture Tientsin and Peiping, which are already surrounded. The time for liberation of these cities draws near, so we should offer some advice with the hope that you accept it.

Oppressed by Chiang's government, the people cannot breathe. Industry cannot flourish. The people cannot make a living. We think you have endured much suffering. Those who care not for the welfare of the people will be despised by them.

Final victory will be to the armies of liberation together with the people. Within the past three years we have not only firmly maintained our liberated areas, but have enlarged them. We have formed our own government based upon democratic principles. Now Peiping and Tientsin are soon to be liberated. Do not fear. Do not depart. Do not allow lawless elements to commit acts of sabotage to installations. In obeying these precepts you will not only preserve the fruits of victory but will also have had a part in the revolution.

If factories are destroyed, the workers' means of livelihood are likewise destroyed. If you should find persons destroying property, advise them to cease. If they still do not desist, find out who their leaders are, keep the list of names, and we will punish them according to the provisions of 'martial law' first promulgated October 10, 1947, and reissued November 1, 1948, after we have entered the municipalities.

The dawn of the new day is near. Maintain your factories intact.

Further instructions were included and signed by Chu Teh (Zhu De), Commander in Chief, North China People's Army of Liberation and Peng Teh Hwai (Peng De Huai), deputy commander.

The story of the exodus is told by William from the perspective of a young boy:

The winter of 1948 was cold and dry. I was seven years old and was in Grade Two, which made me a veteran now, after the first traumatic year of entering primary school and dealing with the nickname of the "Big Nose Boy." Since I never liked to get to school early, I walked at a slow pace noticing everything along the way. Ellen, age eleven, had gone on ahead to meet her school friends.

The usual twenty-minute walk to school was dragging into half an hour. I first stopped in front of the big house across the street where the huge poplar trees were shuddering in the cold. The big tough leaves had already fallen and one could still find a few crammed in the corner where they had not been swept away. The dog wasn't barking and not a stir could be seen in the house. Well, Kong and his family have really left, I thought, remembering the times I had come here to play with my classmate under these trees. We pretended we were at sea in a pirate ship and the rustling of the poplar leaves providing the sound effects of the waves. Their silence now reminded me of the bewildering change that had been going on these past few months. Everybody had been in a stir.

"The Communists are coming!" Kong had said, his eyes as round as the black marble we used to fight over. Kong's father was a high-ranking official, with a wife and two concubines, one of which was Kong's mother. "My father says they will kill all of us, even the children."

I meandered up another block and came across the compound with four buildings forming a square with a six-foot wall around it. The usual hustle and bustle on this compound was muted, only a bored-looking servant at the gate. From time to time, I had been inside with Nini who often came to visit her friend. Those who lived here all belonged to the family of a Manchu prince, who came to Tientsin to live after the Emperor Pu Yi was driven from his palace in the early twenties. I wondered where they had gone. I did not ask but only nodded my head when the servant greeted me with: "Liu Shaoye (Young Master Liu) is going to school."

Then a few doors up was the home of one of Mother's best friends, Bertha, who was the widow of one of Homer Lu's brothers. We were always glad whenever Sun came in and announced that "Mistress Lu" had come to visit. Bertha was a warmhearted lady who giggled often and was dearly loved by our whole family. Now she was somewhere on the high seas. Mother could not see her off at the docks, so she had sent Sun to give Bertha two of Mother's lemon-meringue pies. Bertha also took with her two of our beautiful Persian kittens. I still had a difficult time imagining Aunt Bertha carrying two pies and two cats as she "fled" on a boat to Formosa [Taiwan].

A few more steps and I could see the Min Yuan Athletic Grounds. Something strange was happening there. I saw not the athletes marching in formations, with cheering crowds in the bleachers where Daddy took us nearly every Sunday

afternoon to see the soccer and baseball matches. Instead I
saw soldiers milling around and guards keeping any passersby
away from the various entrances to the grounds. Although I
was curious, it was getting late and I quickened my steps to
our school another block away.

"Wei-han! Wei-han! Over here!" Ellen, with her two classmates, was waving at me. They were standing on the edge of
a big crowd of students; none seemed to be going through the
gate of our school. As I approached them, I could see some
soldiers standing guard at the gate and many more soldiers on
the school ground, some even at the windows of the second
floor classroom.

"What's going on?" I asked in a hushed tone.

"Don't you know? They said that martial law has been
declared and our school has been requisitioned."

"What is martial law? What does it mean?" I asked, confused. I was scared by the presence of the soldiers and the
unfamiliar words.

"Stupid second grader," one of her friends taunted me.
"They are going to use our school as barracks to fight the
Communists. Schools will be closed and people are not
allowed to go out at night."

"What about school?"

I still could not understand what they were saying.

"Attention students! There will be no school today," one of
the teachers was shouting through a paper megaphone. "You will
be notified when school will start again. Please go home now."

In a daze, the children walked away in small groups quietly
and hesitantly, in sharp contrast to the usual exuberant caper
when they were free from school.

"Are you going home?" I asked Ellen.

"We might go to Wang's house. You better go home and
tell Ma what has happened."

Before I left, I turned around and took another look at the
school. How strange it looked, full of stern-faced soldiers,
quiet, ghostly, in the long shadows cast by the early morning
winter sun. Strange as it might have seemed, none of us had
any inkling that when we returned to school, it would be
another era.

Sun, our cook, was just mopping the living room floor
when I got home. Mother looked up surprised from her

unfinished breakfast. Before she could say anything, I blurted out, "Martial law, Ma, and no more school."

"So it is coming closer," Mother said, sounding worried. "Daddy hasn't called from the Water Works. I hope he doesn't have to go to any of the pumping stations outside the city. I wish Nini were back home."

Nini was then at a boarding school run by missionaries in the Native City, beyond the ex-Japanese concession. Mother sighed. It was just a little over three years since the Japanese had surrendered after the horrors of the occupation. The uneasy peace was coming to an end.

Had they made the right decision, the decision not to flee, not to evacuate with the other Americans, not to be refugees? I knew my parents had had many discussions on this. It was one of the recurring themes of their life and had had horrendous consequences the last time around. It was not a decision they made lightly.

But Grace and F. C. had no time to worry about whether or not they had made the right decision. The battlefront was approaching rapidly. Another communiqué was issued by the People's Liberation Army (PLA) right after the schools were closed. The circular tried to reassure the citizens of Tientsin that the transition would be a peaceful one. F. C. received a second message at work, as did other city leaders. Grace had the document translated into English and sent it home, where it was found years later with her letters:

PLA NOTICE TO PEOPLE OF TIENTSIN

December 15, 1948

BE CALM.

Tientsin is surrounded, and victorious armies are on the march. Make your decision now between destruction or cooperation. The following precepts are addressed to all our brothers:

1. We will be responsible to protect lives, property,
   and liberty of all classes. Don't listen to rumors
   or propaganda.
2. Our army will protect the citizens' industries,
   factories, and private holdings. We will not interfere with private enterprise, banks, shops, and
   warehouses, but they are to continue business
   as usual.
3. Kuomintang government factories etc. will be
   investigated and put in order. Bureaucratic capitalists will be assimilated into the democratic
   government. Should private capital be involved,
   it will be recognized as such and put to the good
   of the democratic government. Accounts, sketches,
   and plans must be preserved. Those who assist
   in their preservation will be rewarded. Present
   workers will continue in their usual employ-
   ment and be paid as usual.
4. Directors, managers, presidents, superintend-
   ents, professors, teachers, priests etc. of public
   works, schools, universities, hospitals, churches,
   museums, post offices, and recreation centers
   will be protected and will continue work as usual.
5. With the exception of leading criminals, Kuomintang municipal officials, police, "pao chia"
   etc. will not be detained provided they do not
   take up arms and resist. If they obey the orders
   of the Army of Liberation and the democratic
   government, protect property and do not shelter
   criminals, they may be placed in new government positions.
6. All foreign consular staff members and foreign
   residents who obey the orders of the democratic
   government, refrain from damaging the government, and from sheltering war criminals will

have their property, etc., protected.

7. Both before and after the Army enters the city,
all the people should maintain order. The good
will be rewarded; the bad will be punished.

8. Our Army will not extract even one needle or a
piece of thread from the people.

Carry on your work well. Do not cause unnecessary disturbance. Be calm.

signed: NORTH CHINA PEOPLE'S ARMY OF LIBERATION

William's story of the Kuomintang retreat continues:

Our family always heard the news first because the workers at the pumping stations kept in touch with F. C. at all
times. Each phone ring, day or night, would signal some crisis caused either by the retreating troops, bomb explosions,
or injuries of workers by the mines planted by the KMT.

Our cook Sun became terrified to go out at night. The
retreating troops were press-ganging able-bodied men into
service of the army and once he barely escaped. Other families had been storing food and supplies for the past few
months now. One day when I visited one of my schoolmates,
I found that their family had stacked sacks of flour in front of
the window facing the street, creating a bulletproof wall and
a source of food supply. But my family never thought about
such practical things. Sun still had to go out to buy food daily.
Food was getting very scarce as the peasants and the farmers
fled their villages.

Then, suddenly, another ring of the phone—the Deputy
Chief Engineer, Mr. Tuan, had been taken away by the KMT
soldiers. F. C. searched all around the city to find him. He
finally found out that someone had reported seeing Communist signals being fired from one of the pumping stations. The
KMT had arrested Mr. Tuan, holding him accountable. After
much negotiation at the KMT Headquarters, F. C. was able to
secure Mr. Tuan's release.

One day the water main was blown up. The KMT planes,
trying to bomb the PLA, dropped bombs instead on their

own troops and disrupted the water supply to the city. My father was called out in the night to try to repair the big pipes. We woke up the next morning with black smoke blocking the sun, and we heard that the KMT had set fire to the villages surrounding the city to create a "no-man" zone so that it would be more difficult for the PLA to sneak into the city.

During these frightening days and nights, Grace was worried sick about F. C.'s safety. She tried to remain calm with us when F. C. was gone and tried not to show anxiety when he was home. But all of us were conscious of waiting for the phone to ring with another crisis. We frequently gathered around the radio to listen to the Voice of America, but we could only get the official KMT radio station and it only broadcast "victories," with no hint of the impending defeat.

As the battle around Tientsin grew nearer, attempts were made to destroy the Water Works and other public facilities. F. C. was constantly in touch with the other workmen to protect what they could. Come what may, there was no turning back. The People's Liberation Army was already at the gate. The streets were deserted.

GRACE'S MEMOIR PICKS UP the story from here of that day, January 15, 1949, that changed their lives forever:

The clear, icy blue sky and bright sunshine made it one of North China's beautiful midwinter days. But a biting wind was sweeping down from Siberia. It rattled windows, shook doors, and dashed through the deserted streets taking with it all the rubbish it could gather. Standing on a chair at my dining room window, I tried to peer over the courtyard wall and look into the empty street, listening to the unnatural silence between gusts of howling wind. With the bombardment going on outside the city for the past month, I had grown accustomed to the rumble and roar of gunfire; now the silence was eerie.

Suddenly there was the sound of running footsteps and three deserters came racing into my line of vision, throwing off whatever they could of army uniforms and desperately trying to pull on some civilian clothing; another second and they were gone, leaving the discarded uniforms lying in the middle of the street like dead birds. Two stray dogs came along, sniffed at the uniforms and went their way. *The gate!* I thought. *Had F. C. bolted the gate when he left? Deserters could be desperate!*

Early this morning F. C. had left me alone with the children and I was expectantly looking for him out the window. Yesterday he had received a phone call from the Deputy Chief Engineer saying that the fighting had reached the pumping station outside the city; the pumping station was intact, having sustained some shots. The PLA would be entering the city the next morning. Our part of the city was still under siege.

Rifle shots, popping in the distance, then the frightening swish and scream of a shell and the boom of an explosion shook the window.

Abandoning my perch, I joined the children and tried to appear calm and unworried. Nini, just turned sixteen, sat with a book open on her lap. Across the room from her, I also pretended to read a magazine, staring blindly at the print, waiting for the next shell to scream its way over our heads or hit the house.

The two younger children playing cards on a low coffee table in the middle of the room appeared absorbed in their game, but at the sound of the explosion, Ellen, now eleven, dropped to the floor and seven-year-old Wei-han gave a gasp, covered his ears and shut his eyes in a painful grimace. This annoyed his big sister.

"Stop it!" Nini snapped.

"I don't like to hear that noise," complained Wei-han.

"Make him stop it, Ma."

"Oh, Nini, let him hold his ears, it doesn't hurt you."

"It makes me nervous."

Suddenly the terrifying shriek of a shell apparently speeding straight at us brought us all to the floor, eyes shut tight and hands over our ears. A deafening explosion shook the whole house, and all the windows burst open. Cautiously I opened my eyes. I was alive, the house was still standing and the children were looking at me shocked and wild-eyed.

The cold wind was blowing through the house. My magazine was fluttering in the wind but there was no other sound.

"Quick!" I said. "Help me close the windows."

Nini and I went from room to room shutting out the freezing wind. The dead silence between the anguished howls of wind gave me the uneasy feel of something holding its breath, getting ready to spring. The street beyond the gate had a shut-up and waiting look.

Then I heard the gate open and footsteps! Before I had time to panic, Wei-han cried, "It's Daddy! Daddy's here!" And as soon as F. C. had entered the front door Wei-han pummeled questions at him, "Did you hear the big guns, Daddy? Did you see the explosion?"

Ignoring him, F. C. came straight to me. "Are you all right? Were you very frightened?"

"Of course I was! Who wouldn't be? But we're all right. Did you see what was hit?"

"No, I couldn't tell. I came as quickly as I could. They don't seem to have hit anything. But the explosion blew out a lot of windows. There's broken glass all over the streets."

"What's going to happen now, Daddy? Why have they stopped shooting?"

F. C. now looked at his son and said, "I don't know what's going to happen. I don't know anything except it's not over."

Something had hushed the big guns. The foreboding silence continued.

"I'm hungry," blurted Wei-han. "Let's eat."

I almost laughed. He was used to having lunch when his father came home, but today nothing was routine. The city had been surrounded for days and no food was coming into the city. Sun had not even attempted to make his usual trip to the market.

"There's nothing to eat," Nini snipped at her brother.

"You'll have to have sardines."

"But I don't like sardines!" Wei-han objected.

"Spoiled brat! Don't complain."

"You know there's nothing else in the house," reasonable Ellen tried to placate him.

Despite the uselessness of my actions, I went to the kitchen to see what kind of lunch Sun and I could put together. I was glad to have the semblance of normalcy. Sun sat on his kitchen stool hunched over the table apparently doing his accounts. The amahs sat quietly in a protected corner of the kitchen which had no window on the street. But it was already too late. We would never eat that lunch.

Rapid shots not far off sounded like the pop-popping of hundreds of strings of New Year's firecrackers. The gunfire was interspersed with loud explosions. Food was forgotten. I hurried back to the living room.

"Machine guns," explained F. C., "and hand grenades—coming this way. Listen—they're coming right down this street."

The children ran to the window and Nini climbed up on the windowsill. She wanted to see what was coming down the street.

"Come away from that window!" shouted F. C. "Bullets can come over the wall into the room."

He herded us into the windowless corridor under a cement stairway where stray bullets couldn't reach us. The staccato barking of the machine guns and crashing explosions of hand grenades came closer and closer until it seemed that the battle was directly in front of our house. I held tight to F. C. with one arm and to Wei-han with the other as the choking smell of gunpowder began seeping in.

Gradually the sounds receded up the street and when the noise of battle seemed safely in the next few blocks, the children ran to the windows. Nini, being the tallest, climbed up on the windowsill and hollered, "Ma, come look!" I expected to see nothing but an empty street. I stood on my tiptoes and could barely see over the six-foot wall in front of the house.

What I saw startled me. Stretching from curb to curb and as far up and down as I could see, an army was marching. The sound of the tramping feet was so blended with the noise of the wind that it created the impression of a phantom army surging silently on, wave after wave. It was more hair-raising than the shooting.

I felt compelled to see for myself, but unable to see over the wall and with the children on the windowsill, I turned, as if driven by some deep impulse, snatched up the nearest coat, which happened to be a spring coat—it was very cold and I was bareheaded, wearing only a housedress and spring coat—I unlocked the door and without saying a word, without thinking even, rushed out. I was surprised to find the courtyard gate unbolted. I pushed it open—and suddenly a bone-piercing gust of wind with a strong smell of gunpowder snapped me to my senses.

I looked around. There was no other courtyard gate open, no other person on the sidewalk, no faces at the windows—only me—face to face with the People's Liberation Army.

CHIANG KAI-SHEK RESIGNED as president of China, on January 21, 1949, and two days later Peking surrendered without a fight. While the Communist army gathered its forces on the northern banks of the Yangtse River, waiting to move further south in the spring, the administrative arm of the army focused on creating a provisional government in the North. To avoid the disasters that faced the Nationalist government after its return to power in 1945, the Communists maintained strict orders to occupy the cities of North China peacefully, to keep businesses and industries operating, to reopen schools and hospitals, and guarantee safety as much as possible. Food and fuel were stabilized and stockpiled supplies made available. A new currency, called the *renminbi*, was exchanged for gold, silver, foreign currencies, and the despised, fluctuating CNC notes. Orders were issued to round up but not to harm former KMT officers and soldiers.

Mail service soon resumed and Grace received back issues of American magazines. In the January 1949 issue of the *Saturday Evening Post*, she saw an editorial cartoon which she described as a "pitiful figure of a Chinaman, representing the 'Chinese people' sitting on a heap of rocks in a barren waste, with the smoke of burning cities in the distance. Out of the sky descended a hammer and sickle just about to cut off the head or beat out the brains of the Chinese people." The cartoon stirred her to pick up pen and paper.

Grace's letter to the editors of the *Saturday Evening Post* in April 1949 is a ten-page description of her experience immediately after what the Chinese called the "liberation" and what the West called the "Communist takeover." The details of this letter were in such contrast to what the American media was portraying about China then that Grace sarcastically wrote: "It would seem that one has a clearer view of things from a ten-thousand-mile distance. We here in Tientsin are perhaps too close to see what is going on or too close to interpret it properly. . . . After three months of observing the Chinese Communists, I wouldn't have the least worry if it weren't for the things I read in the American magazines."

Not sure of mail service out of Tientsin, Grace sent it through a friend to his brother in Hong Kong and told him to send it to the *Saturday Evening Post*. When it got to Hong Kong, however, it created quite a stir. One of the people who read it was the editor of the *China Digest*, an English publication favorable to China. The next thing Grace knew it had been reprinted in Singapore, San Francisco, and wherever there were overseas Chinese. One of F. C.'s engineers studying in Paris at the time said he read it there in English and French and Chinese.

//

Tientsin, April 22, 1949

Editor of *Saturday Evening Post*
Philadelphia, Pa.

Dear Sir,

. . . It's now three months since the *Pa Lu Chuin* took
over the city. *Pa Lu Chuin* is a sort of nickname for the communist army; it means literally "Eighth Route," and *Chuin*
means army. And what follows is my personal version of the
plain truth about things here in Tientsin before and after
the advent of the *Pa Lu Chuin*.

All my years in China have been lived in an anti-
Communist atmosphere. Tientsin is a cosmopolitan port
city: the home of foreigners of all nationalities, rich
Chinese landlords, and businessmen, the families of old
warlords who had squeezed whole provinces dry; wealthy
officials and bankers—a hotbed of anti-Communism. We
were steeped in anti-Red propaganda. The Chinese
Communists were godless, murdering, torturing, thieving,
liberty-suppressing bandits, and before December 1941, I
took it all to heart and was one of the most convinced of
antis. But the Japanese occupation cured me of swallowing
any kind of propaganda whole, for I heard the Japanese
turn the Americans into all sorts of human fiends, and from
that time I take all propaganda with a large dose of salt.

When it was clear that it was only a matter of a very
short time before Tientsin and Peking would be in the
hands of the Communists, there ensued a hectic scramble
to get out on the part of those afraid of what might happen
when the Communists took the city. We determined to
remain in our own home and face whatever came—hoping
it wouldn't be too bad! We expected to have our way of
living perhaps radically changed. We expected to be
behind some form of an "Iron Curtain." We'd heard much of
the Communists' anti-American feeling and I thought it
likely that things might not be altogether pleasant for
Americans. We'd heard that everybody would be forced to
work and all would have to eat the same sort of food. One
friend of mine, a wealthy young Chinese widow, flew to

Formosa because she'd been told that Communists did not approve of widows or idle women and she was afraid she would be forced to marry some comrade and set to hard labor.

I expected that American books and magazines would probably be banned and that surely no more American movies would be shown. I expected to have to give up my American coffee and American tomato, pineapple, orange, and grapefruit juice and V-8! . . . that my children could no longer drink Borden's Hemo and irradiated Pet milk. It was a dreary prospect but it couldn't be as bad as the Japanese occupation we'd lived through and almost anything was better than being a wretched refugee!

My first sight of the *Pa Lu Chuin* was not reassuring. Dogtrotting down our street, the square, squat, fur-hatted soldiers had a wild and savage look. The Attila-the-Hun type hats they wore were huge and long-haired with earpieces and tails flying in the wind. They wore padded uniforms and padded overcoats and their legs were wrapped beyond any semblance of legs. What with the big flopping hats on their heads, the machine guns on their backs, and the pistols, knives and grenades, shovels, and pots and pans hanging around their middles, it's no wonder they appeared short and squat! Suddenly I heard a shrill whistle and the line halted, and the soldiers leaned against the wall "at ease." When I saw their faces the Hunnish horde changed before my eyes into a crowd of jolly, red-cheeked Chinese boys, laughing, scuffling, and kicking at each other like schoolboys on a lark. Any fears I might have had of a fierce, ruthless, conquering army evaporated.

Nini described what happened immediately after the Pa Lu Chuin came into their neighborhood:

> When Mother ran outside, the cook was horrified and called to F.C., "Tai-tai is going outside, going outside!"
> F. C. said, "Let her alone. They won't hurt her."
> In a few minutes we all ran outside, first us children, then father, and the cook and the amahs. The soldiers stopped and had a break and it was very cold. They sat along the wall on

the other side where the sun was coming down very brightly. The cook was so polite. He offered them some hot water and things, but they refused.

Willy began prancing up and down mimicking the soldiers marching. I was afraid that maybe they thought Willy was fighting them so I called, "Stop it, Willy." He came back and stood with us.

We lived in a very upper-class neighborhood with bankers and industrialists—who were all afraid. Our neighbors came out slowly into the streets. About two or three o'clock, the soldiers had gone and the shooting had stilled. Everybody came out and chatted, wondering what the next step was. People were even more friendly to each other than usual, after so many days of staying off the streets and imagining the worst. One neighbor had sandbagged up his door, because he was afraid of the fighting. When the soldiers came, he refused to open up. All the neighbors came by and shouted at him that it was all right, everybody was safe and the fighting was over. Finally he took away the sandbags and opened his gate.

The PLA came back in the afternoon and searched each house for KMT soldiers. One neighbor had an officer who had gone in the day before and changed all his clothes. I had seen how the KMT soldiers had acted, looting like bandits, and I had seen how the Marines had acted sometimes. The PLA commander, when he found the KMT soldier, treated him nicely, tried to console him, even carried his bundle on his back, and was saying, "Now don't be afraid. Nobody is going to hurt you. Come along. We'll go along with the rest of them." This gave me a big impression. And then later, when more KMT soldiers and dependents were rounded up, they were all weeping and complaining, and the PLA soldiers were consoling them and helping them. It was almost funny.

Grace recounted in an interview an exchange with a soldier in her bedroom:

When I stayed out on the street watching the PLA. I got chilled. I was shaking and couldn't get warm. So I went to bed with a fever. I was in bed when the PLA soldier came back to search. The cook came in my room

and whispered politely, "Tai-tai, there's a comrade here."
He learned quickly to say *comrade.* "He wants to search
the house for deserters. They're picking up all the KMT
soldiers that were left behind or hiding somewhere."

I said, "Well, of course, take him around, Sun."

"Well, he wants to come in here."

"Certainly. Bring him in. Let him come in, look in the
closet, under the bed—anywhere."

So then I looked at the door and I saw a big hat, a
big fur hat coming around the corner, and two round
eyes peeking out at me, two red, red cheeks like apples.
He looked just about fifteen years old to me. And so the
cook very politely told him to come in and said I wasn't
very well. I smiled and said something, I don't remember
what, in Chinese. Then he tried to tiptoe and he had on
these enormous boots. I tried not to laugh. He walked
through the room on booted tiptoes into the bathroom
and the other rooms. I told him to look in the closet and
look all around so he would be sure that there was nobody hiding. He just went all around, made the circuit,
and then went out, still tiptoeing in those big boots.

Ellen, age eleven at the time, remembers other details when the
Red Army was billeted in the neighborhood:

Afterward the soldiers stayed with the families. They
stayed in the hallways, wherever there was room. No soldiers
stayed with us, but many, maybe a whole platoon stayed on
our street. The first thing they did was to sweep and clean and
straighten things up. I asked, Why don't they put one in our
house? We have a hallway. We have room. Was it because of
the foreigner [Grace]? I wanted to have one because I often
saw when I was walking down the street that these soldiers
were so useful. They swept the courtyards, they made the
fires; they took care of the children. I saw many of them walking up and down the street, carrying a baby or strolling a
baby. One day I went past a house, and I saw the *Tai-tai,* the
lady of the house, just leaving and she was saying to the soldier who was holding the baby, "Now you feed it at such and

such a time and do this at such and such a time." We had never seen anything like it. No one believed it.

They only stayed a short while, but what won over the people was the army's discipline and the contact between soldiers and the people. You can talk and talk and talk, but what means the most is the contact. Anything borrowed was always returned, anything broken was always paid for. Kids in the neighborhoods took to them like they were heroes. We watched them in the stadium practicing climbing, drilling, crossing a swinging bamboo bridge they had rigged up to get ready for the south. The stadium was full of kids watching the soldiers. They stayed for a few months before the next big battle came and they left, before the weather became warm.

In Grace's letter to the *Saturday Evening Post*, she compared what she was observing in China to the English civil war as described in Macauley's *History of England*, one of the few books that had been available to her during the Japanese occupation:

> Since that day [January 15, 1949] we've had plenty of opportunity to observe this amazing army that has something of Cromwell's Ironsides and something of M.R.A.— The Moral Rearmament Association! There have been as many as four hundred thousand soldiers in the city at once. They come and go; as some go out to the south, others come in to take their places. They are not quartered away off somewhere in barracks but are billeted on the people. Nearly every family with extra room has a few soldiers. Most of the people we know have or have had them at some time or another.
>
> Of course not many people are overjoyed at having soldiers billeted in their homes, but there's not much grumbling, and no one can complain of the soldiers' behavior. They all seem kind and courteous and good-natured. There's no stealing in the army—no liquor and no "wimmen"! Any soldier caught going into a house of prostitution would be shot. I heard an American say it was the first chaste army he'd ever seen and it got him down. As Lord McCauley said of Cromwell's army. "In that singular camp, no oath was heard, no drunkenness or gambling was

seen, and during the long dominion of the soldiery, the property of the peaceable citizen and the honor of woman were held sacred." Only the "no oath" clause would not apply to the Pa Lu—swearing is too important a part of Chinese conversation.

Every morning at 5:30 insistent blasts of a police whistle sound up and down our block for about ten minutes. Then all the soldiers in this neighborhood gather in a field two doors away from us and start the day with calisthenics and song. During the day when they are not working or drilling they play in all the vacant lots, fields, and playgrounds. They play basketball, practice broad and high jumps, and swing like monkeys on bars. In the Ming Yuen field they have built tall structures and ingenious contraptions that they have to climb over and around and down to perfect their agility and balance. It is marvelous to watch what they can do, how far they can jump and all sorts of gymnastics. They run across a high narrow slippery plank that is kept constantly in motion. They run back and forth on a swinging log, and they practice scaling walls and dropping from the top.

Of course Grace noticed the music she heard, but more importantly, she observed the changes in her own children:

There's a great deal of singing and dancing that the children enjoy enormously. The Pa Lu have taught all the children in the city how to do the "Yang Ko"—the Rice-Planting Dance. It is much like ballet in that a song is acted out in movements that have meaning such as drawing water from the river, planting rice, sowing and picking cotton, reaping grain, etc. When my children are home the house is filled with the sound of dancing feet and singing voices. My small son, imitating the clash of cymbals with his hands and chanting the onomatopoeic "ch'ang, ch'i, ch'ang, ch'i," dances the Yang Ko through the house with the verve of a soldier going to battle, while my daughter practices the inspiring song and dance in which the growth of the revolution is pantomimed, from the farmer's reaping and sowing motions in the field to the soldiers' bayonet charge like a ballet dancer. The movements are beautiful and, at the same time, very strenuous for exercise.

They kept some of the KMT prisoners in the old Empire Theatre. One time when I was passing that theater, I saw them—several hundred sitting outside the theater with the PLA singing revolutionary songs. In the evening after their early supper, the Pa Lu gather in squads in the street and, led by a combination of cheerleader and orchestra conductor, they fill the air with lusty, vigorous, joyful harmony. It's quite an experience to pass through street after street of singing soldiers.

. . . Our pre-liberation fears have not materialized and there's no change in our way of living so far. If there is a curtain, it certainly is not iron, for I've received my February and March [subscriptions to] *Good Housekeeping, Ladies' Home Journal, McCall's, The Woman, Your Life, Journal of Living*, and an assortment of movie magazines. My husband has received literally stacks of engineering news records, and the doctors are getting their medical journals and the journals of dietetics and nutrition. I've gotten mail from my home in Tennessee and from Formosa and Shanghai. I am still buying Chase and Sanborn and Maxwell House coffee, Hemo, evaporated milk and all the juices! I even bought two cans of Wesson Oil yesterday, the first I've seen for nearly ten years. Somebody had been hoarding it all this time! Our diet has not changed; our wardrobe has not been altered; we visit the same places and see the same friends. That is true of most of the people I know.

American movies are still being shown. I saw Frank Sinatra and Jimmie Durante in *It Happened in Brooklyn* last week. Two rows of Pa Lu soldiers sat in front of us and enjoyed Jimmie Durante enormously, and we were enormously amused at the little Pa Lu who couldn't make up his mind whether or not to put his bayonet back on his rifle during the intermission. He finally decided to put it back on in case some emergency should arise. The great decision made, he relaxed and had a good time gaping at the "big city" audiences.

Those who had the hardest time adjusting to the changes were the ones whose livelihoods were dependent on previous conditions. In this regard, Grace described her own neighbors and associates in the letter to the *Saturday Evening Post*:

Only a very few have anything to complain of and they are probably getting only what they deserve. Money shops have been closed and speculation stopped. Things look dark for the bankers and many of the private banks have closed. Bankers and brokers, speculators and owners of shops that catered to the wealthy are very unhappy, but they are by no means suffering; they can't go on making a lot of money. I must confess that their plight arouses no compassion in my bosom!

Take our landlord, from whom we rent our flat, for example. He comes from a very wealthy family and is the manager of a bank. He married three wealthy women— one at a time though as he is a rather decent sort—and his eldest daughter married a grandson of Yuan Shi-kai [President of the first Republic, 1912–16]. So he is connected with big money in every direction, but his bank is folding up and he is terrified and has taken to his bed with high blood pressure and what he calls a nervous breakdown—not just because of the bank, for he never even pretended to be able to live on his salary as bank manager, but because he feels the foundations slipping out from under the only way of life he has ever known. That is the case with many of his class. They have not been mistreated or even bothered, but they feel that their day is done. Some of them feel lost and unhappy and some have the good sense to try to adjust to changing conditions.

I was talking to a clever Cantonese export-import man the other day and I asked him just what did he think of the situation in a business way. He said business wasn't so good; nobody was making any money, but seemed to be just getting by. However prices were more reasonable, ending the leaps and bounds that had made everybody nearly crazy for the last few years, and money was worth something again. He had no complaints; he had done a piece of business with some Communists from Manchuria the day before and said it was the quickest deal he had ever transacted. They gave him a check, he handed over the goods. He sent the check to the bank and he got his money immediately. Formerly, he said, red tape would have strung out that business at least a week. He was cheerful and optimistic and declared he was truly thankful that he had not run off to the South.

. . . One evening last week we had dinner guests, Mr. C. and his wife from Peiping [Beijing]. Mr. C., who has a Ph.D. from Columbia University, is a former Central bank of China man who was sent to Peiping several months ago to be a financial advisor to General Fu Tso-yi. His wife, a Stanford graduate, taught economics in a Shanghai school. Both are now in the Communist People's Bank in Peiping, working with wholehearted enthusiasm in the Research Department, and had come down to Tientsin to inspect the factories, flour, and textile mills and other industries.

They were late for dinner because she had been so far out in the Chinese City going over a cotton mill. A girlish looking woman of forty-four, and so tiny my five foot three towered over her, she came in with slacks on under a long Chinese jacket, dusty shoes, and hair wisped from the wind. But her eyes were sparkling and her face beaming with satisfaction at having found some of the factories producing even more than formerly and also at seeing what a friendly spirit there was between the "old" people and the "new" people.

The relationship between the "old" people and the "new" people, that is, between those who had already been there and the new Communist representatives, was not always so friendly. Lacking trained personnel to run the cities, the challenge to the new regime was to gain the cooperation of the educated, technical, and professional people as well as urban laborers. A team of military representatives were sent to each workplace to manage the transition. These recruits were usually drawn from the PLA forces who were young men from rural areas of northern China. Grace's letter continues:

To all business, except the strictly private, to the schools, public works, and industries, two, sometimes three or more, political workers called "military representatives" are assigned by the Military Commission that has charge of the City

Government at present. These military representatives are sometimes green young country fellows without any experience in dealing with a large city's established organizations, and ignorant not only of the city but in a large measure, of the rest of the world. Situations arise that they cannot handle and they create unnecessary complications.

In the Tientsin Water Works there are ten of these military representatives. Their leader is a young man such as I have described. He is zealous for doing good and means well, but he made the mistake of doubting the work of the General Manager and Chief Engineer, who is a Shensi [Shaanxi] man. Now the Shensi *pi chi* (disposition) is notoriously stubborn, independent, and hot-tempered, and besides this man is a Cornell graduate and learned his waterworks trade under Allen Hazen in New York City, which means the ultimate in waterworks training. So while the Assistant General Manager and Secretary stood palefaced and horrified, the Shensi *pi chi* blew up; the table was pounded and the military representative was treated to a thorough dressing down.

Then not waiting to see what effect his speech had on the comrade, the furiously angry man left the place. He did not know what serious consequences his action might have but he said to his wife, "They can shoot me, hang me, or cut off my head but no *so and so* farmer is going to call me a liar."

His wife watched him go away to work the next morning not quite sure whether or not she was ever going to see him again. At noon he came home beaming, his *pi chi* unruffled and serene. The Communist representative had come into his office all smiles and apologies, "You know," said the young man, "we are just *tou bau tze* (country jacks). You must be patient and teach us so we can study and learn."

I know this is a true story for it is my husband who is the General Manager of the Water Works. From that time he has been treated with the greatest respect by the comrades.

F. C.'s conflict with the peasant leader was not merely one of class differences—F. C. was also from rural China, and his accent showed his origin. He was angry at being told how to run the water company by someone who knew nothing about it. He had suffered for years under leadership that knew less than he did and his tolerance had grown thin.

Soon after the incident with the military committee in charge of the Water Works, the Lius were visited by a leading Communist assigned to be head of the public utilities in Tientsin. Mr. Ching had the responsibility for making the system work for the whole city. Liu Fu-chi was in a critical position, and he was known to be difficult and principled. Mr. Ching desperately needed F. C.'s cooperation. Grace continues:

> Last night we had a most interesting session with the man responsible for not only the Water, Light, Power, and Tramway Companies but for all the factories. He is a Whampoa [Military Academy] graduate and has been a Chinese Communist Party member since 1927. He told us that the Water Works will finally put into effect the Extension Works Plan. This plan was made by my husband in 1935, but he was never able to carry it out. But now it looks as if some honest intelligence and common sense have taken control and things are going to be accomplished in China at last.

The proposal that Mr. Ching made was to construct the first citywide water system designed and built solely by Chinese from products made in China. Such massive public projects were among the first developments begun in the cities while land reform remained the primary focus of rural areas. Grace and F. C. were stunned, and delighted, by his announcement that evening. Grace described the significance of this event in an article entitled "My Husband is a Model," published in *China Reconstructs* in 1953:

> During the first years after we came to Tientsin in 1934, long before he became chief engineer of the Tientsin Water Works Company, he had designed and blueprinted plans for extension work to increase and improve the city water supply. At the time until after liberation, only about forty-five percent of the people of

the city had piped water. In districts where the workers lived, people had to use water straight from the river or dirty ponds, and there were frequent outbreaks of waterborne diseases. Fu-chi's early plans provided for the gradual extension of pipelines to every part of the city, gradually eliminating the use of harmful sources of water.

But those plans stayed locked away in a safe for fifteen years. The former Water Works directors and Kuomintang officials, concerned only with lining their own pockets, could spare no money for service to the people.

Mr. Ching explained to F. C. that it was the policy of the new regime to purchase industries from the former owners, even the former directors that Grace so disparaged. He asked F. C. to help negotiate the purchase of the Water Works from them before the expansion project was put in place.

William recalled the special relationship he enjoyed with his father during this period:

F. C. used Sundays to visit and inspect the various work sites while the project was under construction. The family often tagged along for the outing. The Hai Ho project and the Chieh Yuan Pumping Station were located in the countryside northwest of the city, nearly an hour's drive from the city center, in the area outside of the old foreign concessions. The drive to Chieh Yuan Pumping Station was through narrow and tortuous lanes, filled with throngs of pedestrians, bicycles, and rickshaws. The chauffeur-driven car (an occasional jeep) often caused a sensation, with people peeping and pointing at the car and commenting on the strange foreign woman and children inside.

I went off with my father nearly every weekend, watching F. C. confer with the other engineers and workmen. It was huge, as large as a college campus, with sediment basins, like little lakes, and piles of sand to filter the water. To me it was like a giant park; I loved to play in the sand piles by the huge sediment tanks and climb on the gigantic concrete pipes.

When father and I walked through the village on the West River bank to the work site, bystanders would point at me and whisper, "Look, a little Russian boy!"

F. C. would laugh and say, "What Russian boy? That's my son."

In the early fifties, very few visitors went to China, and so when they saw my "big nose" they assumed I was Russian.

Grace described F. C.'s pride in his work in "My Husband is a Model":

One Sunday afternoon Fu-chi took the whole family out to the Hai Ho construction site while the work was going on. Around the Hai Ho pumping station all was intense and bustling activity. Wei-han went off with his father to watch new pipes being laid in trenches while the two girls and I climbed up on the old reservoir embankment to locate the source of the singing and chanting we heard. From there we saw the singers below—hundreds of workers, digging away in the new basin, pushing small cars full of earth over miniature tracks. Bright red stars on their shoulder-wide straw hats were dashing in the sun.

From our height we could look down at Fu-chi standing by the pipeline in a characteristic pose with feet planted wide apart and looking broader and shorter than ever beside the very tall, lanky, Shen Ta-nien, one of the engineers.

"I could tell Daddy a mile away," laughed Nini, "just by the way he stands. He looks so determined and unbudgeable!"

Fu-chi called to us to come down and see the new pipes. These tall white cylinders arranged in rows while waiting to be laid in trenches were an impressive sight and were the pride of the whole Water Works. Knowing the story of how they happened to be made, I could fully sympathize with the feelings of the worker I saw proudly patting the smooth white sides of the pipes.

The making of these low-pressure pipes of reinforced concrete is a good example of the new way people have begun to work and think and cooperate after liberation. Several hundred of such pipe sections were needed.

They could not be bought in China and were too expensive to import. When Fu-chi suggested that the Water Works make their own pipes, opinion was divided. Such pipes—each section was eight feet long with an inside diameter of four feet and a five-inch wall and weighed around three and a half tons—had never been made in China. Was it possible that they could be made without modern machinery?

Failure could waste a lot of time, effort, and money. Many meetings were held to discuss the idea thoroughly. Fu-chi and the engineers were confident of success and discussed everything with the workmen and painstakingly explained exactly how it could be done. The Party organization appealed to Party and Youth League members to be courageous and take the lead in helping others to break away from old conservative backwardness. After a few pipe sections were made and tested under pressure, the whole company was seized with enthusiasm. Everybody wanted to help—even the clerical workers went out to Hai Ho and dug trenches, mixed and carried concrete, and helped to bind and wind the steel. The pipes were a great success.

The pipes that the Water Works built were more than just a simple manufacturing success. They were a symbol of the Nation, proof that China had come of age. They represented the Nation's independence from the colonial powers, its ability to design and build what it needed using its own resources, labor, and technical know-how.

Liu Fu-chi training workers and engineers at control panels of Water Works, 1953.

紅吹不定幽趣在濠梁

馬不嘶綠亂寧風行常長落

NINE

I N THE YEAR immediately following the Communists' entry into Tientsin, Grace witnessed sweeping, yet orderly, changes, much welcomed after the previous ten years of harsh and unpredictable conditions. Grace's family fared better: F. C.'s workplace became productive and the schools improved. She relied on her husband and children's experiences for information but she could also see for herself what was going on. To her it was like having a firsthand view of history. Grace wrote later that year: "Since the liberation of Tientsin on January 15, nine months ago, we have been gradually learning to live a new life—and we like it! We feel that we are living where history is being made and where great things are taking place under our very eyes."

What worried her most was uncertainty as to how these changes would affect her children's lives. Grace had long been concerned about their growing up in a semi-colonial and semi-feudal society with complex and contradictory sets of hatred and prejudices. Amerasian children had been looked down upon by Europeans and Americans and both envied and despised by the upper-class Chinese who associated with them.

According to Nini, Grace had strict ideas about raising interracial children in China:

> Her fear was that children like us, half-half, can very easily take the bad from both cultures. She spent a lot of time, at least with me, reading—always Western classics; that way I learned what was best from the Western culture. As our father was Chinese and we lived in China, she thought we ought to take the Chinese part more, that we shouldn't be left straddling a fence, you might say. I think my mother's viewpoint that way was correct. Since you live in a society, you're part of that society and you must have your loyalties to one or the other. You must know what you are. We stand with China, with her people. Yet the good part of having another culture is that it leaves you broader minded. You can get the benefits of the good things of another culture.

Now Grace faced a new set of circumstances and prejudices. The new regime brought with it heightened uncertainty about the treatment and education her children would receive. Because she had three school-age children, one child in middle school and two in primary, the character of school life was of the utmost importance to her. The choice of schools had been a difficult one before liberation with divisions by nationalities, languages, class backgrounds, and religious instruction. She hardly knew what to expect after liberation.

Grace's description of the schools her children attended is presented in an article appearing in the *China Weekly Review* in December 10, 1949, entitled "An American Tells of Her Children's Education in New China":

If I had to choose one thing that impresses me above all the others, I would say it was the revitalization of the schools, the injection of vigorous new life into the dead, dried-up, conventional Chinese educational system . . . I feel left behind and passed over by a whirlwind that has swept my children out from under my undoubtedly too-hovering wing—the children I used to coax out of bed, whose lessons I had to supervise and for whom a tutor had to be engaged occasionally. All that is a thing of the past. They now get *me* out of bed, and they must do their share of tutoring.

When my twelve-year-old daughter says she must be in school before seven, I set the alarm for six; but she is usually up before it rings. And why does she have to be at school at such an hour? She is on patrol duty! My daughter wears on her coat a shoulder patch bearing the Chinese characters "Fu Wu." That means she is on duty serving the school and her fellow schoolmates— watching to see that the small children do not get hurt, that the schoolyard fights do not become too violent, and that wastepaper and trash are not thrown on the floor or in the yard.

She is also the "tzu chang" (group leader) of her "hsiao tzu" (small group or unit); a group of three boys and three girls of the same class who meet to discuss their own and each other's shortcomings and how to "kai kuo" (change). But the most noteworthy and useful thing about the "hsaio tzu" system is the help the pupils give each other. Those who excel in their studies must help those who are having difficulties. The group pulls together and solves its problems whether scholastic or disciplinary. It is excellent training in teamwork and cooperation and automatically does away with much of the old selfish striving for individual superiority.

In the home, roles were reversed; the parent became pupil and the child, instructor. At night the usual helping with homework became a learning opportunity for Grace:

A few weeks ago I had a very instructive talk with my eight-year-old son. He is the deputy group leader. Their "hsiao tzu" has nine children. I asked my son to tell me about their "tan pei hui" (a meeting in which the children speak out honestly concerning their mis-behavior in school).

"Well," said he, "everybody says what he has done that wasn't right. Then each body says he must do what to make him remember not to do bad again." (His English is a somewhat literal translation from Chinese.)

In other words each child imposes his own penance and carries it out immediately. I asked my son, "And what did you say you had done that wasn't right?"

"I talk sometimes while the teacher is teaching the lesson." For that misdemeanor he penalized himself five extra pages of "big letter writing" (writing about one-and-a-half-inch square Chinese character with a brush).

"And did you do it?" I asked.

"Yes," he said, "I must do it."

"Do they all do what they say they must do even if the teacher is not there?"

"Of course! We say we do what, we must do what"—directly from the Chinese: "Wo men shuo shen mo, wo men i ting tso shen mo."

In answer to my question about the books they are using now, he said, "Now our books are much better than before. Now they teach us good things."

When I wanted to know what sort of "good things," he got one of his books and translated several small stories for me and explained the lesson each taught. Here first is the countryside—all the able-bodied adults are hard at work in the field, the children are carrying food and water to the workers, and the old grandpas and grandmas are sitting taking care of the babies or making shoes. Each has a job according to his strength and ability. As my son explained it, "Even the little people and the old people can do something useful. Nobody must be lazy!"

Then comes the story of the ants and the dead dragonfly. One ant cannot move the least little part of the big creature, but when hundreds and thousands of

ants combine all their tiny efforts, short shrift is made of
the great dead body and it is soon stored away for the
ants' winter food.

"You see," explains my small instructor, "one person
cannot fight the Kuomintang all by himself, but many,
many people together have much strength and the
Kuomintang is soon finished."

Perseverance and persistence are illustrated in the
next lesson. The rain of many years has worn a hole in
the stone step and persistent filing has abraded away a
piece of steel to the fineness of a needle.

William also applied his new point-of-view to Western literature:
"Every time my mother would read books to me, I would ask her what
was the significance of the story. Everything had to have a meaning.
When she read *Treasure Island*, I asked who were the good guys and
who were the bad. In this book, the good guys are the squire, the doctor, and the boy. And the sailors and the workmen were the bad guys.
Yet in school it was different. I couldn't see how landlords could be
good guys. Grace thought it was amazing that we were being taught
not only to hear the story, but to think about it and ask questions."

Grace recognized the obvious political implications of the lessons, but at the same time, the stories carried values of hard work
and perseverance that were not so far from her own upbringing.
She decided to withhold judgment and see how these lessons were
carried out in practice.

The girls' middle school, where sixteen-year-old Nini boarded,
was about twenty minutes away by bicycle. Nini would rush home
in the afternoons to collect extra food or items and listen to the five
o'clock news on Voice of America then rush back to school, dressed
in a black, padded-cotton jacket over wool slacks and Chinese
padded shoes. Grace's article described Nini's experience in the
former school for upper-class girls:

The same class of girls attend the school but they
have ceased to be languid "hsiao chiehs" (pampered

young ladies). They have become energetic, hardworking, hard-playing, enthusiastic school girls who
run the school themselves in a most progressive, democratic way.

Shortly before liberation, the KMT troops occupied
the school, and left it in an almost ruined condition. In
one part, all the windows were broken and the floors
torn up. The part that wasn't damaged was left filthy.
After liberation the damage was repaired, and the
superintendent called for volunteers from among the
students to clean up the place. A surprising number
turned up willing to work but many of them had no idea
how to launch an attack on the really appalling filth,
and they wandered around aimlessly flitting dust cloths
about. Although somewhat of a "hsiao chieh" herself,
my daughter was not a complete stranger to
housecleaning. She organized a squad of the most
enterprising of the young ladies and they rolled up their
sleeves and went to work. They took home blistered
hands and aching backs. But they went back every day
until the job was done. Now they take great pride in the
"slick" appearance of their school. On holidays they
wash the windows and scrub the floors and desks with
hot water and washing soda.

Judging from my daughter's spirited reports, school
life is more interesting than ever before with something
exciting always going on. Earlier in the fall there was
the election of the school committee with its week of
election campaigning. The girls took a lively interest in
making campaign speeches and composing slogans
extolling the virtues of their candidates. . . . Out of
thirty candidates—three from each of the ten classes—
fifteen were elected by vote to make up the school
committee. The girl with the highest number of votes
was chairman of the committee, the girl with the next
highest, the vice-chairman. Of the remaining thirteen,
each became the leader of one of the school groups or
units, such as: the recreational activities group—taking
in athletics, singing and dancing; the social workers'
group—in charge of the small school for the very poor

children of the neighborhood, taught by the girls themselves; the co-op group; the inter-school relationship group; the class "hsueh hsi" (study) group; and eight others. One of these fifteen girls is later elected to represent the school in the All-Tientsin Schools Union.

On the school grounds there is a wall the girls call the "Min chu ch'iang" (the Democratic Wall). Here a girl can paste up any complaint, protest, or suggestion she pleases provided she signs her name to it. When the pupils do not like a certain school policy and paste up enough protests with valid and reasonable arguments, something must be done to change the objectionable policy.

Interviewed more than two decades later, Nini described her experience in basic terms: "Nothing changed and everything changed. The outside was the same, but the essence changed. The teachers were the same, but we were taught completely differently than before. We learned new songs, the meaning of liberation. It was more interesting, more exciting. We had never had folk dancing and singing in school, but now we did. I learned to play the waist drum. You could air your opinions in the student union more freely than before. Teacher/student relationships were quite good at this time. It gave us new ideas. There were lots of new ideas. We heard them on radio, at school, in the newspapers."

While these changes were underway in North China, General Chen Yi led the Communist troops across the Yangtse River in April 1949. Meeting little resistance, they captured Nanking, the former capital of the Nationalist government, on April twenty-third and Shanghai in May 1949. With amazing speed, the Communist forces moved west and south, consolidating their hold on the country as Chiang Kai-shek's forces evacuated to Formosa. In late September, Mao Tse-tung, leader of the victorious army, assembled in Peking a "Political Consultative Conference," echoing the name of the body instituted by General George Marshall in 1946 and giving the appearance of finally succeeding in establishing a democratic coalition government. At first, the consultative conference bore representation from many different parties, although they were outnumbered by the Communist party representatives. This body elected the members of the central government of a united China, with Mao as the chairman. They declared October 1, 1949, as the date for celebrating the founding of the the new government and gave it the new name of the People's Republic of China, to distinguish it from the first Republic of China founded in 1911.

A massive parade celebrating the founding of the People's Republic of China took place in Peking. Miles and miles of smiling faces marched past Mao and the other Communist leaders in front of the Gate of Heavenly Peace at the entrance to the once Forbidden City. Smaller parades, but no less grand in celebration, took place all over China.

Nini's part in the October 1st celebration parade in Tientsin became a formative lesson in Grace's article:

> Nini's school distinguished itself in the huge thirteen-hour parade celebrating the establishment of the new government last month. On the night of the big celebration parade, around 1 A.M. some reactionary element attempted to create a disturbance in what they thought was a weak spot. A gang, thought to be KMT sympathizers, tried to break through the marching column of girls and their Yang Ko groups. But the girls stood firm and fought back. Some of the girls were knocked down and my daughter, one of the twenty-six Yang Ko dancers, was hit on the shoulder and knocked unconscious. Carried to a nearby ambulance, revived, and sent immediately back to the school; she suffered no worse injury than a bruised nerve in her shoulder. The disturbers were quickly subdued by the armed postmen who came to the rescue of the girls.
>
> Wearing her arm in a sling all the next week, my daughter was smugly proud of herself. Now she could swap parade stories with her father who once in 1919 couldn't sit down for a week after getting "whammed"

across the seat of his pants by a soldier's rifle butt
during a striking students' parade in Peking.

Indeed, Grace was the only family member who did not fare well
in these first months after liberation. What she did not yet know
was that she had tuberculosis. The dreaded disease which had
killed Mrs. Holmberg and many of the family's best friends during
the war had now taken hold of her. It was only diagnosed later, but
during this time, just when she was wanting to be active, she found
herself confined to bed. She wrote in a letter to her brother in 1950:
"The children are well and F. C. is well and weighs 165 pounds! But
I have had a lot of asthma and bronchitis again, just like last fall and
early winter. It has kept me confined to the house more than I like
and I'm much too thin again."

Because of her confinement she relied even more upon her husband and children for knowledge of the transformation taking
place around them. But in that first year, she was still actively
engaged in learning about the new society. She read and studied all
that she could to interpret what she was observing. She found herself often writing to dispel what she read in Western publications.
The following description of Tientsin was sent to her brother in
January 1950:

Six months or so ago the Voice of America was quoting
"China Experts" as saying that the Communists could never
run a big city, that they would run the cities into economic
chaos, etc. Just to mention one thing, the city has been
literally cleaned up. The streets which have been in
dreadful repair since the 1939 flood have been repaired, old
eyesores (tottering buildings, garbage dumps, etc.) have
been removed. Garbage boxes are never left standing,
overflowing with garbage on the sidewalks for days, but are
taken away every morning at 6:30. In the summer it used to
be a nauseating sight to see in front of the courtyard gate,
beggars, mangy dogs, and flies swarming over the odorous
garbage boxes.

And to see the traffic, that hopeless China traffic, efficiently and kindly (none of the Kuomintang kicks and blows) regulated is a marvel to behold! The Kuomintang policemen used to kick and beat the rickshaw men and still the traffic was a hopeless snarl. Perhaps it's not as picturesque and "so typically Chinese" as formerly but it's a lot safer.

A few weeks ago, neighborhood cleanliness campaigns were held all over the city. The police inspected all the courtyards, kitchens, and servants' quarters and the cleanest places had red stickers stuck on the door and dirty places got black stickers. We got a red sticker! The accumulated filth of decades was raked out of some places.

Now that the railway lines are open and clear from Peking to Nanking to Shanghai and from Peking to Canton, we can get food from all over the country, things we haven't had for years. For instance, I didn't taste an orange for eight years and now they are coming from Canton and Szechwan and we eat up a dozen a day!

I have to laugh when I hear over the radio and read in American magazines and papers things that are supposed to have happened in Communist China. Our friend who came back here from Formosa said he heard over there that F. C. had been put in prison, and another friend from Hong Kong was surprised to see *Life, Time, Newsweek, Saturday Evening Post, Reader's Digest,* and *Ladies' Home Journal* in our living room. He'd heard in Hong Kong that the Communists had stripped the houses of furniture and allowed no imperialist literature to be read. There is not and never has been from the very entrance of the "Pa Lu" Army into the city any force, or any terror, nothing but the most Christianlike kindness and patience I have ever seen—a lot more than I would have under the circumstances.

A year after the advance of the People's Liberation Army into Tientsin, conditions had improved so dramatically that Christmas could once more be celebrated at the Liu home. No longer in hiding from the Japanese. No longer dependent on supplies from the U.S. marines. No longer hostage to the chaotic postal service, which delivered boxes from home too late. Salaries were stabilized

and money had value. It was the first time in William's life that the
family had been able to celebrate Christmas.

Grace described the celebration in the letter to her brother:

> We had a wonderful Christmas—the best since 1940.
> F. C. has had an eighty percent increase in salary and we
> just splurged. He bought Ellen the bicycle she's wanted for
> a long time and Nini a black lamb jacket and two books
> she'd been begging for—*Les Misérables* and James Body's
> story of the American Revolution, *Drums*. Wei-han's heart's
> desire was various and sundry small items among them a set
> of Chinese story books. I got two beautiful pairs of nylon in
> a lovely dark shade, an American wool rose-colored scarf,
> plum-colored silk-padded satin jacket lined with silver grey
> silk. F. C. bought himself three new shirts—collar 16½!—a
> pair of new shoes and two new gay neckties.
>
> Christmas eve we had a dinner party—our family and five
> guests made a table of ten. Our guests were a doctor and his
> daughter (Nini's best friend), another doctor and his wife (my
> best Chinese friend), their little son, and a young man from
> Shensi (F. C.'s province). We had roast duck and apples—
> duck to the Chinese is like catnip to cats, they almost roll in
> it—but we had braised chicken for me and Ellen and Wei-
> han because we do not like duck. For dessert we had "pa pao
> fan" (eight precious rice), a glorified rice pudding containing
> raisins, lotus seeds, dates, walnuts, lichi, a sweet bean puree,
> and several other ingredients. I made a luscious eggnog with
> eggs, sugar, and whipped cream, the kind you eat with a
> spoon. It tasted so exceedingly good that we all ate a lot,
> fairly licking the bowl clean.
>
> Nini went to midnight mass at the Kung Hsang Chapel
> with our amah, a Catholic, and her friend and schoolmate,
> a Presbyterian! Nini is at present a weird combination of
> Catholic and Communist, she's pro-American, anti-Russian,
> and a very enthusiastic supporter of the Chinese
> Communist Revolution. But she's got plenty of sense and
> nobody can tell her what she must believe.

Drinking eggnog and attending midnight mass at Christmas
may not have fit the Western perception of what was happening in
China in 1949. The description of her daughter as both Catholic

and Communist must have alarmed Grace's family back home. To them both Catholicism and Communism were equally intolerable—and to proclaim them so forthrightly as a parent was unthinkable. When Grace said, "Nobody can tell her what she must believe," she was speaking, not just for her daughter, but for herself.

⟋

GRACE'S COMMUNICATION WITH HER American family grew more tense, while antagonism between China and the United States increased. Before the next Christmas, the two countries were at the brink of war. By 1950 Grace had been in China for sixteen years without returning home. Adding her eight years in New York, she had been gone from Chattanooga for twenty-four years. Sadly, she realized that she did not really know the adults her brothers had become. In a poignant letter, Grace began to wonder about their lives and the things she had missed. At first, she blamed herself for the loss of communication:

January 5, 1950

Dear Tom,

I haven't heard from any of the family for more than six months. I wrote Sam early in the spring and got a rather prompt reply asking me to write only about my family and not about China. He used to write me so faithfully and now I haven't heard from him for such a long time. It's true that during the summer months there was a lot of confusion about the mail to and from the States, but for several months now, mail has been coming straight to Tientsin.

I know I've been very bad about writing. I am lazy still and prefer thinking my letters in my head after I go to bed rather than getting them down on paper and mailing them. Sometimes one doesn't write because there's not much to write about and sometimes there's too much. Mine is the latter difficulty. To pick just enough to put into a letter out of all the upheavals and interesting events we have been

experiencing is not easy and I can't sit down and write only
ordinary family events.

I often wonder what you are like now. The last time I
really talked to you was 1926, you were getting married—
the year I went to New York. Remember packing your trunk
in the Jones' house and the white kitten went up in the attic
and got her paws black and came down and walked on your
clean white shirts? As far as I am concerned you are still a
boy of twenty-four. I know nothing about a middle-aged
man with grown-up children. And we used to be pretty
good friends and thought just alike. But twenty-four years
lived in such different environments have probably made a
difference in our thoughts and ideas.

I often get myself mixed up in my mind with Mama now.
I look so much like her—my hair is getting noticeably gray
and my cheeks have hollows. And I have to argue with Nini
so often the way Mama used to argue with me. In many
ways Nini is very much like the girl I used to be. She always
has to be hauled out of a book and prodded to her studies,
and she never wants to dress warm enough or eat
properly—where is Mama now?

America's attitude toward China was split at the time between
two very differing points of view. President Truman issued a statement declaring "disengagement" as the official U.S. policy: "The
United States Government will not pursue a course which will lead
to involvement in the civil conflict in China . . . [or] provide military aid or advice to Chinese forces on Formosa." Dean Acheson
replaced George Marshall as Secretary of State and his report on
China supported Marshall's view that the Nationalist army had "disintegrated" because the Chinese people had no faith left in the
Nationalist regime. Further American aid would be pointless.

Even though high officials knew the Marshall/Acheson analysis
to be true, the "hands-off" policy was not accepted by others, some
of whom had strong ties to the U.S. media and Congress. The
"China Lobby," as the advocates of U.S. aid to Chiang Kai-shek
came to be known, attacked the Chinese Communists as pawns
of the Soviet Union. The argument of Soviet domination of the

world, made through magazines like *Time* and *Life*, owned by Henry Luce, son of missionaries to China, had a powerful influence on American thinking and foreign policy.

In December 1949, Mao had gone to Russia, his first trip outside of China. His protracted negotiations with Stalin had limited effect and eventually resulted in a bitter split between the two nations. But this split was not yet evident as Russian advisors returned with Mao to China, adding to an illusion of alliance with Russia which spurred dread of a Communist world bloc. As anti-Communist fervor flamed in America, Grace was in the "belly of the beast," writing home as passionately of America's wrongs as Americans spoke against the evils of China. Grace's communications with her family became strained in the early fifties. Her letters became longer and more strident. She was frustrated. It seemed to Grace that the torrent of anti-Communism which bombarded her brothers swayed them more than the eyewitness experiences of their own sister.

Grace's letter of January 1950 blasted the assumption of Soviet domination:

> All this yip yapping in the American press and over the Voice of America news broadcasts about "foreign domination" in China . . . is complete nonsense. The two hundred much advertised Russian advisors visited Peking, Nanking, and Shanghai and now have apparently evaporated into thin air or returned to Russia. Nobody sees or hears anything further of them. The only one I've heard of in Tientsin is a Russian woman—Chinese born—who is helping out in customs. They say she's marvelous at statistics.
>
> F. C. went to Peking with the Director of the Public Utilities (a former Communist General) and met the Deputy Mayor of Moscow and the Moscow Water Works engineer. F. C. said the Deputy Mayor of Moscow was a pleasant, witty fellow who talked of the marvels of the Ford plant in America, and the Water Works engineer was quite impressed with F. C.'s Allen Hazen background and

expressed desire to visit the Tientsin Water Works if he could get permission from his "higher ups." About a month later, after a visit to Shanghai, the engineer did stop off in Tientsin a half day. F. C. took him, accompanied by some Municipality officials, to the Chieh Yuan pumping station, where he was shocked at the thick, "muddy soup" of the Grand Canal that had to be changed to clean drinking water. He was impressed with the American-type rapid filters that F. C. had designed and built; and when he saw the clear, clean drinkable water flowing over the weirs, he delivered a lecture to the municipality officials standing around about the difficulties and hard work attending the miracle of obtaining pure water from such a source. He ended with the Russian equivalent of "good, very good" to F. C., thereby giving that already complacent person much face.

Naturally I'm pro-American and dislike the Russian propaganda we've been subjected to for the last few months, although I know it's mostly for Russian and American consumption. It's annoying but nothing to worry about. The Chinese "lau pai hsing" (ordinary citizen) just shrugs it off. Stalin would have to have an army a hundred times bigger that the one he's got to force anything on the Chinese. They don't force easy! They have more "resistibility" than any people in the world, I think. The people in the street greet Stalin's and Lenin's pictures with "Here come the poor old Russians!" followed by expressive Chinese vulgarities and much laughter.

At the height of the propaganda furor, Russian classes were started in most of the schools, but Russian was elective and had to be paid extra for while English is required. In Nini's school at first there were eighty teachers and pupils who signed up for the Russian classes. It gradually dwindled to forty, then twenty and now Nini says there are only five or six faithful ones who go merely to save the Russian teacher's face.

. . . What a waste of time and money, to say nothing of human life, it was that the powers that be in the U.S.A. made up their bright minds that Chinese Communism was synonymous with Russian aggression. That false idea led to the stupid and unprincipled U.S. policy toward the Chinese people. If those in authority in the U.S. had not been, and remained, adamantly hostile to the Chinese Communists whom the people were backing, and had not been determined to bolster up the enemy of the Chinese People, cynically disregarding the wishes and welfare of the Chinese People—there would have been no exaggerated Soviet propaganda in China and Mao most probably would not be in Moscow now. Heavens, I hope you were able to make that jump. I get so wound up and involved I forget which sentence I'm on.

I listen to "free" nations' broadcasts and read "free" nations' papers and magazines and I compare the plight all the "free" nations are in with the almost unbelievable progress that China has made in the short two years that the Chinese people have been really free—free from *all* foreign imperialism and ancient Chinese feudalism!

For the first time in hundreds and hundreds of years, China has a government that has the interest of the people at heart—and forsooth, the United States does not approve of it! Well, that's just too bad, for it is here to stay—

We were glad to hear the other day President Truman's very emphatic announcement of his "hands-off" Formosa policy. What a mess of trouble those antiquated old dodos Hoover and Taft would like to precipitate.

The China Lobby's cry—"Who lost China?"—presumed that someone in America was responsible for China turning Communist. It targeted State Department officials and sometimes Truman himself as "soft on Communism."

On February 9, 1950, Senator Joseph McCarthy flaunted before the press a list of 205 "subversives" in the State Department as being known members of the Communist Party and shaping U.S. foreign policy. His press conference set off a wave of national hysteria and "red baiting," which led to a witch hunt that flamed the rhetoric of the Cold War and mirrored the practices he condemned.

The conflicting forces in America soon weighed upon President Truman, who commemorated Washington's birthday with an impassioned speech on freedom, democracy, and the right to self-determination—from the American perspective. Grace heard the speech over the radio and immediately dashed off to her brother a less than subtle response:

February 23, 1950

Dear Tom,

I am writing this at 7:30 in the morning. Ellen and Wei-han left for school about ten minutes ago. F. C. hasn't gotten up yet and Nini is still sleeping—her spring holidays aren't finished yet. The house is very quiet, but my thoughts are far from quiet, for at seven o'clock I listened to President Truman's Washington's Birthday speech broadcast on the Voice of America. And it stirred me up to more anger than I've known for a long time.

He talked of freedom from oppression, freedom from coercion and force, the freedom of a nation to choose its own form of government. And he ended with the words, "freedom and justice for all."

As I listened to the nice sweet words that flowed from the radio I got hot with indignation and I wanted to yell back at Mr. Truman, What nation spent billions of dollars trying to force the Chiangs and their government on the Chinese people, although acknowledging how rotten he and his regime were, although admitting the knowledge that the Chinese people were sick of them and had repudiated them? What nation still refuses to the Chinese people the right to choose their own form of government?

Mr. Truman warns the world against Communism and the Soviet Union. I have lived under Communism for a little over a year and I have seen and heard of none of the dreadful things with which the press and radio frighten the American people morning, noon, and night. There's no "iron curtain" here—we hear the A.F.R.S. from Manila and San Francisco, the Voice of America (so called, I'd hate to think that it really spoke for the American people) from New York, the BBC and Radio Australia every day, several times a day. I read the *Reader's Digest, Life, Time, Newsweek*, the

Saturday Evening Post and the *N.Y. Times* and I don't wonder
that Americans are jittery! . . .

The Nationalist army began bombing the harbor of Shanghai in
1949 with the backing of the United States navy and supported by
U.S. aid. She feared that if the bombings came closer to Tientsin,
the Water Works, and therefore her own family, would be targeted.
From her perspective, the Soviet threat paled in comparison to the
American one. Her letter to her brother continued:

> The Shanghai air raids have caused death, destruction,
> and misery. Nanking was bombed yesterday, and Formosa
> announces they're building a new air base on an island only
> four hours by air away from Tientsin. So the city is getting
> ready, anti-aircraft guns have been placed in different parts
> of the city, the windows of all the houses are being pasted
> with strips of paper to help keep shattered glass from flying
> all around, dark curtains are hung over the windows and
> we are just waiting, hoping we won't get any of the
> "American aid to the Nationalists on Formosa." As far as Mr.
> Truman's warning against the Soviet Union is concerned,
> our greatest danger of death and destruction comes from
> the United States.
>
> Do you wonder that I don't appreciate Mr. Truman's
> noble sentiments? To talk to the Chinese people about
> "freedom from coercion," freedom from force and
> oppression to the Chinese when they all know that
> American bombs dropped from American airplanes using
> American gasoline have killed whole families in Shanghai—
> and not Communists either—is doing the cause of
> American Democracy no good. If Tientsin is bombed,
> the Water Works and Power Company will certainly be
> targets. Naturally I thought the bombing of Shanghai
> and the killing of perfectly innocent civilians was dastardly,
> but the prospect of Tientsin being bombed at any time
> now selfishly upsets me a great deal more, because I
> might be one of those innocent civilians or my husband
> or my children.

Well, my house is no longer quiet, so I will have to bring
to an end this outpouring of my indignation on your
innocent head. I hope you got my other letter. If we don't
get bombed I'll write you a more cheerful letter next time.

The cheerful letter never came. Grace's brothers thought she had
turned against her American family. To Grace, it seemed that her
American family, and not she, was behind the censoring curtain.
Only her sister-in-law was still willing to listen:

April 18, 1950

Dear Mary Hills,

I am writing to you because you are the only one of my
rather numerous connections that has expressed the
slightest curiosity as to what has been taking place in
China. Although it is of such great importance to the whole
world, no one has been interested enough to even comment
on things I've written in my letters. Your one letter asking
for information was the only one that showed any desire
for firsthand information on a great historical revolution
and rebirth.

I think you don't realize what an iron or rather "brass"
curtain there is in the States. The ordinary American citizen
is kept just as ignorant of the truth about the rest of the
world as they think the Russian people are. The American
press and radio are pretty tightly controlled. Americans are
carefully "protected" from knowledge that might bring
about a better international understanding and a peaceful
solution to the present unnecessary world complications. I
will tell you just a few instances of proof of this fact—
instances that I know personally. I was naive enough a year
ago to believe American papers and magazines would like
to hear the true story. Well, I know better now.

Last summer, after listening to a particularly vicious and
nasty broadcast by the Voice of America, I wrote a letter to
the *N.Y. Times.* I did receive a reply and got my letter back.
They said they regretted their inability to use the material I
had sent. I wrote to *Life.* They printed part of my letter in an
issue of the "International" edition, but followed it of

course, with a "slap down" and refutation by the editor who evidently knew more than I did! I wrote another to the *New Republic*, but even such a liberal paper as that was afraid to print it. Finally I wrote to Edgar Snow [author of *Red Star Over China*], and he had my letter printed in the *Nation* last November, of course with all reference to himself cut out. The last of January I wrote a short letter to the *Washington Post*. To my astonishment they printed it—probably because I said I knew they wouldn't. Several days later the *Post* printed a letter from the director of the Bureau of Far Eastern Information who "put me in my place." He said I had to write that letter in order to avoid the "miserable existence" of every American in Red China!

Characteristically, when she was bombarded by confusion, Grace decided to educate herself. She was in a unique position to read the literature of both sides. She wrote to her sister-in-law of her discoveries:

> Concerning the American people's distrust of the Soviet Union, I will tell you a little of my own experience on that line. Although I knew they were lying and distorting the truth about China, I believed they were telling the truth about Russia. The true facts in China were in front of my eyes; Russia was far out of sight. Like most people, I never questioned the dreadful things I heard. Gradually I began to see how inconsistent my attitude was . . . I made up my mind not to be a political illiterate any longer. I bought an armful of Lenin, Stalin, Marx, and Engels and went to work. And I meant really work. I found the going very difficult at first, but I read and reread and studied until I had gone through seven of Lenin's most important works—they're small—and one big one of Stalin's, some Marx and Engels and then the *History of the Communist Party of the Soviet Union*, and then back to Lenin again. Now it was much easier to understand . . . Next I got out my old *Reader's Digests* of the last ten years, also old and new *Saturday Evening Posts, Life, Time, Newsweek,* and *Colliers* and I studied diligently and with an open mind and critical eye every article on Russia. And I made discoveries that completely changed my ideas on the

Soviet Union and the menace of Russian imperialism and aggression. I found discrepancies and contradictions galore, deliberate tampering with quotations, fixing them up to mean what they don't, a half of a sentence put together with the half of another, sentences and phrases taken from their context and made to sound altogether different. But in the '45, '46, and early '47 issues there were articles more favorable to Russia (because they were our allies in the war against Germany) . . .

It would take a big book to tell you all my mental comings and goings, but this is where I am at present—I believe at least three-fourths of the things told against Russia are false. Maybe one-fourth is true; the Russian communists have probably made great mistakes, as the Chinese communists admit they have and as they most likely will again. But I think . . . the people of the United States and the people of the entire world have more to fear from whatever very powerful element is in the States that is backing this "Cold War" than from Russia.

Because of the bombings of Shanghai, the foreigners remaining in that city could not leave. The last ship left in September 1949. Another ship had been promised by November but Chiang's bombings and his blockade of the Shanghai harbor had prohibited the boat from entering. By April 1950 the remaining foreigners in Shanghai were told to go to Tientsin to catch the *General Gordon* as their last chance.

April 21, 1950

The city is in a pleasant dither of excitement. All the Shanghai foreigners are pouring into Tientsin to wait for the *General Gordon* which is coming to Taku Bar. One or two parties have been straggling up separately for the past few weeks, but now they are coming wholesale on every train. The hotels are overflowing and many are staying with Tientsin friends. Tientsin shops and eating places will certainly make money for a few days. Fortunately for the

Americans, commodity prices are down and the American dollar still up, so I think there will be an orgy of buying.

Last Saturday F. C. and I were invited to dinner to meet some of these people. Everybody was "overcome" when one of the women and I each discovered the other was from Chattanooga! Can you believe it? Her name is Jenny Lea and she had been teaching in the Shanghai American School for three years. She had come up from Shanghai with Mr. and Mrs. Douglas, an American newspaperman and his wife. She seemed to know all my old school friends. She said she would look everybody up when she got back, especially my brother Tom, and tell about seeing me well and happy in this "unhappy land" (quoted from Dr. Jessup's report).

Another thing causing excitement in the town is Laurence Olivier's "Hamlet" which is on for eight days. Nini and Ellen went yesterday afternoon. *Hamlet* is Nini's favorite "piece of writing." She came home in ecstasy and got out her copy of *Hamlet* to read her father the most effective passages. Wei-han insists on seeing it because it has a *kuei* (ghost) in it. F. C. will take him tomorrow. I will have to miss it as there is too much smoking in the theater and I can't stand, or at least my bronchial tubes can't, that tobacco-laden atmosphere.

F. C. and I have never had time to become bored with each other. The years have gone by so fast, and exciting event has trod on the heels of exciting event to such a degree that we've never had time to settle down to being an old married couple.

I have got to stop before I write you a small book. When I write with a pen I get tired, but writing on a typewriter is like thinking with your fingers. You think, and the thoughts flow throughout your finger tips and on and on—

The Liu family, 1955. This photo was taken for Grace's article "My Husband is a Model."

Liu accepting congratulations upon being named a Model Worker, 1953.

TEN

THE 38TH PARALLEL was drawn across Korea in 1948, separating the Republic of South Korea and the Democratic People's Republic of Korea to the north. On June 25, 1950, North Korean troops crossed the 38th parallel and marched into South Korea, overrunning the country in a few weeks. President Truman responded by shifting U.S. troops from Japan, and fifteen other nations joined suit under the auspices of the United Nations' newly formed international forces. On June 30, the United States announced it would give all necessary military and economic aid under the leadership of General Douglas MacArthur. Army reservists were called up in America.

By August the U.N. forces in South Korea were having little success in regaining territory. On September 15, U.N. troops under

MacArthur's command swarmed ashore at Inchon, winning back Seoul and moving on toward the 38th parallel. Confident from the victory, MacArthur told Truman that he could be finished by Thanksgiving—but his optimism had not counted on Chinese intervention.

Mass rallies throughout China called for volunteers in defense of Korea against U.S. aggression. When U.N. troops captured Pyongyang, the capital of North Korea, on October 19, Chou En-lai threatened Chinese military involvement if MacArthur proceeded to the Yalu River, the border between China and Korea. Hundreds of thousands of Chinese volunteer forces moved toward the border undetected by U.S. surveillance. Despite warnings, MacArthur continued to press toward the Yalu. Heavy fighting took place under the worst winter conditions. By January 1951, the U.N. forces were stunned into a wrenching retreat and were driven back to Seoul.

Grace's letter of that month reveals that she is bedridden after finally being diagnosed with tuberculosis. But her own health is of less concern to her than the war:

January 17, 1951

Dear Mary Hills,

I am writing in bed so I can't use my typewriter. I'm now left with only a pencil—the children have "borrowed" all my pens.

I've been in bed for two and a half months—resting, and have nearly another month to stay. I felt so well and energetic during the summer that I really didn't expect any asthma last fall, but with the first cool weather it hit me more viciously than I've ever had it. The ephedrine and codeine I had to take in order to breathe destroyed my appetite completely and the asthma exhausted me. So I lost eleven pounds in six weeks. When I started having a very high fever around the first of November, I got carted away to the hospital for all sorts of tests. An X-ray discovered very tiny spots of T.B. up in the region of my shoulders. I had two shots of streptomycin a day, and after the second day my temperature was normal and has remained so. I stayed in the hospital twelve days. The doctor said I was not infectious and no danger to the family. After I came home I had four more weeks of streptomycin. The doctor came every morning and gave me a concentrated shot—the equal of the two a day I had in the hospital. The shots are rather painful. I feel restless now in bed, because I feel perfectly able to get up and go about my business. F. C. scolds and fusses so when he sees me up that I wait until he's out of the house and I get up and listen to the radio.

I've been wanting to write to you for a long time, but I have hesitated. Not having heard from either you or Tom since I wrote last I have thought that perhaps you didn't think it wise to have any further communication with Red China.

The instigators of this frenzy of war preparations in America and Europe do not fear attack by Russia. It's something else they fear entirely—and they want to strike before it's too late. The Korean strike was a bad miscalculation and has increased their madness. The U.S. administration is taxing the American people billions of dollars to create weapons of destruction when nobody wants to or intends to attack the U.S.A.

The way the U.S. government has acted in Korea, it's practically taking over Formosa, and the bombing of Chinese on Chinese territory in Manchuria has been the last touch, the final "chemical" agent needed to bind a mixture of many different elements (Catholic, Protestant, Buddhist, business, workers, intellectuals, rich, poor, all kinds) into one Chinese People, solidly and enthusiastically supporting "Aid to Korea and Resistance to Imperialist Aggression." For all Chinese understand now from where this aggression comes from the big financial Empires interlocked across national boundaries—and at present with the power concentrated in the U.S.A.

The effect of the Korean War in China galvanized the Chinese people in the same way that the common enemy of Japanese aggression had created a united front in earlier years. Use of the war as an internal propaganda tool was immense. First it gave the

Chinese reason to praise the heroes of the war, those new young revolutionary volunteers who had held off a great power, far superior in military technology. Movies, speeches, novels, and plays, acted out with music and song, praised the brave soldiers. Secondly, the war also gave the Chinese clear evidence that the United States was a hostile enemy, no longer a friend. The evils of U.S. imperialism were trumpeted as broadly in Chinese propaganda as the evils of Communism were in America.

The Korean War also rid China of its remaining foreigners. The "Resist America and Aid Korea Campaign" resulted in the closing down of foreign businesses, searches for spies, and arrests of foreigners for possessing radios or firearms. By 1951 only a few foreigners remained in China.

From the outset of the Korean War there were differences between President Truman and General MacArthur, but their disagreements intensified as the war escalated. January to April 1951 witnessed the heaviest fighting. Although Truman advocated a "limited Korean war," MacArthur wanted to bomb supply lines in North China. MacArthur conferred independently with Chiang Kai-shek, thereby positioning himself in opposition to Truman's authority. MacArthur accused Truman of supporting "those who advocate appeasement and defeatism in the Pacific."

On April 11, 1951, Truman stunned the nation by firing General MacArthur as commander of the Pacific forces.

Meanwhile, Senator McCarthy's purges of the State Department had spread. No one was exempt from suspicion. The "liberal" media came under attack. From newspaper reporters to Hollywood actors, anyone could be called to testify. In cities and small towns throughout America, fear gripped the nation. Many were arrested or investigated on the basis of "leftist" comments or membership in targeted organizations. Careers were ruined and lives disrupted.

During this period, Grace's brother Sam received a letter from the government with an enclosed form asking him to identify any family members living in Communist countries. Frightened and uncertain what to do, Sam sent the letter to his brother Tom, who was still working at Oak Ridge. Tom's job had changed after the war from procurement to public relations. One day, Tom received a call from the local newspaper asking about a man who had been taken into custody by the FBI. His arrest coincided with rumors of a Russian spy ring and leaking of top-secret scientific information. These two incidents during the Korean War heightened the family's fears that by writing Grace they could be accused of leaking information to Communist China. Merely receiving her inflammatory letters worried the family, and it was clear that Grace could not limit her comments only to domestic news.

Grace wrote the following letter at the height of the McCarthy era, at the most controversial point of the Korean War. The physical appearance of this letter reflects the intensity of her feelings. It is fifteen pages typed, single spaced, from edge to edge of paper, every empty space filled with handwritten notes, emphasis added through underlining and exclamation points. Grace wrote this note at the top: "Nini typed most of this for me but she rebelled toward the end—said her fingers were sore."

The letter was written to her sister-in-law in response to her questions to Grace. But it was hard to read, not just because of the small, close type with no margins, but because of the forcefulness with which Grace wrote these words from inside China.

April 20, 1951

Dear Mary Hills,

I was surprised to get a letter from you from Washington. And you had just been listening to the Senate discuss foreign policy! Well, I must say that the gist of your letter sounded very much like the Voice of America.

I am feeling much better, practically well, if it weren't for occasional bouts of asthma. However, I still spend most of my time in bed as we are having a raw cold spring and I want to be very, very careful. When the weather is really warm I will go out for an X-ray to see if there's any T.B. left, I don't think so, as I don't feel in the least like it.

Now, I think I had better get down immediately to your
questions as they will require rather long answers. To
answer them all fully is a big order, because you seem, to
my mind, to have everything completely higgledy piggledy.
The anti-American feeling in China is against the
government, the rulers, not the people. American
imperialism is a very real and menacing thing. You are
thinking of imperialism in terms of the old British
imperialism, literally taking over countries openly as
colonies. That is not the American style. You say that the
U.S. did not want to annex China and Korea. It didn't, not
in the manner you have in mind. But think of this—why did
the "powers that be" in America spend billions of dollars
and do everything short of sending in U.S. troops and
making an all-out invasion, to keep Chiang in power?
Marshall, the other generals, and the State Department
knew all about Chiang and his government, even before the
war was over . . . they acknowledged that the Chinese
people had absolutely turned thumbs down on Chiang and
his gang. . . . but the U.S. went right on trying to force
Chiang on the Chinese people . . .

If the Communists had not been armed, and the people
with them, Chiang would have won with American money,
American equipment, and would have ruled China as a
puppet of the American government. And China would
have been to all intents and purposes a colony while the
U.S. could pose as a benefactor and reap rich rewards from
the ground-down Chinese people. You may think this is an
exaggeration, but you weren't here in the first three years
after the war. You couldn't see how the Americans "took
over"; they owned China!

I do not think that the American People are unanimous
in their approval of the Government's imperialist policy. I
think most Americans are completely fooled by the
propaganda that is constantly being repeated in different
ways, and through different agencies. They read it in short
stories, novels, jokes, advertisements, news items, editorials,
articles on various subjects, hear it in movies, sermons,
lectures, and over the radio.

. . . You say it is not clear to anyone in America just why
the Chinese took up the fight in Korea. Until I remind

myself how little most Americans know of the Far East, its history or geography, its races and their relationships, I am inclined to retort sharply that you must know people who are not able to put two and two together and make four. There are two vital reasons why the Chinese had to go to the aid of the Koreans. The Chinese and the Koreans are close kin and are very much alike, much more alike than Chinese and Japanese. It's very difficult to tell a Korean from a Chinese. There's only the narrow Yalu river between China and Korea. During the war many Koreans joined the Chinese 8th Route Army (The PLA) to fight the Japanese and many Koreans fled from Japanese. So there is the natural sympathy and desire to help one's brother when he is attacked by a much larger nation, or by a whole "gang up" of nations.

Now remember that Korea and China are as close as Canada and the U.S.A . . . so wouldn't China be slightly simpleminded to busy herself "living successfully and peacefully in her own country" while a country whose government was openly and adamantly hostile to the Chinese government was sending a large army with super-equipment, accompanied by vast naval and air power nearer and nearer her border, until at last forward units stood on the opposite bank and looked over into China only a few hundred feet away?

The Chinese could see the flames and smell the smoke of the burning Korean villages. But that wasn't all. For a long while, planes had been coming over every day, bombing and strafing Chinese territory and killing and wounding Chinese people, sinking Chinese fishing boats and killing Chinese fishermen. If a hostile army attacked Canada or Mexico and brought their artillery to the American border and sent their planes daily over American territory killing and wounding Americans, I'm sure Washington wouldn't sit quietly saying, "We won't notice them and perhaps they'll go away."

. . . You say the Chinese are "killing us." Just what would you expect them to do, when "we" come with our super-weapons and "our" so many "rounds upon rounds of death" from our huge naval guns and "our" round-the-clock bombing with incendiary bombs, and napalm, that jellied gasoline—marvelous invention—that burns alive, turns to "pillars of flame" everything, women, schoolchildren, and babies, the old and the sick, in villages far behind the lines? Do you think killing American combat troops is something worse than that? After all, the American troops were sent to Korea with every modern death-dealing weapon for the express purpose of killing Koreans. It is quite inevitable that some of them would be killed in turn. A great many Chinese have been killed, too. War is not a tea party. Somebody always gets killed! But for those who order behind-the-lines bombing of villages, schools, of all buildings, of anything that moves, for those who are responsible for the massacre of countless civilians, for the wanton destruction of homes, civilian industries, and the campaign of frightfulness and horror worse than Hitler's, I cannot say with you, "Father, forgive them, for they know not what they do." For that which they do is deliberate, and they should not be forgiven.

. . . Just think a minute. Whose armed forces, whose air force, whose navy is in the Far East? . . . Just what country is actually dominating the world?

Now, about writing to the Senators, as you advise. I used to be naive and believed people really wanted to hear the truth. But I found out that they really don't. Most people only want to be confirmed in what they already think, in what suits them to think. I've written the truth about China many, many times, but the truth doesn't fit the official policy, it's most definitely not what America wants to hear. Now if I should write about how dreadful it was over here, and what a miserable existence I live, as an American in Red China, they'd eat it up—I couldn't write fast enough.

. . . Your last question is do I not believe in God anymore? Well, just whose God do you mean? Do you mean the God of the Protestant Church where I used to go every Sunday? It was very strange when I came to China and went to church with Chinese people where missionaries preached. When I heard American missionaries teach and talk to the Chinese about God, they made their

God so American. Somehow the American God of the American missionaries never seemed right for the Chinese.

I certainly don't believe in the God Americans pray to to keep them safe and comfortable while American bombers hurl hundreds of thousands of tons of bombs and napalm on Korea, killing countless women and children and old people, even changing the courses of rivers and shape of mountains with ceaseless bombing.

I could ask you—Do the American people believe in God anymore? Since the Korean war started, I've not read in any American paper or magazine or heard in any American prayer or speech over the radio any condemnation of the inhuman bombing of the Korean civilians and their homes. Even in your letter you say *"they are killing us,"* not a word of the Korean mothers and babies, little boys and girls burned alive by napalm. The utter hypocrisy of the American policy talking of the sacredness of the human personality and human dignity, the evils of Communism and Russian and Chinese aggression! What's happened to the American people? They've lost their moral conscience and moral sensitivity. Every country has protested against these atrocities and barbarities against innocent people. But American complacency in the face of MacArthur's terror bombing makes me think that the American conscience has dropped dangerously behind the conscience of humanity.

For the well-off Americans, I think their religion and their belief in God is a sort of magic formula that they hope will keep them and theirs out of trouble and discomfort. For those for whom this world is a "vale of tears," their religion is an escape into a future land of everlasting happiness. If the Christians would take Christ's own words literally and act upon them . . . Christianity would be an alive and efficient force instead of the dead and hypocritical thing it has become! It seems to be no longer a power for good. The so-called "Christian countries" are planning to bring horror and death to the world. It is the greatest Christian country in the world that has atom bomb bases in the East and the West. It is from the Christian countries the threats of horrible death are coming.

. . . Don't think I've gone entirely "anti-American." I
haven't, but from this distance I can see that the U.S.A. has
gone off on a dangerously wrong path.

But I still do have faith in the American people. I believe
what I read somewhere the other day, "The future doesn't
belong to Senator McCarthy and the armaments trusts. It
belongs to the people." I'm counting on that.

I think America is the most beautiful of all countries and
the spring and fall in Tennessee is such weather no people in
any other part of the world ever get to see. Two things
besides my family I miss in China—the lovely, lovely climate
and real honest to goodness buttermilk. I have plenty of sweet
milk, but nobody here seems to know how to make good
buttermilk. When I crave some terribly, I let my sweet milk
clabber and beat it with a fork—but it's not quite the same.

Well, I certainly have taken up enough of your time. You
are probably a busy person, but you can easily see that I
have nothing to do but sit in my bed and scribble. I did
appreciate your letter, Mary Hills, and your questions. And
if I've answered some of them with asperity (Mama loved
that word!), it's not aimed at you, but at the whole awful
situation. I hope you will write again, and if you feel like
taking me down a peg or two, go ahead. I love to argue.

So you and Tom are grandma and grandpa now! I guess
I'll have to wait some time for grandchildren. Seventeen,
thirteen, and ten are pretty far from the marrying age.

F. C. has just come back from Changsha in Hunan
province where he went to fix up their Water Works. It's
very far away. It took him three days and three nights on
the train to get there. He had to cross both the Yangtse and
the Yellow Rivers, and he was terrifically impressed with
China's bigness (never having seen anything but Peking,
Tientsin, Nanking, and Shanghai before), with the plentiful
crops and, as he said in his letter, "Our wonderful people."
He came back bringing four beautiful umbrellas with
pictures and writing on them (Changsha is famous for its
umbrellas), a big bunch of writing brushes, another
Changsha specialty, and some multivitamins for me.

I am sending you some more magazines and a great
bunch of clippings. Read them if you have time. Even if you

don't agree at all, and even if they make you angry, at least
they will give you some insight into and understanding
of the other side, and that's never a bad thing to have—
even to argue against it.

I hope you write to me again with more questions, and I
hope you and Tom will both interest yourselves in political
affairs. Those things are left too much to the politicians.
Every American citizen should take a fine and vital interest
in politics—what is more important than the way your
country is run?

With love to both of you,

Grace

As the Cold War escalated, the world became divided into two
camps. Both sides began stockpiling weapons of mass destruction.
On May 12, 1951, the United States detonated the H-bomb, the
world's first thermonuclear device, in response to the rumor that
Russia had begun testing. The H-bomb was so massive it needed an
atom bomb to set it off. Its destructive power was one thousand
times greater than the bomb dropped on Hiroshima in 1945.

The U.S. Congress continued to fund Chiang's actions against
the mainland. The February 1, 1952, edition of the *U.S. News and
World Report* stated: "The U.S. is now pumping supplies and dollars
into Formosa at the rate of nearly a million dollars a day to build
up the Chinese nationalist forces . . ."

Among the Cold War news items that Grace read were articles
from the *China Monthly Review* dated April and May 1952 reporting
the use of biological weapons in North Korea. The North Korean
Foreign Ministry had made a report to the U.N. in May 1951
claiming that smallpox had broken out in North Korean villages
after the retreat of U.S. troops while there was none in the villages
where no U.S. troops had been. The articles claimed that germ
warfare research, based upon secret Japanese experiments used
against China during the war, was now being tested by the Americans in Korea in the form of "germ bombs." The accusation of the
use of biological weapons in North Korea was confirmed in the

June 1952 issue by an international humanitarian group with representatives from Canada, England, New Zealand, Japan, and the United States. With tensions high on both sides, Grace felt compelled to write the following letter:

August 11, 1952

Dear Tom,

I have put off writing this letter to you for many months. I don't enjoy talking of unpleasant truths. I know it's unwelcome and most likely will be dismissed as propaganda. But my conscience won't allow me to keep still about what I know to be true while the American people are being convinced by brazen lies and deceit that they must go to war against a dreadful evil—an evil so awful that they must run the risk of their own and the world's destruction.

The premise of those who urge war and preparation for war is completely false, therefore all their conclusions are false . . . The American people are told they are preparing for holy defense against the evils of communism, which is about to devour the freedom of the world and the dignity of the individual. They prate of moral principles and faith in God! All the while they are committing crimes that would make Hitler green with envy.

And people who profit from the war in Korea and from the preparations for larger war run from the truth. No one wants to admit he profits from an unjust and unnecessary war. So it's more comfortable to believe the deluge of lies and slander so conveniently poured out day after day . . . I hear the Voice of America, the Armed Forces Radio Service from Tokyo, Radio Australia, and BBC from London *every day*. I heard the Republican and Democratic conventions over VOA. I recently read an editorial in *Life* on "The Terror in China." It gives a malicious and deliberately distorted and false picture of China. The truth is just the opposite. The *Reader's Digest, Saturday Evening Post, Colliers, Time,* and *Newsweek* are full of lies and concocted slander.

. . . Do you know a single unselfish, self-sacrificing "Big Business" man who would give up any of his profits to

benefit the majority of the people? Much less run the risk of
losing everything and going to jail for his belief in truth
and justice. You know as well as I that the moral principles
of U.S. government officials and officials of Big Money
interests exist only in their speeches.

I have lived now for three and a half years under a
Communist-led government, and the false lie-inspired
prejudice I had has been swept away. I have seen the
wretchedness and misery due to abject poverty wiped out
of China. The former starved and ragged are now
adequately fed and clothed. Hovels have been replaced by
decent houses. Miles of swamps have been filled in and
dumping grounds leveled, cleaned and planted to make
beautiful public parks where thousands of workers and the
formerly scorned "coolie" can enjoy their holidays.
Illiteracy is being wiped out at an incredible speed. The
whole country is teeming with constructive activity. The
Chinese people have been given faith in themselves,
dignity and self respect as human beings and as Chinese.
They are free with a freedom they never dreamed of before
and that doesn't exist in the U.S.A. Freedom from hunger
and cold, freedom from fear—of the future, of war, of
depression and unemployment. And freedom from fear
of unjust treatment—anyone can appeal to the People's
Court and get a people's justice, not a "ruling class" or a
"white" justice.

This I see with my own eyes and hear with my own ears.
And during the last year and a half, F. C. has traveled from
the northeast to the southwest and through central China,
and he was filled with not only enthusiasm, but with awed
amazement at the marvels the people with the help of the
government have accomplished.

Now, I've told you the truth! Whether you allow
yourself to believe it or not is another matter. If you use
your brains and think a few reasonable, considered,
independent thoughts, instead of thinking what
you're told to think, what you're supposed to think,
you cannot help if you are honest to see the truth of the
present-world situation.

. . . If the American people don't pull their heads out of
the sand, if they countenance or even ignore or feign

ignorance of the evils committed in their name, they are responsible along with the ones who give the orders. An aroused American public opinion can still control government action! But soon it may be too late. Smugness and conceit as well as ignorance of the rest of the world's people give the average American a dangerous contempt for other people and an entirely *misplaced* belief in his own rightness.

I'm forming my opinion by what I read in American publications and hear on American broadcasts, by what I know about people during my 33 years in America and by what I've observed of Americans abroad! I am in a position to see and know both sides of this question of the U.S.A. against the Communist countries—If all Americans knew the truth, there would be no crises and no preparations for war.

I hope you are all well. I am better this summer. My X-ray showed no activity, so the T.B. is arrested. But I must be careful. I haven't heard from Sam for ages. Perhaps my letters became somewhat bothersome to him. I am sending you some clippings and some magazines. I hope you get them.

Truce negotiations began in the Korean War in July 1951, but like the war itself, dragged on for two more years, ending finally in July 1953, with the same 38th Parallel as the boundary between the two countries.

The Cold War had extended its grip until the void between Grace and her family in the United States was as great as the ocean between them. Contrary to their assumption that the Chinese Communists had "rung down the Bamboo Curtain," thereby prohibiting mail to and from China, it was, in fact, Grace's family in America that stopped writing.

The letter of May 1, 1953, just before the end of the Korean War, is Grace's last extant letter home. In the letter, Grace made it clear that she sent and received mail from other people in other parts of the U.S. It was only her family that did not respond. She pushed the point further—that other countries had well recognized China and its achievements. As far as Grace was concerned, news of her family and news of the country were one and the same.

For Grace this was an exciting time. F. C. was at the pinnacle of his career in 1953. He was invited to Peking to view the May Day celebrations. As he watched the joyous parade of China's accomplishments, he had never envisioned such glory even in his earliest, most idealistic days. Grace was angered and dismayed that her own family would cut her off.

May 1, 1953

Dear Tom,

What's the matter with all of you? I haven't heard a word from Tennessee since last spring. Doesn't the post office there take mail for China? I hear often from other parts of the U.S.A.–New York, Pittsburgh, Chicago, Connecticut, Oregon, Minnesota, and California.

May Day parades have been going past the house since eight o'clock—it's now eleven. From where I sit I can see the beautiful huge silk flags, red and gold, pink, lavender, blue, pale yellow, turquoise, jade green, coral, so many colors! And such a noise of singing, drums, and cheering. A bigger noise is coming in from Peking over the radio. F. C. went to Peking yesterday afternoon and is now seeing the parade together with other labor models from the reviewing stand. Also on the stand are about one thousand visitors from all over the world—Poland, Czechoslovakia, Bulgaria, France, Finland, Sweden, Germany, Australia, Mongolia, India, Indonesia, Burma, and other places whose names I didn't hear distinctly.

We are all well. I was sick during the fall and half the winter, but I feel fine now and weigh more than I have at any time since before the war (1941).

I hope all of you are well.

Love,

Grace

The last word that Grace heard from home was a letter from Sam in 1954, informing her that her mother had died. Grace did not write back.

◆

IN 1953, *China Reconstructs*, the Chinese government's English-language magazine, invited Grace to write an article about F. C. as a model worker. The model workers of China were considered labor heroes, and in the early fifties were elected by fellow workers. The recognition was initiated by the government as a way of encouraging hard work at all levels. She wrote "My Husband is a Model":*

> One evening in October 1951, F. C. came home and told us in a manner he tried to keep calm that he had been elected one of Tientsin's "model workers." This unexpected announcement left the children and me quite speechless for a few moments. Then came whoops and cheers from the children. My pride and pleasure were expressed only a little less vigorously. In New China those people chosen to be model workers receive great honor. Their experiences and methods are read about and studied all over the country and they are looked upon as examples to follow, to learn from, and to emulate.
> Soon I noticed the girls looking thoughtful. "Well," said Nini, "this means that we three have got to be better students."
> "Yes," Ellen agreed. "We can't be just 'pretty good' when Daddy is a 'model.'"
> Ten-year old Wei-han then became quite sobered by the thought of the responsibility that devolved upon all of us as members of a model worker's family.
> "Why did you get elected a model worker, Daddy?" he asked. "You didn't invent anything."

---

*See pages 162–163, for earlier excerpts from this article.

"No," F. C. said, "I didn't invent anything. I just used my head a lot and worked as hard as I could." The pride in his eyes belied his casual tone.

Then he explained to his son: "The Hai Ho extension project which we finished this spring meant that all the two million people in Tientsin could have plenty of clean, safe water. And building a strong water tower for Hsinhsiang [Xinxiang] meant that the people there could afford a modern up-to-date water-works plant. So I got elected a model worker because my work is helping the people to live a better life. Understand?"

The children and I were familiar with the two projects Fu-chi mentioned. For years, the one on the Hai Ho River had been a favorite family topic. Now it has been carried out. The new government has put a great deal of money into the Water Works and the original plans have been considerably increased to more than double the capacity of the existing water supply.

A large new reservoir (sedimentation basin) holding one hundred million gallons of water was soon built along the Hai Ho River, and a reinforced concrete pipeline was laid down through which the water flows by gravity to be filtered and purified at the main pumping station more than a mile away. Pipelines are being extended to every district in the city, providing clean, safe water for the nearly two million inhabitants of Tientsin.

A clean water supply was essential to improve the basic standard of living and to develop industrially. While still working on the Tientsin Expansion Plan, F. C. was called on to advise other cities. Grace's article continued:

> While the Hai Ho project was still under way, the municipal authorities of Hsinhsiang, Honan [Henan] province, asked F. C. to design a waterworks for them that would be within their budget—that was a bit of a challenge. A steel or concrete frame water tower would be so expensive that it would leave very little of Hsinhsiang's money for the rest of their waterworks.

F. C. remembered the ancient brick tower-like
structures that are still standing in various parts of
China. Some of them are as much as eight hundred
years old and well-preserved. "Surely," he thought,
"that's durable enough!"

He did a lot of research, reading on the old towers,
discussing the proposition with his engineering staff and
especially with the older workmen, and they all decided
that they could build a brick tower just as well as the
ancients could. So Hsinhsiang now has a brick water
tower and enough money left over to build a small but
very modern, all automatic waterworks plant—one that
is run easily by the girl superintendent, a former normal
school teacher of chemistry, and her two assistants.

Lacking access to modern machinery, F. C. had to design ways
to build the equipment with Chinese parts and labor as well as to
train workers in mechanical and technical skills for maintaining and
running the expanded system. Developing the personnel to run the
new systems was an accomplishment equal to building them. F. C.'s
experience of learning on the job as a construction worker in New
York had prepared him to work closely with his workmen and to
create ways in which they could learn from practice.

Early in the winter of 1952, F. C. started on the new
purification plant for the Tientsin Water Works. This
plant, with mechanical filters having an output of
twenty-five million gallons of water a day and
automatically operated by electric and hydraulic
mechanisms, was a complicated project. Its like had
never been done in China using all-Chinese resources.
Many factories cooperated with the company's
engineers in designing and making all the elaborate
equipment.

Workmen had to be taught and trained to read complicated drawings, weld steel tanks, lay complicated
pipings, use slide rules, install automatic apparatus,
and make steel pipes from steel plates made in China.

The workmen were divided into groups. Each engineer took charge of one and after work hours would give his group some fundamental technical instruction in the line of work they were doing. The engineers worked closely with the workmen. As the workmen began to acquire technical knowledge, they gained a more intelligent understanding of the work to be done, became more enthusiastic, and felt ready to tackle any difficulty.

The entire project, including a big mixer and coagulation basin and the handsome four-story building housing mechanical filters, automatic equipment, pipe galleries, and a large chemical laboratory, was completed in ten months.

The overall accomplishments of the newly trained work force inspired Grace to write the following conclusion in another article entitled "Workers Become Engineers" (*China Monthly Review*, July 1953):

They know that the building-up of new China industrially depends in large measure upon them and their fellow workers all over the country. Just this initial step in technical education has been enough to show them what they are capable of doing when they begin to acquire scientific knowledge. They have caught a glimpse of what it will mean when all China's innumerable workers are skilled technicians.

It is an exciting and inspiring vision!

In the construction that took place in the early fifties, F. C. traveled throughout China, helping other cities design and build modern water systems and advising factories on water supply problems. Once when he was in Sian (Xian) near where he had grown up, he looked at the new construction happening everywhere, including the newly completed Lanchow-Sinkiang (Lanzhou-Xinjiang) railway—it was spring and the peach orchards were in bloom—and told Nini later that it made him very proud to see his country moving forward so rapidly.

Grace wrote in the *China Reconstructs* article that she delighted in
the positive changes she noted in her husband's *pi chi*:

> While he was working on this [Water Works
> expansion] project, F. C. always came home late, long
> after the family supper, and although he would be tired,
> we often talked over the day's happenings while he ate.
> We all sat around him at the dining table and would
> discuss his problems and difficulties and sometimes have
> very heated arguments. Although inclined to be
> hot-tempered and stubborn, F. C. had learned to take
> honest, objective criticism [so] that none of us, even the
> youngest, hesitated to speak out when we didn't
> altogether agree with his views or his attitude.
>
> What a change from the old days when constant
> frustrations and fruitless conflicts within a strangling
> environment made F. C. so irascible and difficult to get
> along with! Arguments then usually led to
> recriminations, tears, and hurt feelings all around. Now
> the exhilarating sense of freedom and the joys of
> accomplishment that liberation had brought were giving
> him a new disposition—in many ways making a new
> man of him.
>
> All his best qualities—his clarity and honesty of
> thought, his real kindness and feeling for people, his
> creative initiative and tremendous capacity for work—
> could now grow and expand. Traits I never saw in him
> before began to show—a new humility and patience
> along with a new kind of self-assurance and the ability
> to impart his own knowledge to others.
>
> In 1953 when F. C. was elected model worker for
> the third year in a row, his citation acknowledged that
> he had "saved the government more money than can be
> counted." I thought of those years of frustration in the
> old China. When he was a student at Tsing Hua, he had
> chosen engineering as a way in which he could best
> help China; he went to America to study at Cornell and
> stayed four extra years for practical work in hydraulic
> and water engineering. When we met in New York, he
> shared with me his hope that some day his training

could be put to use by the Chinese people. At last his
dream has been realized.

As a model worker for three years, F. C. was invited to Peking to
view the May Day celebrations that Grace described in her 1953
letter quoted earlier. His accomplishments, not only in Tientsin,
but throughout China, were soon to be recognized with an even
higher honor and responsibility. But for the meantime, it was F. C.'s
family that kept him from having "too much face," as Grace
recounts in the following episode:

> Not long after he became a model worker, F. C. had to
> make his first radio speech. When he left for the
> broadcasting station he denied stoutly that he was the
> least bit nervous, but the family waited around the radio
> in our dining room with dry throats while "special
> model Liu Fu-chi" was being announced. And then we
> heard a perfectly strange voice roaring out into the
> room, speaking faster and faster until when it stopped
> with a final roar, we were all out of breath. When we
> recovered from shock and amazement, we all burst out
> laughing. When Fu-chi came home, grinning sheepishly,
> we told him teasingly that he might be a model worker,
> but he was certainly no model radio speaker!

Nini's middle school class visits workers' home, 1952. Nini is at far right.

ELEVEN

To ACCOMMODATE THE increased numbers of children attending school, many schools temporarily used facilities the foreigners had abandoned. Ellen's middle school was housed at the former horse racing course. The place where the social life of the British and other foreigners delighted in gambling and games, drinking and parties during the heyday of the semicolonial period, now housed not one but two schools. Located outside the former concession, it took Ellen forty-five minutes of fast walking to get there. The makeshift surroundings did not interfere with Ellen's active social life in the middle school years, as she recalled later:

> They made all the horse stalls into classrooms. We played in the walking yards, in the mud, in the creek during breaks. We were often late coming to class. Once I was in the mud and

kicked my leg and my shoe flew into the creek. I got repri-
manded for that. We also played in the hay in the barns. We
had a lot of fun out there. Then in midyear we moved to our
new designate school. I worked hard on my lessons. I liked [to
learn how to run] machinery. We took field trips sometimes
to factories and workplaces. At school I played basketball and
high jumping and running. I was not bad in sports. I represented my school in the relay races. We still went to the
Water Works on Sundays with F. C., but not so often. We had
more of our own lives then—school, friends, other activities.

As the literature of the revolution began to emerge, Ellen read
Ding Ling's *The Sun Shines over the Sanggan River* and other novels
praising the heroic peasants, or diaries of optimistic, fervent young
cadre: "In sixth grade I started to read Chinese novels a lot. Some
were liberation stories and occupation stories, fighting the Japanese, about the underground during the occupation, and some were
about land reform. And there were Soviet novels about fighting the
Germans, and some old Russian classics. I still read some English
stuff, like Shakespeare, but in Chinese."

The next year four new schools opened and Ellen moved to
another middle school, but there were so many middle school students that the school operated in shifts. Ellen and William attended
the same school but in different shifts. The school was built near
Nankai University in a former cemetery whose graves were moved
so new housing could be built.

William attended the early shift. Each morning he would walk
from their house in the former British concession, which was now
incorporated into the city as a whole, through the graveyard to
school. For him the transition to middle school was not an easy one:

The first few weeks were terrible—kids teased me a lot. When
the kids teased me, I'd get upset and my nose would bleed.
Once when I got really upset, my nose bled and I had to walk
home in the cold wind through the cemetery. I didn't have
anything to stop up my nose but my school things, and then
the blood came out of my mouth. When I got home, Grace

was upset. She told Ellen to talk with my teacher. The teacher talked with the class and told them to stop teasing me. After a few weeks it got to be okay again.

Being older, Nini took problems in stride better than the two younger children: "We had some conflicts at school because we looked different. Some people were nasty, and we got teased about being 'foreigners.' Sometimes I let things pass. To me, it was not so very deep. It was always just something I lived with. I have always found that if you are not snobbish and don't hold yourself apart, people very quickly forget about differences. But Ellen didn't let anything get by. Ellen was a little tiger. She fought back with fists."

William soon had many friends and one in particular, Kelin, shared his love of books, movies, and Western music. His description of his activities with his friend gives a fuller picture of the cultural life available at this time:

Kelin and I were very interested in cinema. We went to movies after school and discussed the film techniques as an art form. There were Russian films and still some European ones around. One Saturday, I told my mother I was going to study for an exam at Kelin's house and Kelin told his mother that he was going to study at my house. We met at the cinema and watched films all day. We did okay on the exams so no one ever found out.

We went home after school and listened to Beethoven. We listened to music on the radio and attended concerts. There was a great promotion of art right after the liberation and that is how I got interested in the violin. My father got me a violin and I took lessons.

We all liked to read. During these years my mother used to read us novels like *Ben Hur*. But when she was sick, Nini read to us. Nini was a great storyteller. She would read us books like *Les Miserables* and *Wuthering Heights*. Sometimes she read them in English, sometimes she translated them into Chinese. I think I got my first literary education from Nini. My friends would come after school to listen to her. It motivated us to read ourselves and to learn English.

We all thought we should do well and work hard in school because F. C. was a national labor model. It put a responsibility on the whole family. Ellen was very good in school. She was a model student and was a leader in the Young Pioneers. I got in the Young Pioneers, too, but I was always too undisciplined, always talking in class, too individualistic. At least that was the criticism the teachers gave me. There was quite a lot of homework. Sometimes we would study on our own and sometimes we would meet at someone's house and study in a group. In our textbooks were stories about the anti-Japanese war and landlords and political things. Even our group study and support for homework was political. It was all mixed together.

During Nini's early high school years, she was intensely interested in the political changes in China:

The [Korean] war was still going on, and we became a part of the effort. There was a lot of political study in the classroom, maybe two or three hours a week. In student groups and youth league we studied current events and the movements that happened. We had a movement to keep prices down, and an anti-counterrevolutionary movement. Many students volunteered for work in the more newly liberated areas. I wanted to volunteer, but I was too young. They wanted senior students.

But as Grace's health became worse, Nini had to take on more responsibility at home:

In the early fifties, when F. C. was traveling a lot, I think my mother might have been somewhat lonely. Grace was sick about eight months every year. I think she may have been in a weakened condition during menopause. We didn't know what to do. I stayed out of school most of two years to take care of her. We still had one amah and our cook, but I took care of Ellen and Willy.

During that time, Grace studied. She always had her bed piled up with letters and magazines and books. At first she couldn't understand the Marxist language. She talked with my father about what she read. They were both going through the same process, I suppose. They would discuss books and things they read. We discussed the books with them and talked about political events in China. Both my parents were very democratic that way. Whatever was happening or being talked about, we were always let in the conversation. We got to know their opinions and why they were for or against things. And we began to form our own opinions.

During this time when F. C. was often traveling and Grace was sick, William was quite independent. Most of his time was unsupervised, except when Nini took charge. But he lived with a constant lurking fear when his mother was sick through the long winter months:

> One of the fears of my childhood was that my mother would die. Asthma is an awful thing. It sounds like you are dying. Nini took care of Grace and she took over disciplining me. She was quite a holy terror. I was much more scared of her than my parents. She would yell at me: you must do this, you must do that—she always thought my parents had spoiled me too much, so she was going to set me straight—"Don't make noise when you eat! Don't breathe through your mouth! Stop howling! Don't drink so much tea!"

By the time she was out of high school, Nini had her own strong opinions. Her ardent commitment to the new China grew from her earlier awareness of the need for change. She had seen the extreme poverty and harsh conditions early in her life. She had seen many changes and her ability to communicate them improved. In May of 1952, at age nineteen, Nini wrote an article for the *China Monthly Review*, describing the changes she witnessed in her neighborhood:

> To give a picture of the liberation, let me describe the suburb in which I live. Formerly the wealthiest people of the city lived here, in mansions fortified by ten-foot walls, electrified wire, and protected by huge dogs. Outside the walls, the garbage boxes invited the explorations of beggars and stank to high heaven in summer.

Ashes were dumped carelessly into an empty lot; here the poor children would play and root about for burnt-out light bulbs and other treasures. Streetlights were scarce, and after dark in winter thinly clad women workers hurried home through the pitch blackness, clutching their infants and empty lunch boxes.

One night I saw a woman standing at the gate of a mansion as big as an ocean liner, which belonged to one of Tientsin's worst traitors. I shall never forget how she cried and raged against the owner, cursing him, his forefathers and descendants for the wrongs he had done her.

But since that day when the PLA came through, knocking on doors and calling out, "Don't be afraid, countrymen, this is the PLA!" my neighborhood has changed almost beyond recognition. The mountains of ashes and garbage are no more; nowadays, a bell rings every morning, the residents bring their garbage containers to the street, the refuse is carted away, and the containers are taken back again. Empty lots are filling up with new buildings, lumberyards, playgrounds.

At the spot before the big gate where the poor woman stood cursing the traitor, the student union cultural troupe performed a dance to welcome the World Federation of Democratic Youth Delegation. The traitor, to everyone's relief, has been tried and shot, and his huge house is a hostel which has sheltered the Panchan Lama and the Korean people's delegation, among others.

Many more streetlights relieve the gloom at night, and in warm weather groups of people gather under them to sing or talk over current topics and problems. The workers still hurry to and fro, but no longer in haggard silence; they are warmly dressed and well-fed, and many, in the evening hours, carry books as they laugh and chatter on their way to night school.

I know many more people of the neighborhood than I used to. Mrs. Wang is our group leader. The old man who is always in a hurry is our street representative, Mr. Pai. The neighborhood meetings have created a real community for us at last.

ONE AMERICAN OBSERVER OF rural land reform was William Hinton. Working for the U.S. State Department under the United Nations, he was sent to observe a land reform team in 1948 and his notes became the basis for his book, *Fan Shen: Documentary of Revolution in a Chinese Village*, which was published in the U.S. in 1966. Hinton met the Lius when he was working at Lutai, a state experiment farm outside Tientsin, and became a frequent guest at their home in the early 1950s.

Mr. Hinton explained the land reform process to Grace—that to shake up the deeply ingrained feudal system, outside help was necessary from land reform work teams. These teams of five to twenty-five people were made up of a broad mix of Chinese, representing different classes of society, some of them from urban areas. F. C. was among the urban professionals asked to serve on the land reform work teams that fanned out across the countryside. Involving urban professionals like F. C. accomplished two things at once: it created a representative group to address the imbalances of the old feudal system and it educated the urban elite about the problems in the rural areas.

In 1954, F. C. was asked to head the Institute for the Design of Urban Water Supply and Liquid Waste Treatment. He was made responsible for water-related aspects of urban development throughout the whole of China. This national position required that he leave the Tientsin Water Works and move to Peking where he would work directly under the central government. This was an exciting development for F. C. and Grace, but because the move would require new schools for the children and other practical changes, the family decided that F. C. should go ahead to Peking while Grace and the children prepared for the move. F. C. was in South China climbing a mountain with a team of workers when he ran out of breath halfway up and told the others to go on without him. When he returned to Peking, he was busy with his new responsibilities as head of the national water and sewage intiative and ignored the warning signals. While working on the land reform teams, F. C. had begun smoking cigarettes again. In Peking he

smoked with everyone else at the office, but when he came home
to Tientsin, he quit. The family noticed that he was short of breath
and wheezing. F. C. joked that since Grace, Nini, and William all
had asthma, he was just catching up with them. But Grace was worried. She had seen these symptoms before and had even written to
her sister-in-law in April 1950:

> F. C. was the heaviest smoker I ever saw. It was only
> when he was sound asleep that he did not have either a
> pipe, cigar, or cigarette in his mouth. It distressed me so I
> could hardly stand it, yet I sympathized, and understood
> his apparent need for it. The Japanese occupation and the
> year and a half immediately after was a time of almost
> unbearable strain. But I also knew he was literally killing
> himself with tobacco. I talked, I argued, I begged, I pled, I
> threatened. I was just knocking my head on a stone wall.
>
> Whenever I heard a woman say, "I made my husband
> stop smoking" or "I don't allow my husband to smoke so
> much" or sometimes from a friend, a trained nurse, "Grace,
> why don't you stop F. C. from smoking like that? It's very
> bad for him," I would say in desperation, "Please, please, tell
> me how one makes a husband obey. I've tried everything
> short of hitting him in the head with an axe."
>
> Finally nature stepped in and scared him so bad that he's
> never touched any form of tobacco since. He had five
> doctors and they all attributed an inflammation of a nerve
> in the right side of his brain to excessive smoking. Tobacco
> constricts the blood vessels and the nerves are thereby cut
> off from their proper supply of blood. His whole left side
> was affected with numbness and spasmodic jerking, he
> walked like a drunk man, and his speech was thick.
> The doctors said, "No smoking, rest in bed, milk, eggs,
> tomato juice, multivitamins, and vitamin B." The
> inflammation cleared up in about three weeks and the
> distressing symptoms disappeared, but F. C. was not very
> well for four or five months after. He had a stomach ailment
> that looked like appendicitis, and two or three bouts with
> something like flu. He gradually regained his health and
> strength and for the last few years has been quite well, only
> now he's too fat—160 pounds and only five, six and a half!

When his smoking resumed, F. C.'s health problems returned and so did Grace's anxiety. She insisted he go see Dr. Chang, a renowned lung specialist who had been educated in the States and had his own hospital in Tientsin. She had once been friends with his wife and the couple had dined in their home, but their relationship had become strained in recent years. F. C.'s high profile under the Communists had alienated several of their former well-to-do friends.

Dr. Chang took X-rays, treated him for fluid on the lungs and sent him back to Peking without informing them of the seriousness of his condition. When the trouble persisted, F. C. went to the Russian Red Cross Hospital in Peking for observation and continued to work from there. As the weather got colder in October 1954, Grace was unable to travel but sent William to check on his father at the hospital. William recalls the trip with fondness:

> This was the first time I went to Peking by myself. I was thirteen and in my second year in junior high. Before I left home early that morning, Mother gave me a letter she had written to Daddy, a bag of food from Sun, and a list of books to buy at the foreign language bookstore—as I was going out the door, Nini shouted at me, "Don't forget the books!" "I know, I know," I shouted back, "*War and Peace* and *The Red and The Black*. I won't forget!"
>
> To be able to take a day off from school and go to Peking was quite an exciting endeavor for me. Peking seemed much more Chinese than the foreign section of Tientsin that I had grown up in. That Daddy was sick did not seem to be a serious concern then, as he was always very strong and hardly ever had a day of illness as I could remember.
>
> When I got to the hospital in Peking, I was told that F. C. was having a meeting with his colleagues and would not be able to see me until noon.
>
> I left the hospital and went wandering in the bookstores in the Wangfujing area. While looking for the books that Nini wanted, I found the Chinese classic *The Journey West*. My father and I both loved this story and used to read it aloud together. It was compiled during the thirteenth century and

described the Monkey King's journey to escort the famous Tang Dynasty monk to India to bring Buddhist sutras back to China. We used to laugh at the hilarious events that satirized the societies hundreds of years ago. They reminded us of people and events around us. The same was true for books by Jane Austen, which we read out loud. These classics are all timeless. One of us would burst out laughing and would say, "Listen to this. . . . Isn't it just like so and so." If the passage was in Chinese, we would translate it into English for Grace. I bought *The Journey West* and took it back to the hospital with me, hoping Daddy would enjoy laughing again.

When I arrived at noon, the meeting was just breaking up. I recognized two engineers that Daddy had brought with him to the Institute from Tientsin and saw others I did not know. Daddy said to those present, "Ah, here is my son with goodies from home." Daddy looked fine. With a white coat on, he looked more like a doctor than a patient. "Let's have some lunch. I have another meeting in the afternoon."

He had lunch brought to us in his room. While we ate, he asked me about school, about Nini and Ellen and about Grace. He said he was very impatient to get out of the hospital. Although he was working full-time in the hospital, there was still a lot he could not do. He read Grace's letter, wrote a note to her, and told me he would be back to visit in a couple of weeks. When I left the hospital, the others were already returning for the afternoon meeting.

When summer came, Grace recovered from her asthma and bronchitis, but F. C. did not improve. The family could not imagine what was wrong. William described Dr. Chang's callous manner of informing them of the cause of F. C.'s troubles. It was a very hot and humid day in early July 1955:

> The heat was so oppressive that a thunderstorm did not alleviate the heaviness in the air. Right after supper, Mother said that Dr. Chang had called to say that he needed to speak to her about Daddy. Mother asked me to accompany her and, all the way there, she was unusually quiet and nervous and hardly said anything to me.

When we got to Dr. Chang's house, he was eating watermelon and asked if we would like to have some. Both Mother and I refused, and I sat at some distance from them while Dr. Chang talked to Grace sitting at the dining room table, where he continued to eat the watermelon. I could not hear what was being said, but I watched him smugly slice up the melon while talking to Grace. He'd take a bite, juices running down his chin, then spit out the seeds, all the time spitting out his words as well. Grace sat there with her face turning to stone. I watched and waited. They then got up from the table and came over to me. Dr. Chang said that he would drive us home.

As we were getting into the car I asked Mother, "What is the matter with Daddy?" She answered in a very low voice, "I will tell you later."

Fortunately it was a very short ride. We left the car, passed through the courtyard. No lights were on and it was completely dark. As we groped our way towards the front door, I asked again: "What . . . what?"

"Daddy has lung cancer," came the quiet answer.

"How . . . how long . . ."

"Three to six months . . ."

Mother took a deep breath and gave me a quick hug.

I shuddered.

"Don't say anything to Daddy," she said.

We pushed open the door and went in.

There was only one lamp on and Nini was reading by it. She looked up. When she saw Grace's face, she got up from the chair and went with Grace into the bedroom where Ellen was. I stayed in the living room and sat down in the chair Nini had just vacated. I could hear Ellen crying. I didn't know what I felt—all my insides had turned upside down.

Grace was furious when she found out that Dr. Chang knew F. C. had cancer a year before but did nothing. If we had known early enough perhaps we could have done something. But by the time he told her, it had spread throughout his body. Dr. Chang told her that there was nothing she could do now for F. C. except alleviate the pain. He suggested that Nini learn to administer morphine injections. We talked into the night. How could we just keep him at home and let Nini inject him with morphine! We decided to ask the Water Works company for help.

The next day Nini talked to the management of the Water
Works, and they immediately arranged to have F. C. taken to
a hospital that specialized in cancer treatment. They hired
two nurses around the clock. Nini and Ellen took shifts, so
that one of them was always with him day and night. Grace
was not feeling well, so I stayed at home with her at night and
brought her to the hospital every morning.

In interviews in 1979, the three children recalled separately the
last few days of F. C.'s life:

NINI: F. C. talked to me and to Ellen, but I don't think he
said any of this to Grace. He said first he wanted to be cre-
mated. That was new in China. He had designed the first crematorium in Tientsin because the Public Works Department
didn't know who else could do it, so they asked him. Second,
he said that we should not wear mourning. Chinese used to
wear white for death.

Then he said always look forward, never look back. He
had had a great life and he was able to realize his life's dream.
To Ellen he said that Chairman Mao was the greatest man in
the world and to always follow his teaching. He said that he
did not worry about us and that he knew the government
would take good care of us.

ELLEN: He was in a lot of pain. It was very hot and, of
course, there was no air conditioning. The hospital brought
a big tub of ice to put under his bed. We were young, and
didn't know quite—we never saw anyone dying. Then one
day the nurse said, "Are you prepared for anything that might
happen?" His hand was turning blue, and he went in and out
of consciousness.

One night I was there with him alone. There were empty
beds around him and he was awake. He said, "It's late, why
don't you go to bed?"

Later on he called me. I went over to him, but he didn't say
anything at first. Then he said, "Why are you here, why are
you up so late?"

This happened several times.

In the morning around seven or eight I went back home and Nini came.

WILLY: Nini went early to the hospital to relieve Ellen. Then Grace and I went to the hospital not long after eight o'clock. When we arrived, Nini said to Grace, "I don't think there is much time left. I'd better notify people." We walked toward the bed, F. C. was having a hard time breathing and his eyes could not focus. Grace put her hand on his hand, and he held it and tried to put it to his lips and had a difficult time doing it. As he kept trying, tears rolled down Grace's face. She could only murmur, "No, no . . ."

Nini came in. She took one look and beckoned me to the window and said to me, "Mother needs some vitamins. Could you go to the drugstore and get her some? Go past the Water Works and tell them Daddy's situation is extremely serious."

I did not know whether to leave or stay. Nini said, "Go!"

I took a last look back at the room and left.

After I bought the vitamins I walked quickly to the Water Works. I went to see the chief engineer who had taken F. C.'s place after he was transferred to Peking and said to him that my father's condition was very serious. Just then someone else walked into the office. As soon as he saw me he said, "What time did he pass away?"

I must have looked stunned as the words echoed in my head.

"He doesn't know yet," another disconnected voice sounded somewhere beside me.

I got up and walked out in a daze with the words "pass away . . . he doesn't know yet" ringing in my ears.

When I reached home, Grace and Nini were already home and there were half a dozen people sitting in the living room, people from the Water Works and some friends of the family. I didn't know where to go. Just then the door to the bedroom cracked open and Ellen, who had been sleeping, poked her head out and whispered to me with a smile, "Who are all those people?" I blurted out, "Daddy died." The light in her shining eyes dimmed and without a word she slowly closed the door.

ELLEN: You think it will never really happen. Even later, we thought we would hear him coming home for lunch. We never did cry in front of each other. We held everything in ourselves, and didn't let it out to each other—but it was a shock for Grace.

It was decided that the funeral would be too much of an ordeal for mother as it would be long and all in Chinese. Nini and I represented the family and Willy stayed home with Grace.

F. C. was very well known and had worked with people in all walks of life. The funeral was attended by a great number of people. It was organized by the Water Works and his colleagues made speeches. The funeral procession was a street block long. People lined up to say goodbye. Then the body was taken to the crematorium that he had designed.

News of F. C.'s death spread quickly. Some of his former classmates and friends wrote or came to visit. Rensul Yang, a Tsing Hua classmate who had studied in the States and visited F. C. and Grace in New York, came down from Peking and stayed with the family for a couple of days.

He and other friends told Grace that living without F. C. in China would be difficult—now was the time for her to return to the States. But Grace would not hear it. She felt strongly that F. C. wanted his children to grow up in China and be part of the new China. To honor him, she would do whatever she had to do to carry out his wishes.

F. C.'s favorite photo shows him dressed as an ordinary worker.

William, age 14, last photo with his father.

點水萍綠亂牽風行帶長落

紅吹不定幽趣在濠梁

TWELVE

F. C. DIED SEPTEMBER 1, 1955; he was fifty. The cancer that took his life also took from Grace her beloved companion of the past quarter century, a man she loved so much that she chose him and his world over her own career, culture, and even family. She wrote in her memoir of being reunited with him in New York shortly before they married: "All doubt and hesitation were gone now, for both of us. I knew that this was the one man I wanted now and forever to live with and be with, to face life with whatever the years might bring." And the years, beyond her wildest imaginings, had brought life rich in tragedy and triumph. She and F. C. had survived separation, war, flood, famine, and revolution. They had raised loving children in both Chinese and American traditions. They had seen F. C. rise to the top of his profession.

Throughout all, they had remained devoted to each other, friends and lovers. But now he was gone.

In the days to come, writing became Grace's only outlet. Cut off from her family at home and restrained from expressing her feelings even to her own children, Grace chose to express her grief to an older woman across the ocean.

Harriet Eddy was eighty-two years old and stone-deaf. Grace had never met her. Harriet lived in Palo Alto, California, where she had retired after working for the California library system. She had seen Grace's articles in the *China Monthly Review* and had written to her, beginning a correspondence that was warm and personal. A few weeks after F. C. died, Grace poured out the news to Harriet:

> Tientsin
> September 24, 1955
>
> My dear, dear Harriet,
>
> This is a letter I hate to write—I hate to see the words down on paper. But I cannot hide from reality and I feel very close to you and very sure of your love, sympathy, and wise understanding. My summer was a nightmare of anxiety and suffering. For nearly half a year I could see that F. C. was not improving. During the heat wave of July, he became much worse and the doctor was forced to tell me that what we thought was pleurisy was incurable cancer of the lung. F. C. never knew what he had and after six weeks in the People's Hospital he died on September 1st.
>
> I did not know that last fall the Central Government wanted to send him to Moscow, but the Soviet doctors in the Soviet hospital in Peking, where F. C. stayed for nine weeks, said that the Soviet Union did not know how to deal with such an intractable condition except to keep the patient as comfortable as possible. Everything that could possibly be done for him was done up to the very last. The government ordered from Hong Kong at great expense a British preparation made from a Japanese medicine that kept down the worst pain, so that it was not necessary to keep him drugged with morphine. He was fully conscious most of the time. He had five doctors and two special nurses and

one of us stayed with him all the time, never leaving him alone with only a nurse.

Though he never knew he had cancer, during the last week he began to realize that his illness was fatal and he told me to be prepared for his death and to face the future with confidence. He said he had had a full and satisfying life especially during the last six years when he was able to do much work for China's industrialization, and he had hoped to do much more, but if he had to go now, he had no regrets—he had a good and wonderful share of life. He spoke of the children's future in a socialist world and told them always to live as Chairman Mao had taught the young people and children to live.

He did not—noticeably—lose weight until the last few days, but he had difficulty in sleeping, increasing difficulty in breathing, and hated to eat, all of which made him nervous and exhausted. For the last two days he had to have oxygen to relieve the terrible heaviness of his breathing. The growth traveled from his left lung to the right lung and then to the stomach and liver, under the left armpit and around the neck and then finally to the lining of the brain. The morning he died and the night before, he recognized no one and kept calling for old schoolmates he hadn't seen for twenty-five years. But I think he knew me although he didn't speak to me or look at me. For an hour or two before the end he held on to my hand and kissed it repeatedly. He could then no longer talk.

The whole terrible six weeks had so benumbed me that I had the sensation of standing aside and watching myself go through some kind of fantastic scene. It all seemed so impossible, so utterly impossible that F. C. had gone out of my life forever.

Since then constant physical activity—washing, ironing, sweeping, scrubbing, and cooking—is helping me overcome my first frantic desperation and despair. I have to keep myself reminded of the thousands of thousands of women all over the world who have faced the same thing, and worse, so bravely and firmly.

The children are so good and considerate that I cannot oppress them with any excessive grief. Fortunately I have no asthma this fall, thanks to a Chinese medicine, and I can keep active. The government has been very generous and if we live very economically, the government money will be enough for about eight years, until all the children have finished the university and can work. I have dismissed both my domestic helpers and we are moving to a smaller place. I am a good cook and the girls are learning; and we—

I was interrupted and now I don't remember what I was going to say. The only time I regret my cook and amah is when I want to write a letter and have no time. Otherwise I'm very glad to be kept too busy to think.

To make our expenses as small as possible without cutting down on essentials we are going to have to cut out some items that we could afford on F. C.'s salary—We are now planning to move out to Sian within the next year. That is F. C.'s old home where there are quite a lot of cousins. Sian is the gateway to the northwest—the new frontier—the cradle of ancient Chinese civilization and now one of the newest industrialization centers. F. C. was out there a year ago in the spring and he said it was beautiful and fast becoming a modern city, and with a much better climate than Tientsin and Peking.

I must stop now and get lunch for Wei-han and Ai-lien (Ellen). Nini eats in school. We are going to have To-fu (bean curd) cooked with tomatoes and green peppers; eggs with Chinese sauce and Kan fan (dry rice). Very simple but good.

Dear Harriet, I know you are a wise, brave and useful person. I hope you will write and help bolster up my courage, I have confidence in the future and I've nothing to worry about. But my joy, enthusiasm, and interest in life are gone—and I know that is a wrong attitude and a selfish one. I try to combat it with all my might and I think I succeed in at least not burdening the children and the people around me. But here I am burdening you!

With love and thanks,

Grace

Grace had no idea at this point what lay ahead of her. She had little experience with managing money or budgets. William, only fourteen when his father died, was worried over how the family would survive economically:

> During the first two weeks, we were too stunned to think about the future. We didn't know how to manage financially. When I was about twelve years old, I wanted to put some money in the bank for savings and my father said, "What for? Are you going to be a capitalist?" He was the great provider and we were not supposed to worry about practical things. It was an intellectual's attitude—that money was not worth anything and you should not worry about it. That was okay for him because of his highly valued skill. F. C. had one of the highest salaries but he spent all he had. Our cook's salary was as high as a university graduate's. As far as I know, we had no savings at all when F. C. died.

Now twenty-two, Nini was already used to being in charge:

> Grace stopped eating for quite a while after F. C. died. I had really a tough time to make her eat and get her back. It was a terrible shock for her. We didn't have much money, so I suggested we move. We lived in rather an expensive place. I knew that how we lived was not what you call Chinese normal. Even when my father was alive, we talked about it—he said he couldn't have such a high salary for too much longer. I wanted to go to work. After liberation it was new for women to go off to work. It was exciting for me and my classmates to work for China and have economic independence. There was a policy that allowed children to be hired by the same workplace when a family member died, so I went to work for the Tientsin Water Works.

When F. C. died, the Lius still lived in the house into which they moved during the Japanese occupation. It was the same house where they lived when the PLA came marching down the street, where they entertained the U.S. marines after VJ Day. It was a simple Spanish-style duplex, with tile roof and stucco walls, located on the edge of the former British concession. It was not very large by Western standards, but it was according to Chinese ideas. It was rental property and the landlord exacted a good rent. F. C. had never bought a house. It was Chinese policy that the workplace handled pensions and responded to the family's needs. So it was the Institute in Peking, and not the Tientsin Water Works, that actually was responsible for F. C.'s pension. According to William, the family was unprepared for what happened:

A representative from F. C.'s organization in Peking came and said that the government had decided, in honor of F. C.'s contribution to the state, to give the family one year of F. C.'s salary. Since that was customary and since F. C. had such a high salary, he probably considered that a generous offer, although some people expected them to do much more. But then he went on to say that to honor F. C.'s memory, Grace should eschew her former extravagant ways and really live like an ordinary Chinese. They had heard how extravagant she had been and that the family was lazy and had not taken good care of F. C.

I was too stunned to know how to respond. He did not know Grace at all. He had never seen us, had no relationship or history with the family. What could he mean?

Many undercurrents of feelings and resentments made life very difficult for Grace after F. C. died. There were many built-up resentments against F. C. and Grace. F. C.'s principles and hot temper had made many enemies over the years. Some former directors resented F. C.'s role in negotiating the sale of the Water Works. Other overseas-educated upper-class Chinese had never felt camaraderie from F. C. They expected him to prefer Western tastes and extravagant styles, but he always looked down on these indulgences. Some of these people resented F. C.'s high profile and felt that he had gained it only by catering to the Communists.

These old resentmens reemerged and Grace was blamed for keeping F. C. from being truly one of them. He did not do the things that Chinese men of that class did away from their wives. They always accused her of being extravagant, even if it was just "different." Anything that was different from their ways was criticized: She ate expensive foods, read all the time, had servants, and did not take care of F. C. as she should.

The people in authority over F. C. thought it was his foreign wife that made him draw such a high salary. They
assumed that it was F. C.'s wife that kept him from joining the
Communist Party and from being of like mind with them.

I felt that Grace was being punished, for being who she
was. She was being blamed because they thought she was the
reason that F. C. wasn't totally "Chinese."

The first thing Grace did was to take care of the cook and amah.
Wang Nai-nai had already retired and returned to her home. Grace
paid the other amah and reluctantly dismissed her. Then she wrote
a letter of recommendation for Sun Pao-san and he got a very good
job with the Finnish ambassador and moved to Peking. The children began looking for another place to live, one they could afford.

After school, Ellen went to the house bureau and checked out
houses. "Friends helped us arrange a swap for a new place. We
checked out the place we moved to—it was light and sunny and
quite nice. We went and scrubbed it out, cleaned it up. Grace was
in bed; after we moved she remained in bed for a while. I did the
shopping and Nini cooked the meals. We moved to a house that
was shared by other families. To Grace it must have seemed like a
tenement, so many people in the same building, sharing things, no
servants. To me it was just like how all my schoolmates lived."

In early November, two months after F. C. died, they moved.
William described their new home:

> . . . two rooms in a huge dilapidated mansion shared by
> seventeen families, most of whom were blue-collar worker
> families. The building was built in the grand style of the
> twenties and had belonged to an aide of the "Young Marshal,"
> Chang. It was a big square building, like a mansion with a
> courtyard and a wall around it. There were three floors and a
> half basement with windows. Several families lived on each
> floor, and each family had one or two rooms. Two families
> partitioned the parlor and one lived under the stairway. Each
> floor had a bathroom and a faucet. People bathed outside, or
> in their rooms with a pan. From the basement to the third

floor, each family had a small coal stove, for heating and cooking, placed in the hallway in front of their doors. Whenever anyone started their stove, the smoke from the kindling and the coal would go up the stairwell and permeate each room in the building.

We were fortunate—we had the two nicest rooms in the building with a door in the middle and we had access to a balcony which looked out over the courtyard and street and was shared by three families. We had a room that opened onto the balcony and an inner room that opened to the hall. The outside room had big double-glazed windows and a fireplace that wasn't working. It had wooden floors and high ceilings, but the high ceilings just made it harder to heat. The rooms were bright and clean, an oasis from the hallway. Unfortunately the smoke still poured in whenever some family started their stove.

The four families on the second floor where we lived shared one toilet and a bathroom with a faucet and a sink. The bathtub was filled with someone's coal. Of course there was no central heating or hot water. We had to heat water on the coal stove for both bathing and laundry.

Before we left our old home, we had to sell most of the furniture, our refrigerator, and the stove with an oven. We all had to learn how to start a small coal stove, to keep it going and cook on it.

None of us knew how to cook. Chinese cooking takes a lot of work for the uninitiated—just lighting the stove was a challenge. You first put paper and kindling in the stove, then you put soft coal on top and light it from the bottom. You put a funnel on top of the stove if it does not have a chimney to draw the air through and the fire to catch. The "soft coal" is easier to ignite but produces a tremendous amount of smoke. When the soft coal catches, you put the normal coal on top. We actually used a coal brick which was pressed into a round tube with holes in it like a beehive. The whole process produced a lot of choking smoke that made your throat and eyes burn. Sometimes we'd bank the stove at night so we didn't have to make it everyday and sometimes the stove went out a couple of times a day and we'd have to make it all over again. Imagine seventeen families lighting stoves at once!

Grace learned rather quickly how to light the coal stove but seldom tried it alone. As the weather started to turn cold, they were all at a loss as to how to keep warm. Grace had been accused of extravagance for using too much coal to keep her home warm. Since she had bronchial asthma every winter, the house had always been well-heated, and the family was not used to wearing padded clothes indoors. During the day, Grace liked to stand on the balcony to watch the street activity and wait for the children to come home from school. William continues:

One day about a week or so after we moved, I came back from school and found Mother standing on the balcony in the cold with her coat and scarf on—looking very pale and shaken.

"Ma, what happened?" I asked in alarm.

"Oh, I nearly asphyxiated myself with the coal stove," she replied, rubbing her head. "It felt so cold that I brought the stove in from the balcony and then closed the door. It did keep me warm for a while, but then I started to get a headache and felt woozy. I suddenly realized it must be the stove, so I moved it back to the balcony and opened the doors wide to get in as much fresh air as possible."

Our neighbor, Mrs. Wang, asked me what had happened and when I told her, she shook her head and said, "You poor things, you didn't even know that you can't put a coal stove inside a room without a chimney. Go get those chimney pipes tomorrow and I will help you put them up."

Mrs. Wang shook her head again when she saw us trying to cook on the small stove. She shared the balcony with us and heard us fussing over it. She offered to cook for us and said, "I have to cook anyway—it is no trouble cooking for two families."

Mrs. Wang was in her late thirties with three daughters between the ages of eight and twelve; her husband worked as a janitor in a hospital. From then on Mrs. Wang cooked for us and her husband brought his big industrial size mop and cleaned our floors every other day. That made our lives a lot easier as none of us objected to having simple meals. At first

Mrs. Wang refused any compensation for her work, but we insisted on paying her; it was only a fraction of what F. C. had paid Sun and Amah.

After moving, Grace discovered the lives of ordinary people and their way of handling everyday affairs. Here she found an entirely different world from what she had known. Over time she became fascinated with what she learned from the women in her neighborhood, especially from her neighbor, Mrs. Wang.

Nini described the difference the move made in Grace's life:

When we moved, it put her with a lot of people. The neighbors immediately came over to help. They were very kind and I think it sort of got her out of herself. I think that did a world of good for her.

Immediately she learned more Chinese. She understood more than she thought she could. She knew she talked like a foreigner so she was hesitant to speak in Chinese. But she really understood quite a lot. Grace was able to converse in halting Chinese with Mrs. Wang. While washing and drying the dishes, they would talk about what was going on in the neighborhood. If Grace found something very difficult to understand, she would ask one of us to interpret for her. Mrs. Wang would tell about what the neighborhood women studied in their political study group, and Grace was quite impressed with how much the ordinary housewives were learning about the theory and practice of the new society.

Mrs. Wang was from a landlord Protestant family, high school educated. Her husband, we learned later, was a former KMT security chief, and an interpreter for the Japanese. He was born in a poor peasant family in the Northeast, didn't get along with the stepmother and ran away. After liberation he went to find his family. His wife came to Tientsin. When he returned he turned himself in and confessed his past deeds. After that he became a hospital cleaner and worked conscientiously.

Mrs. Wang was also the neighborhood representative then, and was involved in many community events. She represented our house in the neighborhood meetings and would bring us news and ask our ideas and opinions. They might meet up to two or three times a week, whenever things came up. Because the society was constantly changing, the people had to catch up with the changes. New things cropped up everyday and we had to talk about how to deal with it, how to face it.

The following excerpt is taken from an article Grace wrote in 1956, entitled "Election Day in Tientsin":

One day Mrs. Wang and I were doing the dishes on the balcony. She always had some amusing story to tell.

"I've been at a meeting all afternoon," she said, handing me a bunch of chopsticks to dry.

"What was it this time?" I asked, knowing that she was our neighborhood representative and always had interesting stories.

"I talked to the housewives today about the election for people's deputy. The *lau tai-tai* (old ladies) have the funniest reasons for disapproving of some candidate. For instance, one old lady said, 'No, no, I don't like him at all! He didn't speak to me on the street the other day.' And another one said about a woman candidate, 'I don't think she would make a good people's deputy. She drove my chickens out of the courtyard once.'"

Mrs. Wang saw much to laugh over, but she took her duties very seriously. She worked hard to give even the most backward women some knowledge of the importance of the elections . . .

When election day for district representative arrived I watched the women of our house gather in the courtyard, and I could hardly recognize them! They were making a great occasion of the trip to the ballot box and were wearing colorful dresses and jackets, flowers in their hair and makeup!

Mrs. Chai from upstairs, for instance—a bright jacket, red flower in her hair, and lipstick had transformed the thin sallow-faced woman that I was used to seeing every day in black trousers and jacket.

Mrs. Wang was also wearing red flowers, lipstick, and a pretty new gown. They all went off in a group to vote for the five candidates they had approved. These five deputies of our neighborhood, together with the deputies of all the other neighborhoods of our district, made up the district people's congress. Tientsin's twelve districts formed the Tientsin Municipal People's Congress. Thus, the members of the city government were first elected in neighborhood zones . . . I didn't know much about these things until after my husband died—when we moved into a real neighborhood. Everyone was in a group: either you were in a school or a factory or a neighborhood organization. In this way, I saw ordinary people learning to participate and becoming leaders. . . .

That winter was the coldest the Lius could remember since the Japanese occupation. Grace learned to keep on layers of padded winter clothes like all people in China did during the winter. The house was always cold, but this also had its good side: lessening the contrast between the inside and the outside prevented Grace's children from catching colds. But Grace suffered in the cold room where she stayed all day. All her energy had to be spent on keeping warm. Even so, she was healthier than she had been in many years. Perhaps it was the changed conditions which contributed to her health, but just as likely it was her determination.

THE IDEA OF A trip to West Liu Village had been growing in Grace's mind for some time. Well-meaning friends tried to discourage her. She was told that few people, even those much hardier than herself, would undertake such an arduous trip. But she wanted her children to know their father's roots and thus their own Chinese side.

So less than a year after F. C. died, in the summer of 1956, Grace and her children embarked on the roots-seeking journey to the West Liu Village in Shensi (Shaanxi) Province, one hundred and fifty miles from the ancient city of Sian (Xian), in the very heartland of China. The following account of their trip started out to be an article which was published in the *New World Review*, October 1956, about traveling on the new Lanchow-Sinkiang Railway, one of the most difficult engineering feats undertaken in New China. But Grace expanded her account into this longer and more personal description. She initiated the trip for the children, but by its end, it is clear that the journey was for her. She traveled not only into the heartland of China but into her own heart, to the reason that she had come to China in the first place and then chosen to stay. Her journey begins:

> In August 1956, my three children and I were on our way to the ancient West Liu Village in Shensi Province. I was taking them to visit their father's birthplace where their ancestors had lived for hundreds of years. Coming from the port city of Tientsin with its conglomerate population and foreign atmosphere, to the old family village in the lower Yellow River Area, the cradle of Chinese civilization, my children would see and learn something of their Chinese heritage.
>
> It was just seven years after the founding of the Chinese People's Republic and although the tracks of new railways were hourly spreading and advancing all over the country, there were still far too few railway lines, cars, engines, and railway personnel to handle comfortably and effectively the unprecedented crowds of people traveling in China. Traffic was especially heavy on the lines going to the Northwest to the oil fields and new industrial cities and to the land being settled by pioneer families. To anyone unused to traveling it was a daring adventure to join even for a few days—this surging advance into China's fabulous northwest.
>
> I knew it would be a physical ordeal for us as we started traveling just as the majority of the people, workers, and peasants did—on "hard seats," with no

sleeping accommodations. But it would be an experience that I needed to bring me into closer contact with the Chinese *l'au pai shing* [literally, "old one hundred names," ordinary people].

Our plan was to spend a week with one of the Liu "sisters" (cousins of the same generation) in the Shensi capital city of Sian which as ancient "Changan" was the capital of one of the earliest dynasties of China. From there we would travel under her guidance to West Liu Village.

We left Tientsin with much conflicting advice and confusing information. Some friends thought we were very unwise, in fact, "absolutely crazy" to attempt such a journey in the hottest part of the summer, or to think of going to a village that could be reached even after two days and a night on the train, only by ox-cart and foot. But others were enthusiastic and thought it the wisest thing we could possibly do.

From the railway-ticket office, we received vague information on very important points and, of course, ran promptly into what seemed to me at the moment a catastrophe—we missed our Sian train in Peking! All because we hadn't been told of some formality that had to be gone through when changing trains. To such inexperienced travelers as Nini, Ellen, Wei-han, and me, this was a dreadful blow, especially as the Peking ticket office seemed utterly indifferent to our fate, even saying that there was no place on the next Sian train, four hours later.

The waiting room we were in was jammed—every seat was occupied and every inch of floor space, except the lanes where people were lined up to board the next outgoing trains, covered with bags, bundles, baskets, and small children. Perhaps we would have to wait here until morning—twelve hours. Our one seat was piled with luggage and we had just room enough to stand.

However, we were not left long in our wrath and dismay—the station police came to the rescue. The courteous young man in the new summer blue-and-white police uniform who had inspected my traveling permit as we entered the Peking station now came with an anxious face to see why we had not gotten on our train. When he heard our story he said, "Never mind, we will think of something." In a little while we had our tickets for the next Sian train and were settled in four seats in another less-crowded waiting room. For the next few hours I relaxed and observed my fellow travelers.

I envied the composure, calm confidence, and good humor of these hundreds of peasants, workers, and their families, army men and women and students. Those having many hours to wait were as practical and unselfconscious as if they had lived all their lives in a railway station. Bedding had been unrolled and whole families had gone to sleep on the floor, which was kept clean by frequent sweeping and mopping.

I saw a soldier take out his wash basin and give his face and neck a good scrubbing. A group of cadres sitting on their bags were reading and eating watermelon seeds, carefully putting the shells back in the sack. One opened a bundle and changed his shoes and socks.

Though undoubtedly most of them must have been hot, tired, and uncomfortable, I didn't see any cross faces or hear any quarrels; no one looked angry and upset as I had a little while before. By the time the same policeman came to tell us that we could get on the train, I was feeling ashamed of my biting remarks about the whole railway administration and the ticket offices in particular. Nini's reminding me of how the country's rapid development had necessitated sending great numbers of people over widespread distances, before the railways had become able to do the task expertly, made me ready to be more lenient with the railway and its faults.

We met more negative aspects of present-day railway travel in China, things that needed and were getting criticism. But compared to rail travel of twenty-two years ago when I first came to China, I found that the positive outweighed the negative. For one thing, I appreciated the railroad's one hundred percent safety record when we crept across the wide expanse of the

Yellow River, crossed deep gorges, ran along steep
hillsides that sometimes "slipped," and went through
low-lying plains that had been recently swept by a
hurricane. At every station the train was gone over from
end to end by repair crews.

It was comforting to look out just anywhere and see
the faithful and vigilant track-walkers. The citizen
track-walkers spaced themselves at unusually close
intervals wherever there might be danger. These
civilians protected the trains from the kinds of attacks
that F. C. had known as a young man. In his student
days this trip was so dangerous that he attempted it
only twice—once to go to Peking and once to return.

At intervals during the daytime the pleasant voice of
a young woman announced stations over a loudspeaker,
called the passengers' attention to historic places and
famous scenic spots, advised mothers with small
children, and gave some simple rules of hygiene. Every
half-hour or so a man came through with a broom, then
a mop—the cars were never allowed to become littered.

Perhaps I was the only passenger who did not enjoy
the noisy Chinese opera that poured through the
loudspeaker between announcements and hygiene
talks—as far as I am concerned the continuous playing
of music from Chinese operas on trains is definitely a
negative point!

Our car was full of railway workers, going out to
work on the Lanchow-Sinkiang Railway which had then
already reached Yumen, China's biggest oil field, and in
a few years would connect with the Soviet Union's
Turkestan-Siberia Railway; or to the Lanchow-Yinchuan
section, which cuts through the Great Wall to reach
Yinchuan, a major wool, hide, and skin trading center in
the Northwest. Several village woman with their
children were going to join oil-field and railway-worker
husbands in Lanchow and beyond.

A short, stocky young engine-driver, his tall pretty
wife, and their three small children sat across the
aisle from us, and we were soon old acquaintances.
"Papa," as we nicknamed the young man, was a marvel

of efficiency, energy, and good-heartedness. He took wonderful care of his family and, like a mother bird, was always feeding them with chicken, preserved eggs, steaming bowls of noodles and vegetables, apples, and melons. He helped all the passengers around us with his many useful ideas about how to arrange bundles, bags, and children so as to use every bit of space. He soon found out all there was to know about us and passed on the information to other interested passengers. He, in turn, told everybody about himself and his job and what a wonderful healthful and beautiful country it was where he was working in the mountains beyond Lanchow. He had already been there and had gone back to his old home near Peking to get his family. His wife said she knew it would be a good place to bring up children.

From daybreak until dark we never tired of watching the amazing scenery. Fantastic terraced hillsides, like huge red-and-green layer cakes, cave dwellings carved out of red hills, and toy-like villages perched on mountainsides flew past the windows. Something entirely new had now appeared on China's landscape— the wide-stretching collective farm fields of corn, cotton, millet, and soybeans, instead of the patchwork of tiny fields of the old days.

We made frequent trips to the diner to relieve our cramped legs and backs. The diner was open and full all day and most of the night. The people who ate in the diner were the same people who made up the passengers—it was a curious sight to me to see a peasant family eating in a railway dining car—such a thing was inconceivable in the China that I entered in 1934.

The food in both the diner and in the stations was a decidedly positive point for the railroads. Formerly no one with the least idea of hygiene would dare to buy anything to eat in the stations. But now the vendors were dressed in white coats and caps and their wares were packaged and wrapped and carried in glassed-in carts. Some places famous for their roast chicken did a rushing business through the car windows. We bought two—deep-red brown, with a special flavor and

tenderness. Even our vegetarian Wei-han ate not only
all his share, but a great part of mine while I was
absorbed in the scenery.

After two days and one night, we reached Sian three
hours late. Tracks had been washed out in a place or two
by hurricane rains and had to be repaired. Eighth Sister
Liu met us at the station and we spent an exciting time
in the beautiful old city—more beautiful, I think, than
Peking—once the capital of ancient China, and now in
1956, a bustling young frontier gateway to the great
new developments of the northwest.

Now, Eighth Sister told us that our journey had only
begun here. She would accompany us to the township
of Fu-ping, a small county seat about a hundred miles
from Sian. There we would stay overnight with Fifth
Sister (another cousin) and go the next day another ten
miles to the village.

Approaching Fu-ping station, we saw the small city
with its ancient wall and moat, perched like a medieval
fortress on top of the hill facing us. Wheat, millet, and
corn fields were flourishing all around for this was
fertile countryside. We went down the slope from the
station and climbed the road leading up to the city
gate. To the right of the road a little river meandered
down the hill, and beneath a splendid eight-hundred-
year-old bridge of white stone, small boys were
catching river crabs. Beyond the river spread a thriving
vegetable garden.

We walked across a brick causeway and through the
big city gate. There we were met and welcomed by Fifth
Sister and her husband. Their house near the gate was
built right up against the city wall; in fact, the city wall
served as one of the walls of the house. The children
were delighted to look over the wall that was common
to both house and city and see down into the moat.

We spent the afternoon sightseeing around the city. I
think all the children in the place and many of the
adults, too, came along with us. I was quite a sight to
see myself—a foreign visitor who was actually a relative
of one of their neighboring families!

One of the places we visited that afternoon was the school where Third Uncle Liu had taught for many years. In the school yard we saw a memorial stone carved more than a thousand years ago honoring some ancient hero or, more likely, a scholar. As a young boy Fu-chi had attended this school under his uncle's tutelage. My hands lingered a moment on the stone that he had undoubtedly touched.

The next morning the ox-cart arrived to take us to the village. This type of vehicle must be of unknown antiquity—in Bible times, Abraham and Sarah would have ridden in such a thing. It was an open box on two huge entirely wooden wheels. A light wooden framework had been added to the top and sides, covered over with some kind of cloth. The wooden surface on wooden wheels was entirely without springs of any sort. The cloth covering protected the travelers from sun and rain, but nothing would protect them from being bumped and shaken to bits.

The ox and his owner were a well-matched pair. The huge red ox was magnificent and had a calm ponderous dignity that was truly impressive. The driver, a strong young peasant whose red-brown face flowed with health, was Eighth Sister's own brother. He was the farmer of the family. His younger brother was to be a schoolteacher like his father, our Third Uncle. Eighth Sister was going to be a doctor and was a student at Sian Medical School. She is the one that F. C. had stayed with when he visited here. She had been worried then about his condition.

My son, fifteen-year-old Wei-han, sat up on the driver's seat with the driver. Most of the time, the driver walked beside the ox to encourage him over the rocks and ruts. The rest of us, my two girls, Eighth Sister, and I settled ourselves as best we could on the floor of the cart—and away we plodded! The extreme slowness of the pace somewhat mitigated the severity of the jolts and bumps.

We soon came to an almost dried-up riverbed where tiny streamlets of water trickled through stones of all sizes. After being shaken across the dry rocky bed, we came to a place where the water was deep and wide and swift. When the ox found the going difficult, the driver told the younger ones to get out of the cart. They gleefully took off their shoes and socks, rolled up their pants, and waded through. I wanted to do the same, but in China when you're over fifty you must be treated with great respect, so I had to submit to being carried over in the treacherous cart.

By and by we came to a beautiful place. We were going down a long tree-shaded lane which stretched as far as the eye could see. It was lined on both sides with tall trees, many of whose branches met over our heads. It was a very beautiful, peaceful scene, so why, then, did I have such an eerie feeling when I looked up into the branches?

"Ma!" Nini exclaimed excitedly. "This must be the place where Daddy saw the heads hanging from the trees."

Yes, that was exactly what was running through my mind! We were all familiar with the description of this place and we all had a vivid mental picture of a little boy running for dear life, pursued by some fantastic horror—when he saw human heads hanging in the trees.

At last we were nearing the end of our journey. The sky had clouded up and rain was beginning to fall. Just ahead we saw the village veiled in a fog of drizzle with wispy curls of smoke floating reluctantly from noon-time cooking. As we rolled ponderously along toward this scene with its misty look of an old Chinese painting, I felt that our mode of approach was well suited to an ancient place, wrapped in the peace and calm of the ages.

This old West Liu Village, less than ten miles from Fu-ping, lies in fertile country nearly a hundred miles south of the poorer and harsher countryside around Yenan. Because the land is fertile, the village has not been so poverty-stricken and ground down with hardships as those farther to the north. But we knew that it had many times known violence and terror. The

Mohammedan region was not far away and the
eight-hundred-year-old village history records its
partial destruction several times in raids during
Mohammedan rebellions.

In the Liu family after the last big raid there were
only three cousins (called brothers) left as heads of
the family. My husband's father was one of them and
the father of the present head was another. But those
times were long over by 1956 and the Hui people
(Mohammedans) and the Han people (Chinese) were,
on the whole, peaceful and amicable neighbors,
as some of the curly-haired and big-nosed cousins
bore evidence.

The big ox knew when he was home. He stopped
with determination in front of a door in a wall. We all
hurried out of the rain through the wall door into a small
front garden. From there we entered a house where
Third Uncle, Third Aunt, and other relatives, including
our ox driver's wife and small child, welcomed us.

The old Liu home was built around a courtyard rather
like a Peking house—the courtyard wasn't a yard at all
but a shallow green-tiled pool. Under overhanging
eaves a narrow porch or walk ran around three sides of
the pool. As in most Chinese houses, the kitchen was at
the front on the right of the entrance. I never did find
out how many rooms the house had or how big it
actually was.

Ellen and I were given the room my husband's mother
had occupied—the very room where F. C. was born. It
had been a year since F. C. was struck without apparent
warning by a fatal illness. He died in the midst of work
of great urgency, the work to which he had dedicated
his life. And now it was a solace and comfort to my
spirit to be here in this room where he was born and in
the house where he had played as a small boy. I could
feel the continuity of generations that is so strong in
China. Its eternal quality helps to soothe and heal the
sharp pain of individual loss.

That night as I lay next to my daughter, watching the
candlelight flicker on the ceiling, I imagined that

candlelight had flickered the same way on the ceiling when my husband was a baby. I could imagine his young mother holding him. How did she feel in that flickering light? Did she not wonder what would become of him?

He had loved his mother devotedly and when he was older realized her great strength of character and broadmindedness. At the time he left home, F. C. did not know his mother's story, but he heard it many years after: She had been a slave girl in a great landlord family in the south of the province. The mistress of the family loved the little slave girl and brought her up like a daughter. At the proper age, the mistress saw to it that she was married to a respectable man of a good family and came to live with the Liu family of West Liu Village.

His father died a short while before F. C. was born in 1904, leaving his young widow with a two-year-old daughter and a baby son. The little boy was brought up under the Confucian discipline of his three uncles. It was his uncles who decided that he should be sent to Peking, that education was his only hope.

I thought of the thirteen-year-old boy leaving home, leaving his mother and sister, leaving the village that he had known to go to school in faraway Peking. Setting off down the road, over which we had just traveled, did he turn one last time? Did he see her standing by the door in the wall? F. C. told me that she told him not to think of her or to think he must be ruled unduly by the demands of the family—but that he must make his own life when he got out in the world.

By leaving in 1917 at such an early age, F. C. escaped from the more pernicious side of the Confucian, feudal, patriarchal family system with its veneration of authority and its downgrading of women. But he took with him the best of the moral training and discipline from his uncles, the love and devotion of his mother, and the noblest of Chinese character from the people of the village.

At Tsing Hua a new world opened up to him. He stayed at Tsing Hua for eight years, meeting boys from all over China and forming close friendships that lasted his entire life. Those friendships extended to me and the children and are still a source of comfort and happiness to us.

In the summer of 1925, just after his graduation from Tsing Hua, F. C. made the long trip back to West Liu Village for the first time in eight years. It would also be the last time before he left for America in the fall. But a totally unexpected blow awaited him. He learned on his arrival home that his mother and older sister had died. His uncles feared that he would not graduate and waited until his return to inform him. The sudden news of his mother's death shocked him into a realization that he was utterly alone in the world.

There was one last duty that, as an only son, he must carry out. His mother's coffin was still unburied, waiting in the village temple for her son to perform this last rite for his mother—he must go to the temple and sleep beside her coffin every night for a month and he must go alone . . .

Grace slept that night in the room where her husband had been born, thinking of the young boy, wondering how his mother felt when her only son left home, and identifying with the young man, sleeping beside his mother's coffin, alone in the dark, having no family, no home to return to. She realized she had become his only family. Like him, she had left her home and now had no family to return to. She was utterly alone in the world, except for her children—his children. They were her family and China was her home. For his sake, she would stay and raise their children in China.

Grace, in padded jacket, standing by the wall behind her house.

Ellen and William, high school students; Nini, employed at the Water Works, 1957.

THIRTEEN

I F THE CHINESE revolution were a symphonic score, the first movement would end here. Up till now it had been, in Grace's view, a rousing and compelling march, with the different sections of society playing their parts in the great Chinese socialist transformation. After liberation, China had engaged in a patriotic surge of progress that F. C. had hoped for in his youth. The success of those early years led the nation into an ebullience symbolized by Mao's daring dive into the Yangtse River in the summer of 1956. He proudly boasted his robust health at age sixty-two as well as that of the emerging productive nation.

In 1957 attitudes were opening up, evidence of which could be seen in the more colorful fashions, a variety of art and cultural forms, and more learning, even of foreign languages. In May 1957 Mao proposed an openness to new ideas. The march changed for a moment to a light and airy melody, befitting the warm spring weather and Mao's expansive words: "Let a hundred flowers bloom . . . a hundred schools of thought contend."

The Hundred Flowers movement in the spring of 1957 had something in common with the Prague Spring of 1968. Both were heady bursts of open expression in a previously restricted environment. From May 1 to June 7, 1957, an air of openness pervaded the country. People were encouraged to speak their own views "on what are fragrant flowers and what are poisonous weeds"—as long as their criticisms and grievances were intended to strengthen and not weaken the socialist transformation and the leadership of the Communist Party. With some persuasion, individuals gradually responded, tentatively at first, and then with enthusiasm—in newspapers, magazines, circulars, open forums, posters stuck to the walls, and big rallies. The movement, *ta ming ta fang* in Chinese, literally meant "big chirping, big letting loose."

The students of the May 4th Movement of 1919, who had criticized China's backwardness and attacked its institutions and leaders, were now middle-aged teachers, doctors, lawyers, writers, artists, managers, scientists, and engineers. Many were attracted to Mao's revolution because of their patriotism and their hope for China's progress; some had even returned to China from abroad. Many earned positions in the new government and contributed to the nation's rapid development in the first years. Their presence, however, created an uneasy tension in an ideological revolution and their criticisms were now perceived as reactionary.

Some members of the central government feared a rebellion like those in Poland and Hungary in 1956. When the grievances aired mostly by the educated class went as far as challenging the very authority of the party, it became too threatening to the nation's leaders. Those who had spoken out were labeled dissidents or "rightists," and an anti-rightist campaign began. First, the rightists in the party were set straight, and then a rectification campaign spread throughout China.

With an urgent need to galvanize the political energies of the nation, Mao announced in the summer of 1958 the next movement to speed up development. The Great Leap Forward proposed a fantastic goal—to surpass Britain as an industrial force in fifteen years. The vision of plentiful foodstuffs from agricultural communes and self-reliant industries in every village was the expression of the "continuing revolution." Mao was counting, once again, on concerted human willpower to boost the economy.

The momentary light melodies of 1957 ended abruptly, and another march began, in a higher key with a deeper, stronger drum beat.

SOON AFTER HER RETURN from West Liu Village, Grace was offered a job polishing the English proficiency of a group of men and women from the Tientsin Foreign Affairs Bureau. Although contact with the West was limited by 1956, there were occasions when the Foreign Ministry needed cadres who were skilled in English. Grace gladly accepted the offer. It not only gave her extra income but made her feel useful and took her mind off herself.

These students came to Grace's apartment in the former mansion for their lessons. Grace still lived in the area of the British concession which now, devoid of foreigners and the activities which supported them, took on an entirely different character. The area she once described in a letter as "much more foreign than Chinese" was filled with Chinese and their activities, flowing freely between the former concession and the "native city."

The students sat on the balcony that she shared with the Wangs or on the bed or on borrowed chairs. Since these cadres already knew some English, they identified topics and talked about things that were important and relevant to them. As her students gained greater fluency, Grace learned more about them. It was a mutual exchange. But when the rectification campaign set in, the cadres quit coming, to Grace's disappointment. She had grown fond of them, and she missed having something to do. But more importantly, she was developing as a teacher.

By 1957 over three million people lived in Tientsin, with a fast-growing school age population. The demand for schooling had increased 100 percent at all levels; therefore the need for teachers was enormous. Through a friend Grace heard that Nankai University was expanding its offerings and looking for new English teachers. William described her interview with the head of the English Department:

> The head of the department, Professor Li, was a Chinese intellectual of the old school—white-haired, distinguished, well-poised, and professional in his manner, with a round face and well-manicured hands. We learned before she went to see him that he had been a student of Lu-Xun, the most famous of China's writers of the twentieth century.
>
> Grace told me that in her interview Professor Li asked her when she had come to China. When she answered 1934, he replied, "Ah, that is the year I published the first Chinese translation of *Jane Eyre*."
>
> *Jane Eyre* was one of my mother's favorite books. She had always been interested in the Brontë family and replied, "Did you know that Charlotte Brontë wrote that book in only three weeks?"
>
> "Well," he said, "it took me considerably longer to translate it."
>
> They had a good laugh. I think that broke the ice. They began to talk about their experiences. He had started teaching at Nankai the same year that she came to Tientsin. During the Japanese occupation he told her that he had gone with other teachers and students into the interior. Grace had heard about the students and teachers who had carried their books and equipment and set up in the hills until the war was over. She told him that she had watched the bombing of Nankai from the roof of her building with Adelaide Lin. He remembered the Lins who had taught at the university in the thirties. He was glad that so much of the damage caused by the bombing had been repaired. They had many things to talk about.

When Grace left that day, Professor Li gave her a copy of his translation of *Jane Eyre*, which she treasured.

Grace began teaching at Nankai University in the fall of 1957. She was hired initially as a part-time, temporary teacher of second-year English students. The difference that working for an institution, instead of teaching in her home, made in Grace's life at this point is best explained by her description of her former cook, Sun Pao-san, in an article she wrote for the *New World Review* in 1959:

It was lunchtime at the "Willow Forest" sanitarium for T.B. patients. The stout, middle-aged man in white cap and gown was not one of the sanitarium doctors. He was the head cook—and had just shown us over the spotless big kitchen and introduced us to his assistant cooks, one attending a huge cauldron of meat sauce— for noodles—and another frying fish. "Sun Pao-san, the cook, is very famous," I was told. "Cooks from all over China come here to learn from him."

Four years ago, when we started living on a smaller scale after my husband's death, Sun Pao-san went to the Finnish ambassador's family in Peking. Here he managed the other servants, planned the meals, even the big dinners, receptions, and official banquets, and ordered all the food. His wages were high.

Some time later he came to see me. He had gained considerable weight and was looking prosperous. He told us about the famous people he had seen and served at the ambassador's big parties and banquets.

"Well, Sun," I said, "you must feel very satisfied and pleased with such a job."

"No, Tai-tai," he said, "I'm not. I know it's a good job. I never thought of getting so much money before. And the ambassador and his wife are good to me. But I don't feel happy there."

"Oh, you'll feel different when your family moves to Peking," I said. His wife and eight children were still living in Tientsin.

"No," he said. "It's not my family. It's just that I feel left behind. I'm making money. I get to see interesting, famous people. I live comfortably, my family is comfortable. But"—and his voice rose—"I'm not getting anywhere. I'm not learning anything. The whole country is going ahead on a new road. Everybody is studying and learning new things. But I am standing still, learning nothing, belong to nothing—just a cook in a private family!"

"But Sun," I reminded him, "the pay in government places is quite low compared to what you are getting now. Your family couldn't live so comfortably."

"I don't care," he said stubbornly. "I'd rather live hard and feel that I was going ahead with all the people than to live easy and feel the way I do now."

After a month or two he came back, much thinner.

"I'm working for an institution, now," he told me. "The Willow Forest T.B. Sanitarium for workers. It's hard work and the pay isn't much, but I feel I'm really living and learning. We have meetings all the time to discuss our work and how to improve it. And in our study group I'm learning politics and international affairs and what's going on all over the country. And"—smiling proudly—"I belong to the opera group! And I have sung in performances in the biggest theater in Tientsin."

"So you're not sorry you gave up the fine job in Peking," I said.

"Never!" he declared. "Now I'm in step with the whole country."

The next time I saw him was in the late summer of 1958. He had regained much of his former stoutness. The union, he said, had long ago had his wages raised to almost the amount the Finnish ambassador had paid him. He had become a labor model and had been sent that summer for a ten-day vacation to Peitaiho beach, the summer resort only for foreigners and rich Chinese in the old days. His opera group had given several performances in Tientsin and he sang a leading role.

He had come this time to ask me a favor. He wanted some American recipes, especially pies and salads. He told me that he was training cooks from all over China.

The next time I saw him was in the sanitarium dining room. When we said goodbye, I shook hands with a man who was no longer just somebody's servant. He had become a person with dignity and honor.

When Grace went to work at Nankai University, she was no longer just someone's wife, not just a foreign woman teaching at home. Now she belonged to an organization; she had a role, a professional life, and colleagues. She was now a cadre in China's huge socialist work force. In essence, after twenty-three years in China, she had finally become a participant, no longer an outsider looking on. Nini described the change she saw in her mother at this time:

> It must have inspired Grace spiritually a great deal because she worked so terribly hard those years. At the beginning it was a few hours a day, then she went every day. Every day Grace would get up at 5:30 to go downstairs to the breakfast shop and buy fresh, crisp donuts which we ate with pancakes and soy milk. She would come back by the time we were all up. She would tend the stove, heat the soy milk, and we would all eat together. She was healthier than she had been for a long time. After F. C. died, Grace started using Chinese medicine for her asthma. We read in the paper that this new medicine, with arsenic in it, was doing good for people, so she and I took it for a while. I think it did some good, even for me. It made us feel very "hot," as the Chinese say.

After their breakfast together, each member of the Liu family set off in different directions. Nini went to the Water Works as F. C. had for so many years. William and Ellen each walked about forty-five minutes to different high schools. Grace took the bus to work, a thirty-minute ride followed by a twenty-minute walk. Sometimes, if the weather was good, she walked all the way. When the weather was bad, the twenty-minute walk from the bus stop to the university was an ordeal. In the winter, knife-sharp gales from Siberia swept down across the iced-over rice paddies and the campus lotus ponds. Grace, who barely weighed ninety pounds, often had to hold on tight to a lamppost or be blown aloft.

As the demand for English classes increased, Grace's courses did well and she soon became a full-time teacher. It didn't take long for Grace to notice that the style of teaching at the university was quite different from the conversational approach she had used with the cadres at home. The traditional approach to teaching English in China was based on grammar and translation. The professors lectured in Chinese, the students answered in Chinese. Although they were studying English, they did not communicate in English. The teacher gave a detailed description of the grammar in a certain literary text. The students would translate the text from English into Chinese, or from Chinese into English. They took pages and pages of notes in Chinese and analyzed each passage thoroughly. William described his mother's disappointment with the results of this system:

> One night Grace was grading some papers at home and she sighed out loud. "Ma, what's the matter?" I asked.
> "It is so unnecessary," she moaned. Then she read to me what one of her students wrote. He had just come back from Peking where he had seen an English-speaking group with an interpreter from the Foreign Ministry. The interpreter was having a difficult time. Grace's student was very embarrassed for her but he couldn't help her because his English was no better. He was very upset because he had worked so hard for many years and he knew that the interpreter must have worked even harder.
> "My student feels that it is his fault. But it doesn't matter how hard he works, the problem is not his—it is the way he is taught. He can read, he can even analyze the structure of a sentence better than I can, but he can't speak. I asked a senior student the other day what time it was and he could only point at his watch—yet he had just come out of a class where they had been diagramming sentences from T. S. Eliot. Imagine that! What a waste of time!"
> The next day when Grace explained to her student why it was not his fault, word got around that Grace was criticizing the department and especially the old professor whose name was also Li, but he was not the head of the department.

Grace's criticism did not go over very well with Mr. Li or the longtime professors in the English Department.

By early 1958 the whole nation was engaged in "study and criticism" as part of the rectification campaign. At the university as in the rest of China, teachers met in groups for "criticism, self-criticism." The meetings were intended to be a time to correct one's way of thinking and style of work, both in and out of the classroom. William continues:

It came up in these meetings what Grace had said. Grace's criticism caused quite a stir. Some of the students and even the younger teachers agreed with Grace, but the grammar-translation method had been used for years and many of the professors were wedded to it. It was the way they had learned. They had built their reputations teaching this way. And many of the students liked the old approach as well because they were good at it. They felt accomplished when they dissected a sentence in Hardy's *The Mayor of Casterbridge*. They felt inadequate and embarrassed if asked to actually speak. Consequently, Grace was criticized. She was told it was wrong to talk about someone behind his back.

Talking behind someone's back was a question of incorrect political behavior, not one of bad manners. In his essay, "Combat Liberalism," Mao had written that in the process of "active ideological struggle" it was considered a manifestation of liberalism "to indulge in irresponsible criticism in private instead of actively putting forward one's suggestions to the organization. To say nothing to people to their faces but to gossip behind their backs, or to say nothing at a meeting but to gossip afterwards." Changing this kind of behavior was what Mao called "shedding one's bourgeois skin."

Part of the process of shedding one's bourgeois skin was self-criticism. Self-criticism was intended as an opportunity to point out your own errors and set forth ways in which you sought improvement. The method, based on Marxist-Leninist analysis, required that people examine their own class backgrounds to understand the ways they had been taught to think . The goal was to break from one's class and to achieve a truly proletarian world outlook.

Grace wrote the following paper as a self-criticism summary during her first year at Nankai at the end of the rectification campaign. Grace was now accountable for her words and actions in a way that she had never been before. She was writing to her colleagues in her group and used the language of the group. This statement was kept as an official record in Grace's files at the university until it was given to the authors, with permission, in 1998.

Grace Liu
August 14, 1958

I began taking part in the political movements after "*ta ming* and *ta fang*" and the anti-rightist struggle—just before the first teaching reform movement. It was the first time I'd ever taken part in political meetings; and during the movements that followed I have gained a great many benefits, although a large part of the time I have been uncertain and confused as to what was being said.

First of all I have learned to estimate myself somewhat more correctly. Formerly I was inclined to overestimate myself in some ways while feeling inferior in others. Because I was a foreigner, couldn't speak Chinese, and had never taught in a university before, I was sensitive, lacking in confidence, suspicious, and easy to feel hurt. This bourgeois, individualist sensitivity is, I realize, only the other side of pride and conceit. These feelings are egoistic, individualistic, and completely bourgeois. I have long known this intellectually, but it is only since joining in these collective political discussions and criticism and self-criticism that I see the way to overcome this self-centered attitude—criticism and self-criticism and the discipline of collective endeavor.

Because I have read and studied Marxist-Leninist literature for several years, I thought I saw things from a working-class standpoint, and that I was very successfully shedding my bourgeois skin! But the criticisms, *ta tze pao* (big character posters), and collective discussions have shown me that just studying Marxism-Leninism doesn't automatically give one a working-class standpoint. I still have many bourgeois feelings, reactions, and attitudes.

During the first movement this year, before the Spring Festival and holiday, I received practically no criticism, but even some praise, and was in danger of being very satisfied with myself. But one incident during the combined meetings in which the students criticized the teachers shocked me out of my self-satisfaction. My student asked me for permission to repeat my remarks to him about Mr. Li and T. S. Eliot, the English poet. It was very painful to me to have to consent. I did not want to appear before everyone as a person who talked behind the backs of my colleagues. So I came face to face with a very ingrained bourgeois *ze yo zhu i* (liberalistic) trait involving both hypocrisy and dishonesty. Later on [the Chairman of the Department] Professor Li criticized me in a *ta tze pao* for criticizing other teachers behind their backs instead of publicly in meeting or in *ta tze pao*. These two incidents caused me to do some very serious thinking. I didn't like to say straight truths to a person's face, especially to someone who was polite and friendly to me. I felt it would be unpleasant and embarrassing. So I excused myself by thinking one ought to be tactful. To talk behind one's back I excused by thinking it a very human failing that most everyone indulged in. But I've come to realize that it is not a *human* failing but a typical bourgeois trait that can be overcome when one's standpoint is changed.

When Grace first came to China, she was expected to act as a foreigner, a member of the elite, an intellectual in essence, in a "typical bourgeois" way. But now she was operating under a different set of expectations. Students had several ways to point out their teachers' shortcomings. They could address the teacher in class, bring it up in a political discussion group or write big character posters.

Anyone—student or teacher—could write any comment or criticism in bold Chinese characters on large sheets of newsprint-like paper and post it on a wall. Grace's self-criticism continues, referring to posters her students had put up about her:

> The several *ta tze pao* that the students put up for me showed up other subtle bourgeois traits that were so easy to overlook in one's self. Peng Tze-mei gave me a shock when he said I'd made a serious mistake in political outlook in one of my classroom exercises. How could that be, I thought. He must have misunderstood the English words. But when I heard his criticism translated several times to me I had to admit that he was right. I had turned the story into a dialogue for the students to practice. My dialogue of the two workers was a far less severe indictment of capitalism than O. Henry's story. Especially to students not so familiar with English, my dialogue actually sounded as if I were softening the evils and the suffering caused by capitalism. This has taught me that I must be vigilant in everything I write and say, so that no bourgeois attitudes creep in. I hope the students will always be very sharp in their lookout for any kind of errors in my teaching and warn me immediately.

Grace does not plead her case in the next section, but simply states her situation regarding salary and job security. She knew that she required a standard of living above that of ordinary Chinese people. She felt bad about requiring more, but given her condition it would be difficult for her to survive with less. She had proclaimed that she wanted to live like an ordinary Chinese so that she could change her old ways, but it was difficult for her to carry it out.

> There are two other questions on which I've only rather recently begun to realize my wrong way of thinking. They are the question of my salary and the question of security—that is having a position as a regular teacher.

Up until only a month or two ago I have considered that unless I am paid a salary every month I do not have enough to get along on. My reasoning has been this: I am fifty-seven years old and not strong physically and I have been afraid to lower my living standard any further for fear of getting sick or breaking down in some way. However, even without my salary from Nankai, we still have, counting my daughter's salary, more than most working people live on (between seventy and eighty yuan a month). Then am I really standing with the working class when I say it's impossible for me to live as a working-class person? I think that this is only a superstitious fact that I and my family can't get by on this amount. I must dare to break old habits and learn to live as a working-class person. I know that to work hard and enthusiastically in a collective social environment is conducive to health and long life.

I have also feared a lack of security. Not to belong to any organization, to be engaged only by the hours of the month, to be temporary or expendable, had made me fearful of the future when within the next two years I have used up the last of the money given me by the government when my husband died. But this attitude— does it not show a lack of faith in the Party and People's Government? Why should I fear the future for myself? If I have a real socialist mentality, if all my interest and efforts are concentrated on doing my utmost to help build socialism and bring about the ideal state of the future, would there be room in my thoughts for concern over my own individual future?

In the next part she criticized her own teaching. She admonished herself for her inexperience, not planning systematically, lack of direction and being indulgent rather than firm with the students. In a spirit of being "open and receptive to criticism" she volunteered to sit in on other teachers' classes, especially Mr. Li's and suggested that he might sit in on her classes as well to offer criticism of her teaching.

In her conclusion Grace responds to the theme set forth in the essay, "Sixty Points on Working Methods," distributed earlier in

1958. At this stage, Mao still advocated "ideological education"—
as opposed to "ruthless struggle and merciless blows"—as the way
to reform the nation. The total workforce was asked to examine in
the small discussion groups what it meant to be both "red and
expert," that is, to develop both politically and in technical skill.
Grace concluded her summary with what it would take for her to
accomplish this goal:

> I think it is the goal of all of us to be both "red" and
> "expert." I've thought a lot about what it means to be
> "red." It is much simpler to be "expert" than to be "red."
> One can apply himself to the study of one or more
> specialities and become an expert within a
> comparatively short time and without undue difficulties.
> But for a bourgeois intellectual to become "red" requires
> not only arduous study, but a deep and fundamental
> change in outlook and character.
>
> To my mind, to be "red" means to have both a
> thorough understanding of the superiority of the
> socialist way and a clear realization of the supreme
> importance of the leadership of the Party—to stand in
> all things with the working class, striving for working-
> class discipline and the communist spirit of self-
> sacrifice, and to have, as Chairman Mao says, "a
> proletarian, communist world outlook."
>
> To me this still seems a far goal—and how shall I
> reach it? In the first place I must identify myself with
> the workers and peasants. The best way to do this is, of
> course, to do some kind of physical labor together with
> laboring people. If I have an opportunity to do any
> physical labor within my ability I will grasp it. In the
> meantime I will continue to take every chance to come
> into closer contact with working people in my daily
> life—to learn their needs and problems and their
> forthright way of thinking and acting. I want to acquire
> a deeper realization of the importance of labor as
> the thing that "created" man has developed, that
> has changed him through the ages and is changing
> him today.

Another way to feel identified with the workers is to keep up with national current events and learn what the workers and peasants are doing, closely follow the great accomplishments they are rapidly bringing forth one after another. I will study again Chairman Mao's "On Practice" and "On Contradiction" and do my best to apply the principles in examining and dealing with problems.

To become "expert" I must increase my knowledge of English grammar and international phonetics and I must make greater systematic efforts to learn Chinese well enough to use it in my teaching. Teachers who are both "expert" and "red" can more fully serve the cause of socialism and help train the great force of working-class intellectuals that is needed to carry out socialist construction. We English teachers must constantly bear in mind that our purpose is to put a keen weapon to be used in the fight against imperialism into the hands of our students.

Had Grace turned the argument that teaching English in itself is a reactionary activity on its head? Twenty years later, Grace described the meeting when she was called before the English Department:

There was a meeting of the whole department, all the teachers and the students, to criticize me particularly. I knew what they were going to say about me, more or less; I knew my bad points and my failings so I got ready for it. I asked to be allowed to speak first. I made a self-criticism and I did it pretty thoroughly. Anyone who wanted to say anything about my bad points after that, well, it was kind of flat because I had already said it. Some of the teachers who really liked me very much felt they had to go along with the rest of them and say something. They really told the truth—that I used material that was foreign, Western, bourgeois, capitalist, and that had been used in colonial countries, that the imperialists had used—some of the British material. I had used those books, you see, but I had changed them.

I don't remember all the details about what was said,
what wasn't said, but in the meeting, the criticism is
often a little overboard—but the people don't really
take it that seriously. Like using foreign materials, well,
we still used foreign materials after that. You have to use
foreign materials. But the criticism is a kind of reminder
that when you use anything like that, you have to pay
attention not to be influenced by the content. Your
attitude is [what's important], whether you are teaching
for the people, for the working people, and in their
interest, and whether you are teaching the students
some bourgeois attitude, which is, of course, probably
quite true.

Grace began looking at herself in a different light, as she had
never been called on to do before. But at the same time, she wanted
to initiate reforms in the way English was taught, based on what she
was learning from her own students' experiences. Her self-criticism
document provides insight into how the process was carried out
in China, by a Westerner who willingly took part in it and saw its
merits. In the scheme of changing ideologies to one that would
enable the individual to better "Serve the People," criticism–self-
criticism was the tool used until the next phase set in.

Grace, as she went to work at Nankai University, 1957.

Grace, her three children, and Enhua, her son-in-law, 1962.

FOURTEEN

IN THE SUMMER of 1958, fearful that the economic reforms proposed by the soon-to-begin Second Five-Year Plan would not reach the goal of surpassing Britain's industrial output, Mao decided that the whole nation needed to be mobilized. He had always relied on the voluntary, heroic outpourings of the masses—like the volunteer soldiers of the Korean war and the peasants taking charge of land reform: it was the power of the human will and determination of the spirit that created the "revolutionary fervor." Hoping to renew political enthusiasms and to step up the pace of socialist transformation, Mao announced the Great Leap Forward.

The Great Leap was intended to transform China into an ideal Communist society almost overnight. Collectivization instead of individual ownership and effort would be the key. The agricultural

cooperatives would be collectivized into communes. Private ownership of land or business would be replaced. Men, women, and children would share work, food, and pay. No incentives other than
selfless devotion would be necessary.

Another reason for the Great Leap was that the relationship
between China and the Soviet Union was splitting. It did not fully
crack until a few years later but the shifting could already be heard.
The Chinese people drew confidence from their emerging independence, the realization that none of the great foreign powers had
succeeded in dominating China—not the British, the Japanese, the
Americans nor, now, the Russians.

A bumper harvest in 1958 fueled the nation's enthusiasm, and a
massive outpouring of industrial activity resulted. By late 1958 hundreds of thousands of backyard furnaces were melting any metal that
could be found in a frenetic effort to increase industrial output by
one-third and reach an unprecedented target for steel production.
Initial statistics revealed fantastic increases and it seemed that the
nation would reach a "high tide" of production through mass effort.

But, indeed, steel cannot be made in back yards. And charcoal
cannot fuel a national industry. Families and villages cannot change
their very structures and functions overnight. And personal initiative needs rewards. Not only did impossibly high targets and bad
management figure into the failure of the Great Leap, but bad
weather added to the disastrous results in 1959, '60, and '61. Indescribable famines were the tragic legacy of the Great Leap.

Nini was working at the Tianjin Water Works during this period.
Nini had been going to the Water Works all of her life and knew
most of the people, the workmen and the managers. She ate lunch
in the canteen and supper, too, when there were meetings at night.
At first she did filing in the technical department and then mapping. It was in the mapping office that she met her husband:

> My husband En-hua and I worked in the same room. In
> China you become quite close to your colleagues. In addition
> to meetings, we both belonged to the Youth League. In the

League we helped carry out the production plan, and if there were social movements on, we helped promote the movements. We did a lot of study, reports, and lectures. We were given tickets to go hear certain people talk. We had amateur plays, singing groups, and dancing. It was very lively and social—I helped with backstage decorations and things like that—it was lots of fun.

About two years after we knew each other, maybe in 1958, we went out together to a movie. At that time, it was fairly common for young people to date, go to movies, etc. But the first time we really got to know each other was during the "anti-pests campaign." Sparrows were considered one of the pests because they ate grain—so we went out in teams early in the morning to keep the sparrows off the ground. We hit pots and pans and gongs together to make a loud noise. The sparrows could not land and they eventually dropped down exhausted and died. En-hua and I went up on a roof to scare them and after we were there someone took the ladder away. We were stuck there together for a while, so we talked.

En-hua was my group leader in 1958, so we were thrown together a lot. I was attracted to him, and thought we might get married. One day he asked me if I would want to be closer friends (a closer friend is a future husband or wife). It was like a proposal. I wasn't so very surprised. I said yes right then.

We got married in 1959 during Chinese New Year. I had to register early because I had lost my cloth coupons. If you got married, you got extra cloth. We had no ceremony, we just registered in the security bureau, the police station. They asked us some questions, we signed the papers. We each got a license. We had a small supper with our two families to celebrate. Things were getting hard to get during this time, and we wouldn't have enough for a big party.

We moved in with his family. They lived in the native city outside the former concessions. There were two families living in a courtyard. It was a long room with a bedroom on either end, and the main living area in the middle where the cooking and eating happened. We had to get water from way down the lane. My mother-in-law had a very strong character, and I learned a lot from her. She had bound feet and I learned a lot about Chinese women in the past. She didn't like my father-in-law at all. They didn't get along. My husband didn't get along well with his mother or father either. When he was around them, he changed. He said he couldn't help it, but when he walked through the door he felt different.

Food became much scarcer in 1959. Rationing began then. There were many discussions about who would get how much. It was decided by how much people ate as a rule. I didn't eat much then, so I had one of the lowest rations. I had about twenty-six catties a month, eight ounces of grain a day (mostly cornmeal). There were not many vegetables. We began pickling parts of the veggies we used to throw away. There was only a few ounces of oil a month, maybe two ounces a month. Very little sugar. Coal was also scarce. Once food is scarce, everything is scarce. Each region had its own quota depending upon how much food was available. It was better for us in the big cities than in the countryside.

People got sick a lot more from lack of food. Work was at half pace—the Party told people to rest a lot because there wasn't enough food. We ate in the canteens more often because there was a little more available and it was prepared to make it seem like more (more water in the rice, mixing in lots of bran, etc.).

The first sign of malnutrition is swelling, so everyone was checked for swelling and enlarged livers. People who were malnourished were given extra food. At the Water Works we went out as a group and collected certain kinds of edible summer weeds. Everyone was in the same boat. Our leaders, too, were on the same rationing. We could see them suffering with us from the effects.

Our family went on those rations and we'd never been that hungry before. Grace discovered that she could eat a little cornmeal. She had been allergic to it during the Japanese occupation. I got swollen and my liver was too big.

Babies born in those years were quite weak—we were all in it together. There was very little black market or "going through the back door."

Our work at the Water Works almost stopped. We went to work everyday, but we just sat around and talked. People were too weak to work, and the leadership kept saying don't work, take it easy.

In the latter part of 1962, we began getting duck eggs. There were more vegetables, a little more meat, and oil. Grain rationing gradually increased until I was getting thirty-one catties.

In 1961 my husband and I moved back with Grace and Willy because I was quite sick at times, and it was so far to my work from where we had been. Willy and my mother slept in the inner room, and my husband and I slept in the outer. We all took care of each other.

My husband went four hours every night to school for six years. He learned civil engineering. He came home around 11:30. On Sundays, he was at school half a day, home half a day. Often we just passed each other in the hall. It wasn't so hard on us. We had no children then.

ELLEN FINISHED HIGH SCHOOL in 1958. Grace and William were in Beijing when notice came that Ellen had been accepted at Harbin Industrial Institute. Nini helped Ellen prepare bedding and clothes for cold weather. Harbin was a city far to the north, in what was formerly Manchuria, a city once controlled by the Japanese and then by the Russians. The scientific and technical program at Harbin Institute had been set up by the Russians, but the Russians had already withdrawn their teachers by the time Ellen arrived. Ellen explained the connection between Russia's withdrawal and the Great Leap:

In Tientsin there hadn't been many Russians, so we didn't notice much change. Some places like Harbin knew what was happening much more because they had to readjust to the Russian withdrawal. The Russians took all their blueprints and plans, teachers, and experts with them. The Russians had been at Harbin beforehand setting up the program. But even by 1958, the Russian experts and teachers had withdrawn from the school, so the Great Leap was partly from necessity too. It all came out in 1962, at the conference in Bucharest—the Russians stood up and denounced the Chinese. The

Albanians defended us, but the Russians withdrew aid and other materials. Anyway, this was the first we knew that the Russians had withdrawn from China completely.

It was a five-year course. We had a lot of basic courses: mathematics, machinery, drawing, physics, chemistry for three years. My major course was precision instruments. The courses were hard. Almost all my time went to my studies. My first year was at the beginning of the Great Leap, so we did things like making iron and steel. We set up stoves on the sidewalks. I was in a group making coal into charcoal. We went to school with black faces from making charcoal. In the higher classes, the students did experiments and had their own factories.

The arts did a great leap too. Everyone was performing in these small groups. We did everything—singing, plays, performances, things we made up ourselves. I sang in a group and went around to the workers and students and did small performances. There were eight girls in my dorm room; three of them came from the same high school I did. We four, more or less, hung together. We all took the same courses together, and we knew each other well. There was quite a lot of mutual help. The ones who were better were always tutoring the worse ones. I always planned my vacations going home, and it was always a big occasion for me.

We ate a lot because we were doing so much work. I came back fat the first year. There was still plenty of food then. When it got really cold, we wore double scarves on our heads, and masks on our faces when we went out. But inside we had double [glazed] windows, with wood chips between the cracks. We had central heat, steam heat, radiators. We had physical training in the morning. We did ice-skating for fun. I did some competitive running, long distances.

When food got scarce the next year, outside activities were frowned on. We mostly studied. Everybody was run down because of the lack of food and because it was so cold. The teachers didn't give many assignments. They wanted us mostly to stay in bed and not do much to use energy. Everybody had a ration, so we were only a little undernourished. It was forbidden to do hard work or gymnastics. We learned Tai-Chi at that time; it's quieter, builds your body up, gets the oxygen going without using so much energy.

In 1962 things started getting a little better. The grain
rations were slightly higher each time. The students had more
rations than others.

I met my husband Rui-sheng in my classes. I didn't much
notice him at first. He spoke loudly, but he was in another
group. He had been a worker before so he worked in the factory, showing people what to do. I was making the charcoal.
I suppose he noticed me. A year or so later we became more
friendly. He was our class leader, then later a kind of assistant
to the teacher because he had work experience. We studied
more together then.

Rui-sheng describes his first impressions of Ellen: "The first time
I saw her, she walked into a big lecture hall with a couple of hundred other students. I almost gasped. She was so beautiful that I was
afraid to look at her. She never wore makeup or put on airs but she
stood out from the other girls. She had a gentle manner yet she
seemed tough. When the other students knew I was interested in
her, they taunted me, 'Who do you think you are to go after the
most beautiful girl in the school?' But some of the authorities in the
Party warned me that her mother was an American and it would
taint my record, especially since I came from a working-class background. But I disregarded them both. She was so serious about her
work I was afraid she wouldn't talk to me. Then I was assigned to
be her group leader—so I offered to help her in her studies."

Ellen gives her side of the story:

> I wasn't thinking of getting married. I wanted to do my
> study, and I didn't want to be bothered by all these things
> Some boys in college wrote letters to me or bothered me, but
> I didn't like it. I suppose everybody else noticed his interest
> before I did. Some of the classmates teased him about me and
> then I noticed that with other girls he was at ease but with me
> he was a little bit stiff. I knew him for more than a year, and
> I knew he really had feelings for me and I for him. He's capa-
> ble, very outspoken, he's not at all devious or tricky. He says
> what he thinks.

You can't get married in the university, but we knew we would later on. I didn't want to think about it then. Sometimes we went out together, boating on the river in boats which we rented by the hour. We studied together sometimes. He was half paid to work, and so he was busy.

Before we graduated we had to work in a factory. I went to Shanghai and to Xian. I went back to my father's old home when I was there. They asked me if my fiancé's family had any money. I said no, but neither do I. Why should I pick somebody for that reason? It was feudal thinking, that you should marry for the best match financially. Rui-sheng's father died when he was a boy of four or five. He had a mother and a brother. They lived in a village in Shantung province and grew vegetables for the city.

After you graduate from the university, the government finds you a job. Factories request workers from the labor bureau. Then they assign each factory a certain number of graduates from a particular school. The graduates decide where they want to be, but you might not get your choice. Because Rui-sheng and I were engaged, they tried to assign us to the same place. I was designing precision instruments for weights and measures, and most of the jobs for my kind of work were in Beijing, and that's where we ended up. Beijing was the closest I could get to Tientsin, so I was happy to be assigned there.

Rui-sheng and I worked in the same city but very far apart. I lived in a dormitory in the science institute. We saw each other on Sundays. I didn't want to get married just after I came out from school. I wanted to start working, do the job well, and spend time on other things. Then he went to study in another factory outside of Beijing for about half a year. When he came back, we were married. He was nearly thirty and I was twenty-seven.

Our wedding was very simple. Our colleagues were there. No family was there. You take a letter of identification from your workplace to the police station and they give you a marriage license. We all went back and bought some candy and cigarettes for our colleagues and sat around for a while. Our colleagues said some words and did a simple ceremony. My husband had an extra room in his dormitory, and I stayed there on weekends and then went back to work during the week. It didn't change my life much, being married.

When Ellen went off to college and Nini moved in with her husband's parents, William and Grace lived alone in the two rooms of the big mansion. William helped to get the water from down the hall and start the coal stove in the mornings. Their balcony became a familiar place, especially in the summer, for William's friends or Grace's students and sometimes teachers from Nankai. Study groups met in her home and she would ask the students how they thought they could learn better. Grace studied at night and read everything she could get her hands on about linguistics and the teaching of English.

William recalls that on these evenings he learned things about his mother he had not known before:

> My friend Kelin and I would be talking and studying in one corner and Grace would be reading in another. She was always there to help us if we didn't understand something, but she really knew how to concentrate. I would have to call her several times, "Ma, Ma, MA, MMAAA!" before she would hear me.
>
> One day Kelin and I wanted to read *Gone With the Wind*. I had heard Nini talking about it but Kelin had never read it. I started reading it to him in English but he wanted to know everything, so I read it in English to myself and said it in Chinese to him. I really noticed the language that way—Southern expressions like "Now don't be so mean and hateful to your sisters" fascinated me.
>
> "Ma," I said one night after Kelin left, "this is the first book I've read where the people in it talk like you!"
>
> I guess I began to contemplate my mother's origins in a different way. She often talked about her upbringing so that it was part of our upbringing too, but it had always seemed unique to mother. I began to realize that she shared a common language, culture, values, and history with others. Of course, I knew that, but in China the subtleties get lost in the generality of being a foreigner. I began to wonder about her life before she came to China.

One day we were listening to a radio broadcast from Shanghai. A Chinese soprano was singing "Depuis le jour" from the opera *Louise*. Her voice was clear and lyrical, with such emotional resonance that I was touched deeply and commented when it was over:

"That was remarkable!"

Mother said, "I used to sing that."

"You did! But it is very difficult," I said, thinking I knew so much about opera.

"Not really," she said. And then she began to sing—in a subdued voice, but with perfect pitch, she sang what I had just heard. I was dumbfounded. I knew that her lungs were shot from years of asthma and coal dust, but it was apparent that her voice had been trained. For the first time I realized that my mother could have had a very different life had she not married my father. But I also knew that even knowing what she knew now she would make the same choice.

Grace read everything in the Nankai library that related to language-teaching. When she exhausted that source, she began to search periodicals and recent publications; these led her to a network of linguists around the world who were developing new approaches to the teaching of English. She wrote for information, textbooks, and manuals. While she conducted her research, teaching at the university did not change much. In an interview years later, Grace described what she did to change the way English was taught:

In 1961 I was very distressed. I saw there really was no hope for the students in learning English. About this time, Chen Yi, who was the Minister of Foreign Affairs, gave a national talk to students at a conference, noting that the Foreign Ministry could not even find enough interpreters for diplomatic situations. This was embarrassing for China. By pointing out the backwardness of the teaching of English in China, he called for educational reform.

I was fascinated by what he said and agreed completely. In my excitement, I sat down and wrote him

a letter—ten typewritten pages. Can you imagine! I
suggested to him that there was a way to change it. I
had read all the books on linguistics and the teaching of
English that the library had. So I made some suggestions
about how to reform the teaching of English. My
thoughts were based on "practice before theory."

I talked to the Chairman of the Department, Professor
Li, and to the other teachers. I tried to convince them of
the need. I told them that it was against Chairman Mao's
teaching, which said that theory must serve practice. I
quoted his essay, "On Practice"—practice comes first;
then you use theory to go back and guide the practice.
The aim is practice, not theory. Theory is the guidance
but you must apply it to practice or what is the use of
theory? If your theory isn't proved right in practice, then
you throw your theory out.

That is how language should be taught—You should
not first teach the theory (grammar) then try to let them
piece up the language with the theory (grammar). They
should get exposed to the language first (the way it is
spoken) and learn some practical things, and then use some
grammar rules to sum up what they have already learned.

[Chen Yi] gave the letter to the Minister of Higher
Education in Peking who sent it to various universities and
experts to have it evaluated. Then the Minister of Higher
Education wrote to the [Nankai] university saying that
these reforms should be supported. During this time I
heard from a well-known linguist, Lu Shuxiang, of the
Language Research Institute at the Academy of Science,
who encouraged my approach. I wrote to him the next
time. He talked to the Minister of Higher Education again.
And so it went. It took a long time to "trickle down."

But I still had to fight for it [at Nankai] because the
conservative professors had vested interests in the old
way. They had learned that way—they had gained their
reputations on the old way—so they did not want to
change. And some students did not want to change
either. They didn't want to really practice English
because it showed their deficiency.

Some of the younger teachers became involved with
me. We studied all the materials we could get our hands

on. The education minister of Australia sent us some
materials; they had made a new book based on this
approach and they sent it to me. We also got textbooks
from England and from America about the structural
approach. It was the way things were being taught then
outside of China, but China had been cut off for so
long. We began to use some of these methods, but we
had to adapt it to the Chinese situation—we changed
the dialogue to reflect what the Chinese students do in
their daily lives.

Despite the obstacles that Grace faced, the work she did to
reform the teaching of English in China at this time was quite
remarkable. She gradually received support of higher-ups in the
university as well as in the Ministry of Education which made it
possible for her to persevere and to obtain materials from abroad.
The people who benefited the most from her endeavors were the
young teachers just starting out in their careers who formed a work
team with her. They were not so wedded to the ways of the past
and were eager to learn what was being taught outside of China at
that time. Grace would teach them pattern drills from the texts and
they would practice the patterns in their classrooms, adapting the
content to suit the Chinese situation. Some of the young teachers
worked with Grace and William to create a manual which docu-
mented their work and became a textbook of the new methodol-
ogy for teaching English in China.

In a letter to a friend in the United States in May 1962, Grace
described her work at the university:

> I haven't written to anyone outside the country for a
> year or more. I have been, and am, very busy. I am still
> teaching at Nankai University and all my thoughts and
> attention are absorbed by the work I'm doing because it is
> new and rather difficult for me. My actual teaching work is
> not only heavy but we are breaking new ground in teaching
> methods. We are trying to break with the old time-honored
> methods of language teaching that have prevailed here for

the last fifty years or so. It isn't easy and requires infinite patience, work, and study. I've never studied so hard in my life, not only teaching methods, teaching psychology, teaching English as a foreign language and language teaching in general, but for the last year, descriptive linguistics both British and American—they don't altogether agree! I'm very interested in Prof. Charles Fries work in the English Language Institute, Ann Arbor, Michigan. I've been studying his "Teaching and Learning English as a Foreign Language" and his "Structure of English." Right now I'm "plowing" through a book by a University of Texas professor. It's really too technical for me but what I can understand of it is very interesting. This year I've made my own composition course based on my recent studies. The old method was so unscientific, time wasting, and useless.

We've had to combat some pretty die-hard attitudes in our English department, but just this term we've gotten the head of the department convinced that we must make some radical changes, so things are going more smoothly. The students are delightful to teach, so intelligent, diligent, and eager to learn! Most of them come from peasant families from as far away as inner-Mongolia and Canton, and some are overseas students from Indonesia, Malaya, and Burma.

We've been having a pretty hard time for the last three years. I'm sure you've heard plenty about it. Although accounts in the U.S. are exaggerated there is no denying that things have been and are pretty tough! But we've turned the corner and things will now gradually get better.

I've been hearing about the remarkable women's movement for peace in the U.S. from Sylvia Powell and Harriet Eddy. It seems things are really stirring. Maude Russell sent me the "China's Case" chapter from Felix Greene's book. I haven't seen the rest of the book, but he certainly did a good job explaining how the Chinese people feel. I can testify to the absolute truth of it! I haven't written anything for the N.W.R. since my October 1959 article [Sun Pao-san's story in the *New World Review*]. I simply have no time.

I go to Peking to visit Anna Louise Strong occasionally.
She says she's getting ready to write a new book but she
didn't say what about . . .

Grace was still in touch with friends outside China even during
the Great Leap. Her infrequent correspondence was primarily with
women. Most of the women that she mentioned in this letter had
interests in China and were active in educating others in the States.
Harriet Eddy, to whom Grace had written after F. C.'s death, was a
lifelong member of the Women's International League for Peace
and Freedom, founded in 1915 by Jane Addams, a well-known
American social reformer. Even after she became deaf, Harriet was
an avid correspondent with friends and members of peace organizations throughout the world.

Maude Russell had been the YWCA secretary in Changsha,
China, before the war. After she returned to the States, she organized the Committee for a Democratic Far Eastern Policy and published the *Far Eastern Reporter*. She was a well-known lecturer and
attracted large crowds on college campuses.

Anna Louise Strong was an American correspondent who had
visited China many times. Her personal interview with Mao Tse-
tung in August 1946 became famous but made her infamous in
America. In the interview, Mao first used the phrase "paper tigers"
in reference to American imperialists. She continued to live in
China and write, as a guest of the Chinese People's Friendship
Association. Grace and William went to visit her in Peking about
twice a year—that's where they were when Ellen received notice of
acceptance at Harbin.

Sylvia Powell was the editorial assistant to her husband, Bill Powell, publisher of the *China Monthly Review* in Shanghai, for which
Grace had written several articles. Sylvia was called a "Communist
propagandist" by the U.S. passport office after she wrote an article
for a Portland newspaper criticizing the United States for its support
of Chiang's blockade and bombing of the Shanghai harbor in 1950.

When the Powells returned to the States after the magazine closed down in 1953, they were accused of treason and sedition and were put on trial in 1956. It was the magazine's coverage of the U.S. use of biological warfare in the Korean War that triggered their indictment. When the Defense Department refused to release documents, a mistrial was declared in 1959 and all charges were dropped. When Harriet Eddy sent a copy of Grace's letter about F. C.'s death to Sylvia, Sylvia wrote back, "[Grace's] courage gives me courage." That was the year that Sylvia's treason trial began.

Just when food supplies were increasing and when Grace's work at the university was progressing, Grace was diagnosed with breast cancer. The story of how she faced and survived radical mastectomy is told by all three children. Nini was the first to discover it:

> Grace began getting weak and tired in the winter of 1962. She would sigh very heavily. I first thought maybe her T.B. had come back. She wasn't getting much protein because of the food rationing. Finally I suggested we go to the clinic for tests. On the way there she told me she had a lump in her chest and had had it since 1958. I was shocked but I saw that she was frightened so I didn't ask her about it. I tried to reassure her. She was pale, and I knew she was scared.
>
> She said that she hadn't told us about it because we were still in school and she thought it would be too much for us after F. C.'s death. At the clinic we were told she needed to go to the cancer hospital for further tests.

The thought of Grace's illness brought back frightening memories to William:

> When Mother and Nini came back from the clinic, they were both very pale. "Ma might have breast cancer," Nini said to me. "We must take her to the Bone and Tumor Hospital." My heart dropped into the pit of my stomach. It was the nightmare coming back again. It brought back that hot and humid summer night, watching the face of the doctor spitting out watermelon seeds, telling her the news that her husband

was going to die. It had been more than seven years now, and it was in the dead of winter, but the feeling of doom came back upon me.

None of us could swallow a bite that night at suppertime, none of us could imagine what the outcome would be. Nini tried to cheer us up saying that since Mother had felt the lump in her breast for a few years now, it must be benign. She went on to say that breast cancer was operable and the Bone and Tumor Hospital had a good reputation of treating breast cancer.

When they went to the hospital the next day, they were very fortunate to get to see a specialist, Dr. Wang, who lived right across the street from us. He gave her a thorough checkup. After a week of tests, Dr. Wang was ready to do the biopsy and if it turned out to be cancer, to do a mastectomy immediately.

I went to see her the night before the operation. She appeared to be calm and cheerful, but I knew she was really scared, staying in the same hospital where F. C. had died and to be struck down with the same disease.

When she saw me with a book in my hand, she asked what I had brought for her to read. I told her I had brought Charlotte Brontë's *Villette* to read unless she wanted to sleep. She said she wasn't tired although they kept her busy all day with a hundred and one tests. She remembered reading *Villette* to me a few years ago when I still had difficulties in reading. Mother had a wonderful reading voice. Although reading often made her cough and sometimes brought on asthma, she always insisted on reading to me as she felt it was important for me to appreciate the spoken language.

That night before her operation, we talked about Lucy Snowe, the main character in *Villette*, and her experience as a foreign teacher teaching English in Brussels and some of the humorous situations she got herself into. Mother told me she had read the first chapter to the young teachers she had been training and that they were so fascinated that they all went to the library to borrow a copy of the book. When I left the hospital and went into the cold winter night, I felt less fearful of what might come.

The next day, our worst expectation came true: "Carcinoma," they said, and it must be operated on immediately.

Ellen was in Harbin and William was at school when the operation took place. Nini and a neighbor were there all day waiting for Grace to come out of surgery:

> I was with Grace when she came to from the ether. She mumbled and giggled, she didn't know what happened. They wanted me to be prepared in case they needed a skin graft, but they didn't need me because she was so thin they just sewed her back up. Later that day, the head nurse told me that they took a lot out—it had spread to the lymph nodes. "These cases," she said, "might live another five or ten years."
>
> In the hospital, she always wanted to do everything herself. She pulled her tubes out and would go to the bathroom by herself . . .
>
> With determination, she recovered fairly quickly. Three days after the operation when Willy and I went to visit her, the doctors were examining her; they were treating her very gingerly as if she were a delicate old lady who had just had a major operation. One doctor asked her if she could raise her feet. She looked at him and then kicked her leg all the way over her head. The doctor was so startled he screamed and Ma laughed so hard the pain in the wound brought tears to her eyes. The doctors talked about it for days. They had never seen a sixty-year-old lady kicking her legs over her head, not to mention one that had just had a radical operation. She was already exercising her arm. I came in one day to the hospital and she was leaning against the radiator holding her arm up, using her body to push against her arm.
>
> Big tears were rolling down her cheeks. I asked her what she was doing. "Oh, it hurts like hell," she said. A week later, they took the stitches out. She regained full use of her arm eventually.
>
> When it came time for Grace to move to another room, the hospital assumed that a foreigner would want privacy and better accommodations. But Grace said she wanted to go to the general ward, a room with about ten or twelve other patients. The hospital staff said it was too crowded there and she would not be able to rest. But she insisted. Grace spent the next two weeks in the general cancer ward of the hospital.

In Chinese hospitals, there is a lot of activity, families visiting, patients helping each other, sharing food. When anybody gets depressed, others try to console or cajole them. People get to know each other quite well and compare how they are doing. Grace thought this atmosphere would be good for her. She did not want to be left in a room alone. She got quite friendly with the other women in the ward. The people there kept her very much occupied. There was always a bunch of doctors around her bed. They all wanted to practice their English so she had quite a few impromptu classes for the doctors. Her students or other faculty would come and they would talk shop. She was never left out of things.

The women patients around her all had had mastectomies. One of them was an old country woman from the suburb of Tientsin. She told Grace that she had to sell her pig to pay for her operation. Her son came to see her every day and brought her food from home, which she shared with Grace and that helped her appetite. There was a woman judge on one side of her and a schoolteacher in her thirties on the other side. We got to know them quite well. Since they all had their operations about the same time, they went through radiation and chemotherapy together for the next whole year. Every time she went for either the radiation or chemo treatment, we would see her "old gang" again. The old country woman did not like to exercise her arm and she was amazed at the progress Grace had made. Grace encouraged her to keep on using her arm, regardless of how painful it was. The schoolteacher told the others how she dealt with the nausea caused by the radiation and everyone compared their white blood cell counts and the burns they had to suffer. The judge's cancer returned around the end of Mother's treatment and everyone supported her when she had to have another operation. The camaraderie with these women was the real secret to Grace's recovery.

Ellen was taking her exams when Grace had the operation and could not come until later:

Nini wrote me a letter saying that Grace was going into the hospital and could I come back as soon as possible. I was very worried. I finished my exams that day and started home. By the time I arrived, Grace was out of the hospital. During the summer of 1963 Willy and I took Grace to the hospital to get radiation treatments when Nini was working. I think we went once a week. She felt weak, out of breath, and her white blood cell count decreased some, but she was able to continue the treatment. She wasn't discouraged. She was quite satisfied with the treatment. She was also reading a lot of American health books and magazines, like *Prevention*, which friends sent her. She took lots of vitamins, large doses of vitamin C. She would talk about what she read. She believed in vitamins. She was always trying to get us to take more vitamins. But we thought that if you weren't sick, it didn't make much sense.

When Grace finished her last chemotherapy treatment, the university offered her a place on campus to live so she wouldn't have to travel so far back and forth. She and William moved to the campus in early 1965. The move was good for Grace. She was close to her work and in the middle of things just where she liked to be. The air was much cleaner and the noise less. There were large lotus ponds surrounded by willows and Chinese locust trees with paths that wandered through the campus in a healthy, park-like atmosphere.

Grace and William had a nice little bungalow in a grouping of faculty housing. There was plenty of space with two main rooms, a bathroom, a kitchen and storage space. Across a field from the bungalow was the main university building, and behind the bungalow was the main road to the campus. There were lots of comings and goings as both students and faculty moved to and from campus. Grace liked to watch people and bicycles go back and forth on the road to classes.

The school gave her a lighter load while she recuperated. She continued training the young teachers, and many of her reforms were being supported. William began working in the language lab and helping Grace write the teachers' manual. Nini came twice a week to visit and was usually there on weekends. There was enough food to eat again and the country seemed to be on the upturn. Both of her girls were married to good men and she had survived cancer. The reward for all she had gone through came the moment she saw her first granddaughter. How pleased Grace was when Ellen brought her baby to visit in May 1965. The air was warm and flowers were in bloom. The lotus ponds were beginning to turn green again. She was a grandmother and her life, at last, had an air of calm and normalcy.

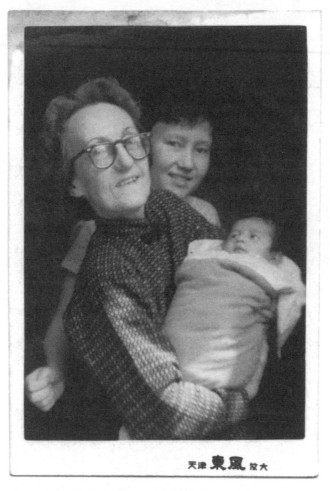

天津 東風 放大

Grace proudly holds her first grandchild, Ellen's daughter, May 1965.

Grace and William in Beijing with English teachers from Britain, Spring 1967.

點水許綠亂寧風荇帶長落

紅吹不定幽趣在濠梁

FIFTEEN

FROM HER WINDOW at the back of the bungalow facing the main road of Nankai University, Grace first witnessed the bands of students from the nearby high schools storming onto the campus. Starting in the summer of 1966, wave after wave of angry students passed before her window, their shouts growing more fierce, denouncing the bourgeois authorities at the university.

The drastic policies of the Great Leap Forward which had brought the nation to the brink of starvation were moderated by 1965, but the push and pull of the political tide continued unabated. Some leaders urged more gradual reforms and less revolutionary approaches toward economic and cultural development. Others pushed for an even greater proletarian vision of the revolution and criticized their opponents for taking the capitalist road. A wave of rhetorical attacks against "reactionary bourgeois capitalist roaders" began to move through the Communist Party and soon spread throughout the nation.

The split in the leadership occurred after the split with the Soviet Union. By the early 1960s, the Soviet Union had completely withdrawn from China at a time when threat from the United States intensified. The U.S. involvement in Vietnam to the south created tension on the border of China and fear of possible escalation. In October 1964 China sent a warning to both world powers by testing its first atomic bomb.

In the sway of opposing opinions, criticism of the nation's policies emerged most noticeably in the arts. Disturbed by the growing trend among artists and writers to criticize the leadership, Jiang Qing, a former actress before she became Mao's third wife in 1939, was appointed to head up the Cultural Revolution group in 1966. Advocating more radical and socialist policies of cultural development, her crackdown on the "bourgeois ideology" of the arts soon spread into education.

The education system itself was criticized for not following the government's policy of promoting workers and peasants. At the crux of the system, the barrier which determined who would be educated and who would not, was the college entrance exam. Grace explained in an interview years later how the college entrance exams were unfair to those from worker or peasant backgrounds: "If they selected students based on the traditional examinations then the students from intellectuals' families got into college and those from worker and peasant families did not. So the Cultural Revolution began with the debate on abolishing the college entrance exams." By 1966 many students from worker and peasant backgrounds had entered the colleges and found the whole system discriminatory. In the spring they began putting up wall posters and criticizing the policies of the university. The challenges to the university posed by students from worker and peasant backgrounds made others in the university feel that the very standards of the educational system were being threatened. By the summer of 1966, schools and universities were shut down, classes canceled, and teachers and authorities of the university targeted as "reactionary bourgeois intellectuals." In some places the fighting became fierce. The more radical students were issued red armbands, becoming known as Red Guards.

The Great Proletarian Cultural Revolution was officially announced by Mao from the Gate of Heavenly Peace in Tiananmen Square on August 18, 1966. Mao's wife, Jiang Qing, stood on the rostrum with him. Her presence at the parade signaled which way the nation was heading. A massive, awe-inspiring parade of China's youth passed before Mao as they shouted "Ten Thousand Years" and called him the "Four Greats": Our Great Teacher, Great Leader, Great Supreme Commander, and Great Helmsman. Throughout the summer and fall of 1966, Mao reviewed millions of youths marching through Tiananmen Square, inciting them to a level of zeal surpassing what had been seen before. Mao gave fuel to the fire by directing the students' rage not just toward the bourgeois authorities at the universities but toward "revisionists" in the leadership of the Party itself.

All schools came to a standstill as the revolutionary struggle came to the fore. Students swept away anything that represented the "Four Olds"—old culture, old custom, old habit, old ideology. In the name of sweeping away, old street signs were taken down and replaced with revolutionary names, art objects were smashed, possessions confiscated, temples or old buildings destroyed. High school students as well as those from universities traveled across the country by train and stayed in hostels for free. They visited sites of the revolution, such as Yenan and Shaoshan, Mao's birthplace, and saw parts of China most of them had never seen before. They met other students and felt an excitement that overcame crowded conditions or lack of food or sparse accommodations.

The tide of revolutionary fervor moved across the nation and left almost no one untouched. Starting on school and university campuses, the attacks spread into the society as a whole, the main targets being the educated and managerial class. Wanting to demonstrate their revolutionary superiority, students attacked anyone who in their opinion retarded the revolution or had associations with "bad" family elements—former KMT, landlords, capitalists, those who had affiliations with the West or were educated in the West, or intellectuals in the broadest sense. Managers, doctors, administrators, teachers, government officials, and authority figures at any level were dragged before jeering crowds or humiliated in public. Many were exiled to the countryside or driven to suicide. Once labeled as bourgeois by the authorities, one's family could be ruined forever.

Grace first noticed that the student attacks had spread beyond the campus on the same day that the great parade took place in Beijing. The day began innocently enough, as William recalls:

On August 18, 1966, I took Grace into town to get a perm, the last one she would ever have. After that perms were too bourgeois and went out with the other "olds." On our way back to campus, we stopped to see our friend Bernice Ko, a Chinese-American woman who was married to a Chinese gynecologist. The Kos lived in a big, gracious house with a lovely garden, a house filled with antiques and equipped with every Western luxury. Two days after our visit, Red Guards ransacked the house, smashing vases, slashing pictures, and carrying out furniture. The young guards screamed at the Kos, "Bourgeois monsters!" Then took what they wanted. The house was sealed off and the Kos were left on the street.

Then we heard that Dr. Fan, a respected pediatrician that Grace knew, had come home one day to find his wife dead, apparently having been brutally beaten. In an abortive suicide attempt, he leapt from a window and was permanently crippled.

Our colleague, a professor of Russian, a mild-mannered man, had jumped to his death from a fifth-story window after the humiliation of being paraded publicly as a criminal. His mistake had been to tear up his diary. On the inside front page of that diary, as in all Chinese diaries then, was a picture of Chairman Mao. The scraps of that picture had been found in his wastebasket when the guards ransacked his house.

From our small bungalow on the west side of the Nankai University campus, Grace and I saw our colleagues being paraded up and down. Some wore placards identifying them as "reactionary academic authority." Grace gasped one day when she saw old Professor Li, the chairman of the Foreign Language Department, his hair shorn in a grotesque manner, doing manual labor, some meaningless task of moving heavy rocks from one place to another. Grace knew that he had a heart condition and worried that the stress would be fatal. We also saw other colleagues in the Foreign Language Department lined up, forced to bend over and get their entire heads shaved except for a strip down the middle, or have chunks snipped out at random. Dunce caps or a wastebasket were placed on their heads before they were paraded outside, with slurs and threats, and sometimes struck with fists and heels. The student guards yelled at them, "Smash the dog heads of the traitors."

We watched as high school Red Guards made a huge pile of "bourgeois and revisionist" books—and that included all Western literature—and set them on fire in great bonfires. The smell of burning books seeped into our windows as the soot fell around our bungalow.

I knew that Grace had only a vague notion of the danger of those days of sweeping incriminations. I had repeatedly warned her to be cautious of what she said and wrote. I even tried to censor her letters, which had, in turn, incensed or amused her. Grace had always spoken her mind and had never had any fear of expressing herself. She had learned through the last few years to be careful of what she said, but I could tell that her patience was growing thin in recent months.

When the revolutionary students fanned out across the countryside, everyone remaining on campus, including me, had to participate in building a monument to Mao. We mixed concrete, dug a huge foundation, and sorted black stones from white ones. One day right after the construction of the statue, Grace and I took a walk around the campus. The statue stood on a pedestal in front of the main classroom building. The whole thing was four stories high. It was a conglomeration of stones and concrete. None of us knew how to build a statue, nor did the construction leaders. Grace commented to me on how hideous it looked and that this was what people put on tombs. I soon forgot about it and had no idea she would mention it to anyone else.

So much of the rhetoric was absurd to her, like calling Mao "the Greatest of the Greatest of the Greatest of the Great Leaders." That was redundant, she insisted; with each added "great" you diminished the meaning of the first one.

But an English teacher's grammatical corrections were not appreciated in this fanatical environment. By the end of 1966, the students had split into battling factions. While one group attacked the "bourgeois intellectuals," the other claimed the more radical stance. Encouraged by the *People's Daily* on January 1, 1967, to "launch a general attack on the handful of people in the Communist Party who are taking the capitalist road," the second group attacked members of the Party itself and called themselves the "revolutionary rebels." They labeled the other faction the "reactionary royalists" because they protected the Party. The two factions began to fight among themselves, each calling the other "counter-revolutionaries."

Grace described how she viewed the conflict between the opposing student factions:

The two sides began quarreling, and the fighting got fiercer. The leaders in the party did not want to be criticized so they instigated one bunch of students against the other bunch. First they debated with loudspeakers. When one side got loud, the other side got louder. One side had ten loudspeakers, so the other side got ten loudspeakers. Then, of course, when you fuss like that, you are bound to get into fist fights. So they got to fighting with sticks and clubs. Brandishing nightsticks, they fought each other long into the night, loudspeakers blaring, "You are wrong!" "No, you are wrong!" With sticks and fists, they staged battles in

open fields in Gilbert and Sullivan comic operetta style
that settled no issue. The campus was a battleground. It
was like a fight you would go see on the athletic field. I
went and watched several of them. It finally got so bad,
the government had to send the PLA in to stop the
fighting. I heard them coming—what was that sound, I
wondered. Three thousand PLA walked onto campus
and parted the fighting students down the middle. They
came with the little Red Book and shouted, "Chairman
Mao said to fight with words, not with sticks."

By February, the PLA had quelled the campus disputes temporarily and called for classes to resume. Local factions became
their own authorities on how to carry out this revolution, most
often whipped up by inflammatory rhetoric. The disorder continued at a bewildering pace throughout 1967.

In August 1967 a burst of anti-foreign resentment was stirred up
in Beijing. Red Guards ransacked and torched the office of the
British charge d'affaires. Radical students took over the Ministry of
Foreign Affairs, and Chen Yi, the Foreign Minister, was taken pris-
oner. He was the one to whom Grace had written about reforming
the teaching of English only a few years earlier. Before becoming
Foreign Minister, Chen Yi had been commander of the Third
Army, leading the PLA forces to victory across the Yangtse in 1949.
Now he was placed under arrest by students.

The few foreigners still remaining in China, mostly in Beijing,
were now under investigation. Anyone with contacts outside China
was suspected of espionage. Letters and papers were searched for
clues to information that could be leaked or personal contacts that
could "cover" for a network of spies operating within China. Grace
had a friend who taught German at the Foreign Languages Institute. Olga Li was a Swiss woman, divorced from her Chinese husband, living with her three adult children in Beijing. Grace and
William often stayed with her when they went to Beijing and cor-
responded in between visits.

The storm of the Cultural Revolution had been brewing for a year and a half before it finally arrived at the bungalow. It was a cold night in January 1968, William remembers:

It was after midnight. I was awakened by a knock at the door. I came out of my room shivering, wondering who could be knocking at such an hour.

Through the glass panes in the door, I saw half a dozen people standing in the small yard, some in the shadow and some clearly visible in the bright, icy moonlight. The closer ones were recognizably college-aged Red Guards. In the back were two adult-looking shadows with military bearing. My heart stopped.

I turned. Grace was coming from her room, securing her robe. "Who is it, Willy?" she asked.

I could not answer. I could only think: So they have come for us!

She saw them through the glass and said, "Open the door, Willy."

Six heavily bundled people stomped in, the cold night air rushing in with them.

"These comrades are Red Guards from Beijing," said the more mature-looking one, who seemed to be from the campus Security Office. He was addressing himself to Grace, "It seems you have friends who are involved in counter-revolutionary activities and espionage." The other guard, a young one who had been identified as from Beijing, interrupted him and said gruffly, "We need to ask you some questions. Put on your clothes and follow us!"

Grace hardly ever went outside in the coldest months and did not have time to fully dress. As we walked along the path between frozen lotus ponds, the piercing wind hit us in the face and nearly took my breath away. She coughed. I looked anxiously at my mother. She showed nothing, only shook her head, her face pale in the moonlight.

One of the Red Guards walked ahead and two followed. The others stayed behind to search the house. The silence of the night was broken only by the crunching sound of our footsteps on the icy path and the wind whistling through the bare branches of the trees.

Beyond the lotus ponds, we came to a group of dormitory buildings and were led into one of the rooms in a dorm, where there were four or five bunk beds with some students sleeping in them. We were told to sit on a lower bunk and wait. The room was freezing and the concrete floor numbed my feet. A student sleeping on one of the bunk beds woke up and looked at us with bewilderment. Nobody said a word.

It got colder and colder as the minutes ticked on. Thoughts raced through my head—which of our friends in Beijing had gotten into trouble? Had we said anything or had we written anything that might incriminate us? Fear turned my stomach into a block of ice. I looked again at Mother. She appeared uncannily serene as she smiled at the sleepy student.

I had told Grace over and over the importance of being cautious, but I had the feeling that we were already implicated. I could not imagine why Red Guards had come from Beijing.

After an hour of waiting, we were taken into another room in which there were only some chairs and a table. Those who had been searching the house had returned. Two of the Red Guards and two men from the security force sat by the table on which were piled stacks of papers and what looked like bunches of letters.

"We think you know very well why we brought you here," said one of the Red Guards from Beijing who spoke fairly good English. "We have dug up some heinous espionage activities from the Beijing Foreign Language Institute. Your friend Olga Li has been passing valuable information to the Swiss Embassy. A lot of the information was gathered by you. You must confess your crimes or you will be dealt with severely."

Grace looked shocked. "That's nonsense," she protested. "Olga would never do anything like that. And I don't have any information of any kind to give to anybody."

The Red Guards looked at each other and smiled smugly. "We have all the letters you wrote to Olga. The ironclad evidence is in your own handwriting. We are only testing you to see if you are willing to confess and give up your criminal activities."

"I only wrote about myself and my children," Grace said indignantly. "How can that be a criminal activity?"

"So you used your children to gather information and then reported what you found out to your foreign friends in Beijing, didn't you? Who else did you supply information to?"

Grace showed the anger welling up in her, but she quickly choked it down. She began to realize what happened to her might have repercussions for Nini and Ellen and their families. Taking a deep breath, she said, "Since you have my letters, you must know that I did not say anything that could cause any harm to the country."

"You reported in detail what had happened on campus and in the city. What about the letters we might not have? What did you report in them?" snorted the other Red Guard. The questions continued until daybreak.

We trudged back over icy ground to the house, stunned by the wind and the badgering interrogation. The stove in the bungalow had gone out, so it was freezing cold inside. We stood with our overcoats on and looked around. The drawers had all been pulled out and their contents strewn across the room. I felt violated and immediately began trying to put things in order around the room. As I did so, I tried to order my thoughts and derive some meaning from the events. I was searching for anything that would give me a clue. It seemed that only our letters were gone. Other papers were still there. Grace, on the other hand, didn't move. She just stood there with her coat on and then she mused, like a teacher who had given a tough assignment, "They are going to have a lot of reading to do! It might improve their English."

Then she sat down, not even trying to clean things up. "Poor Olga," she muttered. "I hope she's all right."

"What could they be taking so seriously?" I asked, trying to figure things out. "We haven't done anything wrong. You didn't say anything objectionable in your letters, did you?"

"Of course not! You always read everything I write."

I paused, afraid to admit it. "Not to Olga."

I had seen no reason to read Grace's letters to Olga. They were good friends, both without their husbands; they talked about their children, events of the day, woman-to-woman sorts of things. What incriminating things could she have written in letters to Olga?

The investigation dragged on until spring. The Red Guards from Beijing returned home, and a faction of Red

Guards from Nankai were put in charge of the investigation. The leader of that group, a Red Guard from Nankai, called T., was one of the students with a "good" family background, meaning from worker or peasant families. He had recently graduated from the university and been hired back as a young teacher. He saw an opportunity here to demonstrate his revolutionary zeal and to further his position on campus. He took a small group of students to Beijing to investigate what the Beijing Red Guards had brought to their attention.

During this lull in the investigation, Grace never left the house. Once you were labeled, no one dared have contact with you. Colleagues at the office stopped talking when I walked into the room. We talked with no one on or off campus except Nini. There was only silence.

The silence came to an end one morning, towards the end of April. The willow trees were just turning green, and the dreaded yellow dust was blowing down from the Gobi Desert. I had just arrived at the Foreign Language Department when T. entered the room and approached me.

T. was a thin young man with small eyes and a large mouth which appeared to be frozen in a perpetual sneer. He was followed by a pretty plump girl, another Red Guard, whom I recognized as a second-year English student before classes were canceled. Although T. was one of the English teachers, he spoke to me in Chinese.

"I want to talk to you about your mother. Come with me," he demanded.

They headed me back the way I had just come. As we walked, he informed me that Grace's actions were much more serious than anyone had thought. They constituted crimes against the Party, against China and its people. She would be taken into custody immediately for further investigation until all her crimes were exposed.

He continued, "Although you aided your mother in many of her criminal activities, you are still young and have grown up in the new society, under the red flag; therefore, you are being considered as one of those who are educable. If you will clearly draw the line between yourself and your mother and do your utmost to expose her anti-revolutionary activities, there is still hope for you to become a new person. Of course, if you should follow in your mother's footsteps, you will end up an enemy of the people."

I did not hear half of what he said. I was wondering where were they going to take her and what were they going to do to her. How much abuse could a frail sixty-seven-year-old woman endure?

Grace was at breakfast, sitting at a little table peeling a hard-boiled egg when I arrived at the bungalow with the two Red Guards escorting me. Two more Red Guards, a man and a woman, and a man from the campus Security Office arrived at the same time. T. gave the orders. The two Red Guards who had just come seized "foreign agent" Liu. The others went through the house again, ransacking it.

"Where are you taking her? She needs . . ." I stammered. It didn't sound appropriate for me to say she needed her vitamins daily.

"She is in the hands of the people now, and she will be dealt with as the revolutionary committee sees fit. You must think about your own sins now!" T. exclaimed.

"But what has she done?"

"You know very well what she has done. Her accomplices have all confessed, so all your evasions will be in vain. Start right now to expose all her evil deeds before it is too late for you."

Two Red Guards stayed to keep an eye on me and to prevent me from having contact with anyone. For three weeks, these guards, whom I had known as English students, watched me and refused to tell me what was happening to Grace. During these long days, they demanded that I write down all the connections our family had or had ever had in China or abroad, the nature of the connection, and the nature of our recent contact. It was a staggering thought. I knew that confessions had to be thorough and complete. Self-righteous restraint or non-cooperative silence could be punished cruelly. If I didn't cooperate they might seek out Nini or Ellen. What could I do?

One day, my guards did not show up. I was relieved just to be freed of the usual tedious tasks. But by afternoon, when they still had not come or sent any message, I became alarmed. I feared that something had happened to Grace and they no longer needed me. But I had no idea where to go to find out and I dared not leave.

Around ten o'clock that night, the loudspeakers positioned at every corner of the campus suddenly came to life. An angry and agitated voice shouted over the public address system: "Revolutionary Comrades, we have won a big victory over the enemy! We have triumphed in catching an American spy hiding on our campus! This evil monster is also a vicious counter-revolutionary that opposes the Communist Party and our Great Leader and Supreme Commander, Chairman Mao! . . . All revolutionary comrades will gather at the Great Auditorium tomorrow morning to repudiate the heinous crimes of Grace Liu!" The announcement was repeated every ten minutes for an hour.

The angry voices, echoing and bouncing off the buildings, mixed with the howling spring wind, left me in mental torment all night. I could not fathom what had happened to my mother.

The next morning, my jailers returned to escort me to the denunciation rally. They wanted to show me how enemies of the people are dealt with. As we walked to the Great Auditorium, I was shocked to see big character posters denouncing my mother, the hideous words written in bold black Chinese characters, "counter-revolutionary American spy." The posters had been plastered on both sides of the main road leading into campus and over the big gate.

The Great Auditorium doubled as the students' dining hall in normal times, but it had been converted into the stage setting for the almost-daily denunciations. It was large and cavernous, so that every sound echoed back and forth, repeating again and again the error of your ways. A crowd of nearly five thousand gathered that morning in the large room. There were two other targets of the "repudiate and struggle" meeting that day, but Grace Liu was the premier exhibit.

To make the greatest impression on me, I was put in the front row, as close to the stage as possible. Since the accused were already held prisoners, the meeting began on time, just as announced.

"Down with Grace Liu," roared the Red Guard on stage, as an opening call.

"Down with Grace Liu," the crowd chanted back. The litany echoed across the large hall.

Up on the stage, two young women guards brought my mother forward, holding her by her arms, one pushing her head down, the other pulling her arms up. If only I could see her eyes I would know if she were all right. But in that position I could not see her face.

"We are here to repudiate this heinous American spy and counter-revolutionary, Grace Liu!" shouted the leader. His voice was amplified on the P.A. system. I knew that meant it was being blasted over loudspeakers all over campus.

Some in the crowd rose to their feet and raised fists in an aggressive gesture of condemnation as they shouted agreement.

I looked up at the frail figure onstage. My mother weighed less than ninety pounds, and she was all but swallowed up by her loose-fitting Chinese-style red corduroy jacket and full-legged, dark blue trousers. It was the same outfit she was wearing the day she was arrested. She did not make a sound or look up. Now and then, her head would involuntarily bob up and one of her guards would punch her on the ear to force it back down.

I had been through enough of these public denunciations in recent months to be reasonably certain that her life was not in danger. Still, I was frightened. Her health was not good and anything could happen. Around me, the shouting grew louder.

"Long live Chairman Mao!"

"Down with the traitor!"

"Long live the proletarian dictatorship!"

My mother was bent over with her arms stretched backward, in the position the Chinese called "sitting in a jet plane." She remained expressionless.

Then the speaker enumerated the crimes of this unrepentant American woman—she was a spy, leaking information to other foreigners. She was a reactionary bourgeois authority, poisoning the minds of young students with Western culture and values. She was a counter-revolutionary who opposed the leadership of the Communist Party and dared to ridicule the "Four Greats" of Chairman Mao.

"Listen to this woman's words! What did she say about our revolutionary warriors?" The speaker's voice grew louder. "This belligerent American woman dared to call the Red Guards 'hooligans' and 'rascals!' She said they should be thrown into a frying pan and fried!"

The crowd roared.

I could not believe my ears. Grace had no way of knowing what was being said and I doubted she had said these things.

"Furthermore, we have it in her own handwriting, in letters she wrote to a foreign agent in Beijing, that she called the monument we built for our beloved leader a tomb. If it is a tomb, then she wishes our Great Leader Chairman Mao dead!"

The crowd jumped to their feet with raised fists and shouted over and over again. "Protect Chairman Mao with our lives! Smash the counter-revolutionary Grace Liu!"

I was breathless. They had found a crime worse than teaching bourgeois culture. Now I realized there was no hope for her. Speaking out against Chairman Mao was a crime punishable by death. I knew people had been executed after being accused of saying things like that. Whether she had said it or not, I feared this was the end.

While the roaring was at a frenzy, the other two "criminals" were brought before the crowd. One was a former Party secretary of the university accused of being a traitor, and the other a counter-revolutionary professor. In precisely two hours, as though anger and emotion ran by time clock, the denunciation rally ended.

As if they had not been humiliated enough, the three accused were forced to walk through a sandbox of dirt and manure to reaffirm their status as sub-humans, before being pushed offstage and led away. The speaker's words were still ringing in my ears—"They will be dealt with severely!"— when I tried to get up. But I couldn't move. I was paralyzed. It was like a nightmare. I tried to get up. I tried to reach her. But I couldn't do anything. The distance between me and her—although in reality only a few feet—was a vast chasm of blackness.

Suddenly a sharp whack on my shoulder stunned me into

reality. T. and another Red Guard grabbed me from behind and hissed in my ear, "Grace Liu is an enemy of the people! You will be dealt with the same way if you follow in her footsteps."

My two jailers escorted me back home and told me to continue to write denunciation material about Grace to show that I had drawn the line and was on the side of the people. I just sat and stared at the walls wondering what was going to happen to Grace, to me, to my sisters . . .

I had not seen Nini since Grace was arrested and I worried about what might have happened to her. Nini had already suffered during the height of the fighting between the Red Guard factions. About a year earlier, she had come to the campus when she was eight months pregnant. We were all excited because it had taken Nini seven years to get pregnant and in those years she had had several miscarriages. She had been extremely cautious with this pregnancy. As the birth approached, Grace was looking forward to having a grandchild close by in Tianjin and gave Nini advice to be careful in the last month.

On her way home—she and En-hua still lived in the old mansion where we had moved after F. C. died—as she left the campus, she was hit from behind by someone riding a bicycle. She was knocked down and didn't even see who did it. By the time she got home, she was hemorrhaging.

En-hua rushed her to the hospital, which was only three blocks away. The doctor examined her and told them not to worry. He said that the baby still had a strong heartbeat and that they would perform a Caesarean operation to save the baby. But the hospital, like all other institutions during that time, was also caught up in the battling factions. While preparations for the operation was under way, the loudspeaker in the hospital came alive with shouts:

"Revolutionary comrades, the Reactionary Royalists are protecting the capitalist roaders in the Party. They are unwilling to give up their power. We Revolutionary Rebels must seize the power from them! Come immediately to the office of the head of the hospital! We must break down the door!"

The operating room doctor and nurses stopped their preparation and ran out, leaving Nini on the operating table not knowing what was happening. En-hua was kept outside waiting, pacing up and down smoking cigarettes as he worried what was happening to her. No one would answer any questions or help them. Nearly three hours later, when they came back to the operating room, they could not then detect any heartbeat from the baby. The Caesarean was performed but the baby was dead.

Nini was released from the hospital and came home. She kept her feelings to herself. En-hua called me to come. She was resting in bed when I got there. As soon as she saw me, she began to cry. With tears rolling down her face, she sobbed softly, "I miss my baby. I miss my baby."

As I waited alone in the bungalow, I did not know that Nini was also being implicated. Immediately after Grace's denunciation, posters went up at the Water Works with slogans saying that Liu Fu-chi had been a bourgeois reactionary authority, tainted by Western "influences" and Western education. Nini's husband En-hua was a leader of one of the production units at that time and he tried to argue with the Red Guards, but they threatened to go to his house and arrest Nini. En-hua left immediately but by the time he got home, the Red Guards were already there. Nini had been found burning English magazines and newspapers. She was afraid that they would be used against her, but before she could flush the ashes down the toilet, the Red Guards had burst into the house. Her actions made matters worse because they accused her of trying to destroy evidence of spying activities. En-hua tried to stop them. He argued that they could still read the words in the print and see that these were harmless magazines. But they did not listen.

No one came near me for another two days. I was kept completely isolated. Finally on the third day, T. and his assistants returned. T. said that Grace's attitude was still not good, but she had confessed to some of her crimes and that she would be allowed to come home that afternoon to continue writing her confession. T. went on to warn me, "If you do not help her to confess her crimes, both of you will be severely punished. You must not have any connection with your co-conspirators and, if anyone should contact you, you must report them to us immediately."

That afternoon, two women Red Guards, both of whom I recognized from the Foreign Language Department, brought Grace back home. She looked paler and, if possible, even thinner. However, she did not look frightened or even depressed. She told me that she had been kept in the girls' dorm for the three weeks and was interrogated every day by a group led by T.

"The accusations were so ridiculous that I could hardly contain my laughter. They accused me of wishing Chairman Mao dead because I had written to Olga that the stature of Mao the students built was 'sepulchral.' It was made of black and gray stones, and I remarked that black and gray are colors used for monuments or tombs of people. T. said in a pompous tone, 'I know "sepulchral" means tomblike. I looked it up in a dictionary, so don't think you can use sophistry to hoodwink the revolutionary warriors.' He twisted his face to show how much he hated me. But I repeated what I had said in the letter—I told him that Mao had specifically said not to make statues and carry out personal worship and that the Red Guards were going against his wishes to build the statue. They were the ones building a monument to him as if he were dead."

I never dreamed she would argue with T., certainly not by quoting Mao. "How did he respond?" I asked.

"He sneered back at me and said. 'We Red Guards built the statue out of our love for the Great Leader. How can you, a class enemy, understand how we feel? It shows just how much you hate Chairman Mao.' I told him that I understood it quite well. I had been in China before the liberation and I knew how unjust the system was and I supported the revolution wholeheartedly. I don't guess it mattered one bit what I said because he twisted everything I said to mean the opposite."

"He said you confessed. What did you confess to?" I asked.

"I didn't confess to anything. No evidence turned up. He had no case against me for a crime so he kept saying I had a bad attitude," she laughed.

As light as my mother's tone was, the situation was quite serious. As soon as someone is denounced as a class enemy, all rights are suspended. As I expected, the next day people came to our house and asked why were we, the class enemies, living in this nice house while the workers were still living in small rooms. So within a few days we were driven out of our bungalow and into a small room in a house on the other side of campus. The house belonged to a former Party leader of the university who had also been denounced and was forced to give up some of his rooms.

The room was about ten feet by ten feet. We crammed into it our small beds, a table, and book shelves which we had to stack on top of each other. There was no chair and no place to sit other than the beds. We shared a kitchen and a toilet with others under the staircase.

We could not bring all our things, but we did take our books. I moved them stack by stack on my bicycle. They had never been confiscated. The book burnings had happened early, before Grace was a target, and had been carried out by the high school Red Guards who overlooked her. The university Red Guards were interested in other issues and so by the time the revolution swept into our home, nobody was interested in confiscating our books.

Instead of being destroyed, Grace's books had been protected. Since Grace had many of the textbooks and research materials important to the English department, some members of the department had approached her early on and offered to put some of her books in a safe place "until the storm blows over." Furthermore, Grace continued to receive boxes of magazines, periodicals, and books from abroad even during the Cultural Revolution. The Tianjin Customs Office knew her well and had always given her special permission for receiving printed material provided there was no anti-China propaganda in it. They knew these supplies were for the young teachers that Grace was training. William tells of an incident that took place during the first time he was under surveillance by the Red Guards:

> Two weeks after the Beijing Red Guards came, packages arrived from a friend in America who usually sent them to us—full of recent *Saturday Reviews* and contemporary novels.

Both of my jailers were former English students. One of them asked to "borrow" the copy of Arthur Hailey's *Hotel* and during the day, while I was supposed to be writing my denunciation materials, he would ask me to explain various English idioms he encountered in the book.

While Grace and William were restricted to one small room, their books and magazines played a significant role in their survival. William's description of their experience under house arrest continues:

We were each given fifteen yuan (less than $3.00 U.S.) a month to live on which just barely kept us alive. I cooked on a small "beehive" coal stove. Fortunately it was summer so we did not need to light the stove for heat. The only time I left the room was to go out to get food. I did not set foot off the campus and I never spoke or looked at anyone for fear of implicating them. Once Grace was denounced, no students or colleagues dared to contact us. We did not know what was happening to Nini and Ellen or any of our friends. The only faces we saw were the sneering faces of the interrogators. T. came several times a week when he was on campus and then he would disappear for several days. We heard later that T. or members of his group were tracking down anyone in China who was connected to us.

During these times when they were busy tracking down other people, Mother and I were left to ourselves. To keep ourselves busy, we would read or do crossword puzzles. It didn't take us long to go through our last shipment of *Saturday Reviews*. When we finished the crossword puzzles and cryptograms in these, we made up new ones for each other. Mother would make one for me and I would make one for her. We used a dictionary when we got stuck. This activity filled the long hours and was good vocabulary practice for me, but it produced a jumble of scribbling with suspicious-looking numbers and letters all over them. I joked with Mother, "We better destroy these as soon as we solve them or our jailers might suspect that we are devising some kind of secret code."

Of course, we passed a lot of the time reading. Mother had many of the classics of English, French, and Russian literature. By reading and re-reading them at this time I gained not only a sense of history, but a deeper understanding of both the uniqueness and the universality of human experience. It helped us look beyond our confinement. One of our favorites was Charles Dickens's *A Tale of Two Cities*. Nini had told me and Ellen the story when we were children to entertain us and later Grace read the whole book to us when we were a bit older. I can still hear to this day Grace's voice reading: "It was the best of times, it was the worst of times . . ." *A Tale of Two Cities* was particularly relevant to me during this period as the story tells of those who were swept up by atrocities of the French Revolution, sometimes mere innocent bystanders.

I mused aloud, after I finished re-reading *A Tale of Two Cities* in our little room, half expecting T. and the investigation group to appear in any moment, "I used to have much more sympathy for Madame Defarge than I do now." Madame Defarge, a character in the book who kept knitting as the accused were executed, had been, in my opinion, well justified in her desire to seek revenge against the French aristocracy, but now I began to identify with some of the innocent people whose persecution she caused.

"Well, Willy," Mother asked me in response to my statement about Madame Defarge, "If you were there and you suffered innocently, then would it mean that the French Revolution was unjustifiable?"

"I suppose not," I replied, hesitantly.

"You would have a choice," she said. "You could cry 'woe is me' and just lie down and die, or if you did survive, you could try to understand and learn from the experience." I was not surprised by what she said. I knew which choice she had made.

We often amused ourselves by giving the people we knew names of characters from the books we read. Grace had commented to me that whenever T. spoke to her he would demonstrate to others his class hatred of her by twisting his face into a sneer. From that time on we nicknamed him "Madame Defarge." One day I looked out the window and saw him coming and said, "Here comes Madame Defarge. I

wonder what crimes we'll be accused of this time." That made
us smile inwardly when his accusations did come.

Another time Grace burst out laughing and said to Willy, "Listen to this!" She read from the book she was holding:

> "There's more evidence to come yet, please your Majesty,"
> said the White Rabbit, jumping up in a great hurry . . . "it
> seems to be a letter, written by the prisoner to—to some-
> body."
> "It must have been that," said the King, "unless it was writ-
> ten to nobody, which isn't usual, you know."
> ". . . Are they in the prisoner's handwriting?" asked one of
> the jury men.
> "No, they're not," said the White Rabbit, "and that's the
> queerest thing about it." (The jury all looked puzzled.)
> "He must have imitated someone else's hand, said the
> King. (The jury all brightened up again.)
> "Please your majesty," said the Knave, "I didn't write it, and
> they can't prove I did; there's no name signed at the end."
> "If you didn't sign it," said the King, "that only makes the
> matter worse. You must have meant some mischief, or else
> you'd have signed your name like an honest man."
> There was a general clapping of hands at this; it was the
> first really clever thing the King had said that day.
> "That proves his guilt!" said the Queen.

William described Grace's amused reactions to the passage:

> Mother read on and we laughed until our sides ached,
> remembering the night we were questioned about Olga's let-
> ter. I knew that *Alice in Wonderland* was more than just a chil-
> dren's story, that it satirized Victorian England, but I had
> never considered its relevance to China, particularly to the
> Cultural Revolution. Now we had another set of nicknames.
> "With the Red Queen around, it is a wonder that any
> heads are still attached!" I said and we both laughed, know-
> ing full well who the "Red Queen" was.
> My mother never thought of the Cultural Revolution the
> way many people did. She understood that when fanatical

thinking takes over, whether it is political or religious in nature, people, particularly young people, act in illogical ways and language loses its meaning, like in *Alice*. She could draw on so many other periods of history through the literature that portrayed them. This was a great lesson to me and enabled us to survive with our wits still intact.

Autumn came and life became more difficult. Although the interrogations gradually dwindled and the Red Guards in the university found new targets to tear into, William noticed that the incessant interrogations and the settling in of the cold weather had begun to take a heavier toll on Grace:

> Her cough and asthma became worse and we had nowhere to turn. We did not have enough money for food and medicine both. By then I had started to visit Nini again. She and En-hua had both been arrested, interrogated, and returned home, so I was not worried that my visits would harm them. Since my bicycle had been confiscated by the Red Guards, I went to town by bus. Nini gave me some money from the little that she had to buy medicine or food for Grace.
>
> By the time the wind came howling down from Siberia, Mother's pleurisy worsened. She moaned in pain with each breath she took. I couldn't take her to a hospital as class enemies were not accepted at hospitals. I just sat there in our one small room and listened to her suffering. Grace would assure me, "Nothing will happen, Willy," she said calmly. "Nothing will happen; otherwise we will never be cleared."
>
> Suddenly I heard her gasping. It seemed like her last breath.
>
> "Willy, the pain-killer plaster, do you remember?"
>
> She had used the Chinese plasters a few years ago when she sprained her wrist. But I had never thought about using them for pleurisy. I had no other choice. I jumped up and said I would be right back. Fortunately, there was a drugstore not far from campus; I came back with a package of these plasters and plastered her back with them. Miraculously they eased the pain and she fell asleep. She slept for a whole day and I

think that saved her life. We both knew that she must live through these times. If she died, it would become more difficult to clear up all these accusations. She was determined not to lose her front row seat on history no matter how much she suffered.

Throughout this time, William was cut off from his school friend, Kelin. Before Grace's arrest he had seen Kelin every week. En-hua had warned Kelin and told him not to contact any of the family. Then one day he saw Grace's poster. Kelin describes his feelings in an interview years later:

Imagine what it was like one day when I was walking down a street and spotted a huge poster on a wall proclaiming some "great victory of the Red Guards" at Nankai University where a heinous American spy had been rooted out. People gathered around the poster and gasped at the shocking accusations of the class enemy and counter-revolutionary who had wished the Great Leader Chairman Mao to be buried in a tomb.

And then I suddenly recognized the picture on the poster—it was my best friend's mother staring down at me, amidst all those lurid accusations!

William's mother had always treated me like a son. I never thought of her as a foreigner. I came and went to their home like a member of the family. I mourned the death of my father at the same time that William mourned for his father. We had been close friends since our school days. I remember when William first came to our school, it was raining, and he wore a raincoat and rain boots. At that time most of our families were poor—we didn't have rain gear. Everybody laughed at him and called him "Big Nose." I was the only person that didn't do it. Our teacher asked us to sit together. Then we became good friends. We went to watch movies after class and we read many books when other kids were interested in other things.

When I saw the poster, I knew how much they must be suffering and I wished I could help. Yet, more than two years went by before I saw William again. And that was only when I ran into him accidentally in the summer of 1970, on the street not far from where Nini lived. I still feel guilty to this day, guilty that I could not give a helping hand to my best friend during those years. The helplessness and hopelessness was like confronting a deadly disease; you knew it would not do anyone any good to go close to the contaminated ones, yet you would forever condemn yourself for not going to their aid. No matter how many books are written about the Cultural Revolution, they cannot add up to more than a snapshot of the terrible feelings we had at that time. Even after so many years, we don't want to talk about what happened. It is a deep hurt in everyone's heart.

Grace's students and colleagues were also torn by their helplessness and hopelessness. One of the young teachers who witnessed Grace's public denunciation described how she felt: "We all had to go. It was required. Yet we hurt so terribly to see Grace Liu on stage, so mistreated. I felt the indignity, the fright, the humiliation, the revulsion. There was nothing we could do. Yet I knew these people accusing her were ignorant. They might have been oppressed in their lives and I understood how they felt, but I could not understand how they could hate someone who was in no way connected to their oppression."

BY 1969 THE TWO factions of Red Guards had taken their conflicts beyond the campuses and into the factories and the countryside. The nation's production was at a standstill. The nation's leaders called for the workers' organizations to quell the "leftist excesses" and bring order to the campuses. For three years there had been virtually no classes and no graduations as the students waged revolution. Grace watched with relief as the Workers' Propaganda Teams took over the Nankai campus and negotiated with the students to continue the revolution by resuming classes.

Gradually classes resumed, teachers returned to work, and those whose pay had been cut were given full salary. With her salary

restored, she and William had enough money for food and medicine. Nini was pregnant again and was able to visit as before. It
seemed that the most difficult years were behind but, indeed, the
long ordeal was far from over.

Without any written notes of this period, William found it hard
to recall the order of things when both he and Nini came under
investigation in late 1969 and 1970:

> It started in the coldest part of winter when Mother's health
> failed. One night I found Grace spitting up blood. I rushed to
> the office of the workers' teams and was given permission to
> take a school car to drive her to the hospital. While she was
> just beginning to recover, I became the target of attacks.
>
> The political climate was as changeable as the weather.
> There was another nationwide surge to "clear the class ranks
> and root out 'bad' elements." This time my mother and I
> reversed roles. I was arrested and Grace was left alone, not
> knowing what was happening to me. A friend of mine and his
> girlfriend were caught listening to Western music in their
> home in the city. The girl panicked under interrogation and
> "confessed" to belonging to a group that opposed the gov-
> ernment. The record player and the records were traced
> to me. I had loaned them out when we were forced to move
> from the bungalow. For the accusers the connection was
> electrifying. It was thought that my role was connected to
> Grace's case and that investigating me would lead to further
> evidence against her. I was arrested in April of 1970. They
> accused me of being a leader of a gang of bourgeois counter-
> revolutionaries plotting to overthrow the government.
>
> Nini was pregnant again when they came to arrest her. It
> was just too much for Nini this time. She sat on the floor and
> cried. She refused to move. Her husband En-hua yelled at the
> guards and told them that she had already lost one child. If
> she lost this one too, it would kill her. Then they would be
> responsible. He didn't let up, he kept yelling and threatened
> them with the lives of his family. Finally they went away
> without taking Nini.

Grace was unable to care for herself alone while William was

under arrest. She moved in with Nini and had to travel back and
forth daily to the campus for political meetings. Even in her weakened condition, she took the crowded bus, then walked the distance to the university, sometimes through severe wind and rain,
often grasping for a lamppost to steady herself.

William recalls his arrest:

> I was taken away under guard and locked in a barred cell in
> a dormitory on another campus that was being used for deten-
> tion. My cellmates included criminals such as a rapist and
> thieves—the association was supposed to impress upon me the
> severity of my crimes. I slept in lice-infested straw on the floor,
> was not allowed to sleep with the lights off, and was interro-
> gated day and night. I was told to write down all the counter-
> revolutionary activities I had been involved in. When I asked
> to be allowed to check up on my mother, I was told, "She is
> not your concern now. Your concern is your own crime."
>
> Even under these conditions, no evidence emerged. Frus-
> trated, my jailers brought in some local high school Red
> Guards to intimidate me into "confession." One day when I
> was poking the fire in the little coal stove in the cell, a Red
> Guard grabbed the poker and slammed it across my face,
> yelling, "It is about time you confess!" A group of others came
> in. I was knocked to the ground and kicked around. The
> guards taunted me, "Look at Big Nose! See if his foreign con-
> nections can help him now!"
>
> After two months, when no further evidence of counter-
> revolutionary activity turned up and Grace's case was no
> longer of interest to them, I was freed, but only after a thirty-
> page confession on the evils of bourgeois literature and music
> was completed.
>
> When I returned to Grace, I told her, "My crime is basi-
> cally that I listen to Beethoven and read Jane Austen."

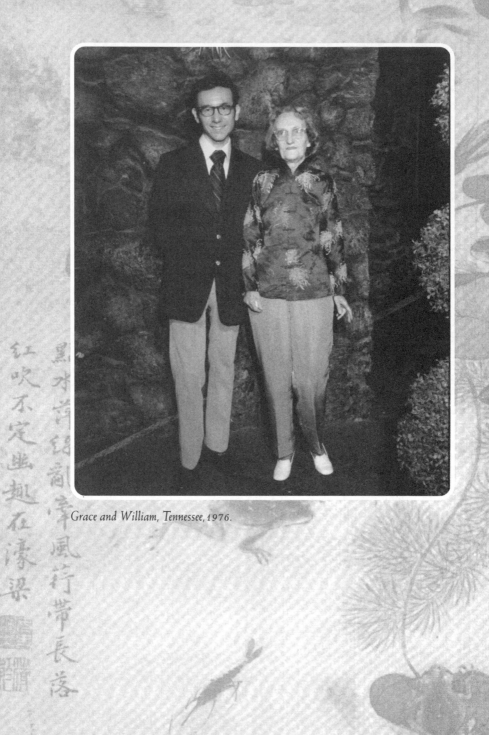

Grace and William, Tennessee, 1976.

黑水茫茫前峰風行帶長落

紅吹不定幽趣在濠梁

SIXTEEN

WHEN CLASSES RESUMED at Nankai University in 1971, Grace, then seventy, continued training the same set of young teachers as before. She had to rewrite the manuals for English language teaching because the texts that had been used before were no longer suitable. William and Grace's assistants first prepared texts for the countryside and then for factories, developing vocabulary and dialogues for activities related to peasants and workers.

Ellen came to visit for the first time in years. Nini gave birth to a healthy baby girl, and William recalled:

> Ellen brought with her two daughters. The second one had been born in 1968, at the time of Grace's denunciation. She told us that soon after the arrest, big character posters

appeared at her workplace, calling on her to draw the line between herself and her reactionary mother. The worst part was not knowing what was happening to Grace. Because Ellen was pregnant at the time, she stayed low and took as much sick leave as she could. She could not contact Grace in any way, even to inform her of the birth. When she returned to work, Rui-sheng's mother came from the countryside to live with them and to take care of the children. Rui-sheng was transferred to her workplace and the five of them lived in one small room in a nearby dorm. Because they worked for the government's scientific institute, the PLA took over their workplace and no Red Guard factions were allowed to fight there. Some cadres went to Tianjin to investigate Grace's case but when they returned they did not speak to Ellen. Political meetings and infighting took place everyday but Ellen was not the target of attacks.

Two years later, Ellen had a third daughter. Since three children exceeded the central government's goal for limiting population, the third child was considered officially "not to exist." The child was given no rations, and the family was not permitted to move to a larger apartment.

In May 1971, the American Ping-Pong team showed up in China. Everyone watched as China's world championship team took on the Americans. The warm reception given to the American team was the first sign that relations between America and China were beginning to thaw. The relationship with the Soviets had become more tense since the Sino-Russian border disputes began in 1969. Public meetings were held on campus to announce the change in foreign relations. The new policy excited the English teachers and students because it meant that English would become more important.

Premier Zhou Enlai handled most of China's foreign affairs. Like many of the Chinese who sought his help during the Cultural Revolution, Grace wrote a letter to him in 1971. She explained that in order to continue her work on educational reform, she needed survivable living conditions. Grace never knew if her letter had any effect or even if it had reached its destination—her request was sent at the same time as the easing of the Cultural Revolution and the warming of relations with America—but one day she was told that she could have another room in the same building and that William's position as English-language instructor would be restored.

Although the force of the Cultural Revolution was lessening, the political tide continued its ebb and flow. Just before China's doors opened, an attempt was made to assassinate Chairman Mao. The alleged leader of the coup, Lin Biao, China's main military strategist, former head of the PLA and designated successor to Mao, was reported to have died in a plane crash with his wife and son trying to escape to Russia in September 1971.

President Richard Nixon arrived in February 1972, when China was six years into the Cultural Revolution. At the height of his revolutionary fervor, Mao welcomed the leader of capitalist world. From the American side, the ironies were just as great. Nixon had built his career on opposing Communism and been confronted by angry students protesting the war in Vietnam. Nixon had released his own "enemies list" reminiscent of the McCarthy era. Now he was being given the red carpet treatment by the leader of the largest Communist revolution in history. Each leader sought the other as leverage against the Soviet Union.

For the first time in nearly twenty-five years, great numbers of reporters were allowed into China. The Western media was caught unprepared. Their view into China for a whole generation had been no closer than Hong Kong or Tokyo. They had been reduced to scrutinizing Chinese newspapers for nuances of words to indicate a political shift or absences of names to indicate a purge. There had been little understanding of the nation's turmoil since the Japanese occupation and almost no contact since 1949—years which were full of twists and turns.

Since television was the preferred medium in 1972, Nixon paid special attention to setting up satellite capability to transmit images of the historic meeting worldwide. The simplistic images associated with television, however, combined with the fact that the Chinese

government did not allow the correspondents contact with ordinary Chinese or free movement inside China, created a superficial
and highly suspect exposure to China. Each reporter interpreted his
experience along the lines of his own political persuasions, which
were received and believed by audiences of similar persuasion.
Because the opening with the West came in the middle of the Cultural Revolution, the impression of a country with a "harsh and
dour reality" underneath its surface is the image of China that was
indelibly printed on the Western mind.

Following Nixon's visit to China, a U.S. liaison office opened in
Beijing in 1973. The thawing of relations between the two nations
was marked by diplomatic spurts and media frenzy. For Grace, now
seventy-two, and forced to stop teaching because she was often
barely able to breathe, the normalization of relations increased her
desire to know what had happened to her American family. When
she and William began talking about the idea of contacting her
family, he reminded her of her experience of writing to her brother
Tom after the war only to find that he had moved to another city.
And that was after only four years. Imagine, he said, what might
have happened after twenty years. And this time there was no
hometown Marine to offer to deliver the letter personally.

Grace wrote a simple letter and sent it to the school in Tennessee
that her uncles had founded, not knowing its address, only the city
it was in. She hoped that the management of the school would
know the whereabouts of her relatives. She had no idea that her
cousin, Spence McCallie, would be the headmaster. Dr. Spence, as
he was called at the school, immediately contacted Grace's
brother, Tom Divine, who was living on a farm outside Kingsport,
Tennessee. Tom had retired from Eastman Kodak, where he had
been employed since leaving Oak Ridge a few years after the war.
As soon as he hung up the phone, with tears in his eyes, his wife
Mary Hills reported, he began writing Grace a long-overdue letter.

In a short time Tom and Mary Hills received a reply from
William, saying that his mother was too sick to write back. William

quickly outlined the happenings in their lives since the time of Grace's last letter in 1953—F. C.'s death, Nini and Ellen's marriages, her teaching at Nankai University, and the birth of Grace's four grandchildren. He concluded with, "Too bad none of us inherited Mother's voice; but we all have her love of music." He did not describe the price he had paid for that love.

As soon as she was able, Grace wrote the first letter to her brother in over twenty years:

March 20, 1974

Dear old Tom,

Yes, you wrote on my birthday—February 23rd.

I am a little better now so I'm going to try to write you at least a short letter myself. How much I appreciate your wonderful letter! But I must read it over and over again many times yet before I can properly digest all the facts. Believe me, I truly never intended to let so much time pass by before I wrote and I was in a panic when I realized I did not know who was living and who wasn't or where anyone was.

I will write what I can now and as I get better I'll write more and more. Right now you'll have to excuse my handwriting. My hand has become quite shaky since my illness. I had very bad bronchial asthma this year. I had to stop all work in September and fight for my breath—always worse during the cold, windy changeable winter months.

Willie's letter gave you a general survey of our family's doings. I will try to gradually fill up the gaps myself—you will understand I'm sure how F. C.'s death seemed to put an end to my own life and to any desire to go on living. But I was responsible for the children who were still in school. I could not allow myself to become bogged down in grief and despair. Only activity—purposeful, necessary activity—could save me. I moved with the children to a different part of the city where there was nothing to remind me of my old way of life. I let the servants go and we went to live in two rooms in a big house with seventeen other families, most of whom had only one room. I tried to do my own cooking and my own housework to make myself too tired to think. This is a long story I can't go into now. How I failed and what rescued me, how good these people were to me and how good for me to live in the midst of them. For the first time since I'd come to China I did not feel like a strange creature and a foreigner. The common people recognized me as another human being. They were very friendly and kind and treated me as one of themselves.

A year later we four went on a wonderful trip to the 800-year-old West Liu Village—F. C.'s old home—in Shaanxi Province. This is another long story that must wait to be told. When we got back to Tianjin I heard that Nankai University wanted an English teacher. I had an old friend here and it was quickly arranged that I should start immediately. I've been here ever since.

I think I've made quite a satisfactory readjustment to life. I've worked very hard and studied harder, because I knew nothing about language and language teaching when I began and had no confidence in my ability. But knowledge gives confidence and I have studied this subject diligently for the last twelve years so I have acquired enough confidence to make the most difficult work exhilarating and enjoyable.

Your family, Tom, simply bewilders me. I can't imagine Mary Hills as the grandmother of ten big grandchildren. The last time I saw her she still seemed just a tiny little girl. I have already read your letter many times, but it's still bewildering. I'm not at all surprised at the many things you have done. I've always believed that you could do anything in the world and do it well, better than anybody else. You and F. C. are the only two people in the world that I've had complete faith and confidence in. I'll write about F. C.'s work later. His death was a great loss to the country—

I must stop now. I'm getting breathless. Don't you all have some pictures? Do send us some and write whenever you have time and tell me more about Elinor—did you say she was a poet? I'm interested in writers.

My very best love to dear Mary Hills and all the children and grandchildren I haven't yet succeeded in unscrambling—

Take care of yourself, Tom, and listen to Mary Hills's good advice.

Grace

When Tom read this letter he was very distressed. There was so much of his sister's life he had missed. He was most concerned about her health. He remembered how Grace had suffered from asthma as a child. He used to stay up with her and prop her head up in the big chair so that she could get her breath. But he thought she had outgrown that long ago. He did not know what kind of medical attention she was able to get now. With Mary Hills's encouragement, he wrote her back and invited her to come to the United States for medical treatment and then stay for the winter with them in Florida. For fear that she could not make the trip alone, he invited her son to come with her.

Tom's proposal that she come to the United States at first seemed preposterous to Grace. How could she possibly survive such a trip? But on the other hand, it was unlikely that she would survive another winter in China. And if William were ever to know his American relatives, he would have to be introduced by her. She wrote to Tom: "I was very intrigued by your invitation to Willy and me to visit you. I think a winter in a mild and wind-free climate would put me on my feet again (respiratorally speaking). I would like to really recover before I face another North China winter. I have already written to our department head about the matter, but I have no idea what the outcome will be. Probably many problems will arise. As you say, things are easier said than done. Well, we will see—"

But Grace had only begun to think of what had to be done. The procedures for leaving the country were virtually unknown to her, or to anyone at that time Grace's American passport had expired in 1951 and there had been no U.S. embassy in China to apply to for renewal. Not wanting to be a "stateless person" she had applied for and received Chinese citizenship in 1957. She was not certain now where to apply for visas or passports. And in fact, there were no flights, since international air service to China was not yet available. And then there was the problem of money. With hardly any salary at all for the last few years, she had no way to pay for such a trip.

William had to take on most of the responsibilities of writing letters, filling out forms, and seeking permission from one place and then another. William made several trips to Beijing to the newly opened American liaison office, where he met with James Lilley. Mr. Lilley told him that Grace had to apply in person, a request that was reasonable, but not easy to accomplish.

As early as May, Grace reported that the university had granted approval and a few months later had agreed to advance her salary in order to pay the travel costs for both William and herself. By September all of the applications for passports and visas had been made and approval seemed likely. Just when it looked actually possible that they might make it, a swift cold wind ripped through northern China. Grace was readmitted to the hospital. At the same time, William heard from Mary Hills that Tom had had a heart attack. William was worried as to whether his mother could survive such a journey, even if she were able to begin it. He knew it would take four hours from Beijing to Tokyo and twelve hours from Tokyo to San Francisco, but he had no idea how long it would take from San Francisco to Tennessee.

When Grace came out of the hospital, she convalesced at Nini's, where Grace had lived after F. C. died. When the neighbors heard that she was going to America, they all came to see her and bid farewell. Her former cook, Sun Pao-san, brought her food he knew she liked and she began to rebuild her strength. Her appetite was returning when she wrote her brother Tom: "Your letter about the corn and okra made me so hungry. Okra is the one vegetable the Chinese don't have and I used to love it fried."

Uncertain, but hopeful that her weak body would sustain her, Grace wrote her last letter from China on September 22, 1974: "I can hardly wait to get there and hear all the family history and eat!"

GRACE HAD DOUBLED RIP Van Winkle's record in years, lived through a revolution instead of sleeping through one, and crossed half the globe in a matter of hours. It would not be surprising if she felt dazed when she landed in the United States on October 25, 1974. Grace wore Chinese black pants and black slippers with a white silk overblouse, the only "formal" attire she brought. Her short, grayish white hair was cut off bluntly. Her face was thin and gaunt, with no makeup. She seemed small and frail, not like a heroine returning from distant shores.

Wearing a Western-style suit that was several sizes too big for him, William extended his arm for his mother to hold as she exited the plane. Grace took his arm and walked steadily and with determination.

Mary and Bob Ware, who had fled China in 1937 as the Japanese attacked, met them at the San Francisco airport and sent them on to Tennessee where Tom and Mary Hills greeted them. The last time Grace had been in Tennessee was to say good-bye to her family before she set sail for China. Tom remembered how little Nini as a toddler had reached out to hug him and all his resentment of Grace's marriage had melted away. There were many hugs again this time.

How disorienting it was for Grace. The older members of the family were no longer there, and the ones she had known as children, younger than she, had aged beyond recognition. And so many younger ones had come along, bearing names and resemblances to those she had known before they were born.

The world she had known forty years earlier had changed in many bewildering ways. When Grace returned to Chattanooga, she went looking for the home she remembered from her childhood on a hill outside of town. She wrote this passage in her memoir about her experience of looking for the past:

> "But the hill," I exclaimed. "The house was on a hill with beautiful big trees."
> "Sure, the hill was right there. But they 'dozed it," I was told by a workman.

"*Dozed* it, what do you mean?" I'd never heard of such a thing.

"The bulldozers, ma'am, they 'dozed that hill right down."

"But . . . why?" I asked.

"For a highway, ma'am."

I stared at that low, flat piece of ground with nothing on it but wild grass and weeds and thought how unwise it was to go hunting up one's past. Time can do shocking things—the world of my youth was gone.

As we drove back into town, pictures of my childhood on that vanished hill filled my mind. I saw the white house under the big oaks and the huge mulberry tree at the left of the house. A gravel walk bordered with white narcissus curved up the left slope from the small gate at the foot of the hill to the porch steps. To the right was the big gate the cows came through on the road to the barn as the sun started down.

In the peace and quiet of the late afternoon, a little girl about eleven years old was sitting in the swing on the porch, swinging back and forth. I knew what she was feeling. I knew what she was going to do—I could feel the songs filling her throat.

I remembered so clearly that long-ago me. How I loved to sing from the top of that hill—to launch my voice out into the air and listen as it floated and soared through the trees and over the road and the car line below, and in the pauses came echoing back to me from the top of the opposite hill.

I hear Mama calling from the doorway: "Sister, sing my favorite song." Then I hear the wistful words go sailing over the trees in my eleven-year-old voice:

"Believe me if all those endearing young charms / which I gaze on so fondly today / were to change by tomorrow and fleet in my arms / like fairy gifts fading away / thou wouldst still be ador'd as this moment thou art / let thy loveliness fade as it will / and around the dear ruin, each wish of my heart / would entwine itself verdantly still."

There was no one in sight when I began singing. But when I look down the hill, I see some of the workmen and people from nearby coming in twos and threes to sit

on the crossties stacked beside the rail line. Inspired by
the audience, I sing contentedly through my store of old
songs until it grows darker and darker all around

———

GRACE WAS HOSPITALIZED, AND when the doctors finally examined her, they said that her lungs were as black and damaged as
those of someone who had smoked for forty years. Her lungs were
irrigated, and she convalesced in her brother's Florida home. As
soon as she could, she wrote back to the head of the department
and her colleagues at Nankai:

December 28, 1974

Dear Professor Li,

I thought I would have gotten around to writing to you
long before now, but I ran into difficulties soon after
reaching the U.S.A. I stood the flight from Beijing to San
Francisco very well indeed, in fact, better than Wei-han
did. He lost his appetite, but I never missed a meal. The
San Francisco cold, damp weather and talking too much
started me coughing again, but I still felt quite energetic
when we arrived in Tennessee. Then relatives came from all
over to see me in Kingsport and so much excitement and
talking began to wear me out.

We started south by car after about a week. We had a
terrific day in Chattanooga and I had a wonderful time
seeing people I hadn't seen for forty years and more—
nearly all of them had thought I must surely be dead! But
thank goodness I was very lively and energetic for that one
day at least, then we had two more days to travel south by
car. Everybody here goes either by plane or by car. The
railroads have almost disappeared in the United States. I
find car travel exceedingly tiring and by the time we
reached Naples in the south of Florida I was completely
exhausted. I had a fever for two or three weeks and then
stayed in the hospital for thirteen days. I am much better

now but the doctor insists on my taking an antibiotic that
makes me feel quite awful or at least it did at first. I'm
getting more used to it now. I walk on the beach every
morning and have had a boat trip out on the bay.

I hope Nini has shown you our letters and pictures.
What we write to her is really for everybody. Please give
the department and school leaders my warmest and most
grateful greetings for the New Year. And remember us to all
our colleagues.

All the best to you and your wife.

As ever,

Grace

By 1974, the year that Grace left, it was already clear that
changes in China's leadership were ahead, but no one predicted that
the changes would take place so fast. After Premier Zhou Enlai died
on January 8, 1976, one event after another left the nation reeling.

During the Qingming Festival in April when the Chinese tradi-
tionally pay homage to deceased ancestors, a spontaneous demon-
stration occurred in Tiananmen Square. Personal expressions of
mourning, wreaths, poems, messages, and gifts, intended as memo-
rials for Zhou Enlai, were laid in the square. Many people, like
Grace, although she never knew if he actually intervened
on her behalf, felt a great loss at his death. Vice Premier Deng
Xiaoping had praised him at his funeral as one who "maintained
broad and close ties with the masses and showed boundless warm-
heartedness toward all." He was noted for living in a plain, hardworking way. On the morning of April 5, 1976, when the people
discovered that their tokens of grief had been removed during the
night, a spontaneous protest erupted into violence, resulting in the
arrest of thousands. Deng Xiaoping himself was removed from
office on April 7 and held accountable for the outbursts.

There was a belief in Chinese culture that profound natural disasters accompany the end of dynasties or other major political tran-
sitions. Although this old way of thinking had been "thrown out"

during the Cultural Revolution, few in China missed the significance of the event that occurred on July 28, 1976. All of northern
China was ripped by the worst earthquake in China's known history. Its epicenter was only sixty miles from Tianjin. When Grace
heard the news, she wrote immediately. It was a very long two
weeks before she received the following letter. Nini was living with
her husband En-hua and daughter Yun in the same two rooms of
the old mansion.

August 9, 1976

Dear old Ma and Willy,

I got your letter of July 28th, asking me about the
earthquake. What a day! I shall never forget. That night
[July 27th] I couldn't go to sleep because of asthma: so I
stayed up and wrote you two a letter till 1:30 A.M. [28th]. It
was raining cats and dogs. Then I read a while, and about
3:45 A.M. I turned out the lights and suddenly saw a flash of
reddish purple light which I thought was lighting. Then
came a roar and the whole house began jumping up and
down for about four times. By this time I had turned the
lights on again. When the jumping stopped for a few
seconds, I heard what I thought was hail and rock raining. I
later found out it was house tops falling down. Then we
started to rock back and forth.

En-hua was sleeping in the outer room and for the first
time we had the door between the rooms shut as I did not
want to disturb him with my reading with the lights on. By
this time Yun had wakened. I was still sitting in the bed
holding her and telling her not to be afraid and we'd go
down to the basement when the rocking stopped. But the
rocking seemed to get worse, and then I heard the wood
frames of the windows began to crack as I said to Yun I
think we better start going and I got off the bed and tried
to open the door. It wouldn't open. I pulled and pulled;
then I put Yun down on the floor and pulled with all my
might. It was stuck tight. Then the lights went out. I heard
En-hua shouting on the other side of the door and I called
out that I can't open the door, and I heard him kicking the

door and he finally kicked it open. When we went into the corridor, all the neighbors were in the corridor.

You can't imagine what happened to En-hua. I didn't know whether to laugh or to cry. He had been very busy and had had little sleep for quite a few days, and he had the door shut so he was sleeping very soundly like the dead. Well, he said afterward, he didn't know what hit him: he jumped up, opened the outside door, and dashed out. When he got to the stairs he said he didn't know what happened; he seemed to have stepped in a hole and went rolling down the stairs, hurting his arm. Then he jumped up and dashed outside, the most dangerous thing he could do. So many people were killed by going out too soon and were crushed by the falling debris. Outside, the cold rain on his bare skin woke him up, and he thought what am I doing here and he dashed up into the house and ran up the stairs meeting Mrs. Mopsy [her neighbor who mops all the time] dashing down the stairs. She said later on she wondered where he had been. Instead of going into the basement through the hallway, Mrs. Mopsy also dashed into the yard and then couldn't find the gate. That was just when the lights went out and the loose wire of toppled poles came coiling around her. People in the basement yelled at her to come into the house, and if she had been a few seconds later she would have been electrocuted.

We then went into the basement in Fat Mrs. Liu's room; she is the chairman of our courtyard. There were about six or seven children and I don't know how many grown-ups. Although frightened herself, Mrs. Liu started her stove and made what seemed to be pots and pots of mong bean soup. She kept saying: "Oh, I am so scared! Drink! Let the children drink the soup." I will never forget the kindness people showed each other. People were giving each other their last bit of things.

Our part of Tientsin was one of the hardest hit. When dawn came and everyone came out into the streets, I could barely believe my eyes. En-hua left soon afterwards for his office, returning around three in the afternoon. Then we went to Shengli Road [the widest street in Tientsin]. The rain was still pouring down. There we met one of his colleagues who welcomed us into this little tent in which were his family of five or six. I don't know if I would have had the kindness in me to have welcomed other families in so graciously. While we stayed there En-hua went to the Water Works. He came back around five, saying the Water Works said for us to go there, but we must hurry as there was going to be another quake around six. So to the Water Works we went and have been staying there off and on ever since. The forecast was really accurate, and the big aftershock came at 6:50. Food and water are easy to get, and the shops began to sell necessities the very next day. The Water Works workmen worked like mad fixing up the pipes in three days time, while the earth was still quaking. It is not over yet. Yesterday there were six medium-size ones.

I've been home the past three to four days living in front of the house; it's not so safe here so we are going back to the Water Works. We might be able to live in the outer room in the winter if no more big quakes occur. We are thinking of sending Yun to her grandmother's for the next six months. Her kindergarten's building is badly damaged.

Willy, all your friends are safe: Kelin and his family are well. Old Dr. Ko and his family, Professor Li and his wife all came through with flying colors; remember how the little quake last year nearly killed Mrs. Li! People with heart trouble seemed to come through all right. I have seen Mousy often [a friend of Willy's, nicknamed after the way he knocks on the door]. His uncle and aunt were killed and their three children are living with the Mousies now.

Things are so well-organized. These old ladies of the neighborhood are really something! They work night and day patrolling with the militia, seeing that everybody has food and care, looking after the old people—those who have no family. They know exactly in what condition every-one in their neighborhood is in. Many people have gone off leaving all their things in the care of the neighborhood committees. To the bad elements who want to plunder and steal, the punishment is both fast and drastic: so I haven't seen a single incident around here. You can leave things on the street for days and no one will touch it.

I must stop now as I'm very busy. I still have asthma and I have chest pain. I will have to ask for some medicine to be sent. I'll tell you in my next letter.

Love,

Nini

Zhu De, the builder of the Communist army, died in July at age ninety. Then on September 9, 1976, the Great Helmsman himself, Mao Zedong, died. While thousands passed before his casket at the Great Hall of the People, the nation watched in stunned silence as his wife Jiang Qing and three others, known as the "Gang of Four," were rounded up on October 6, and the Cultural Revolution came to an end.

The previous fall, at Tom's suggestion and with his assistance, William entered the College Scholars Program at the University of Tennessee with a focus on linguistics. Grace joined him in Knoxville when her health improved. While William was at the university, a sea change began to happen in U.S.-China relations. Students and professors began the first wave of exchanges that were to gain momentum in the next few years. One of Grace's nephews was among the very first student groups to enter China in November 1976. Grace and William heard from Ellen that one day at work, her boss informed her that an American cousin had come to China and had asked to meet her. This simple, yet remarkable, family reunion marked the beginning of many academic exchanges that William was soon to witness.

In February 1977, William was invited to Philadelphia to meet with Dr. Labov, head of the Department of Linguistics at the University of Pennsylvania. He spent two weeks in Pennsylvania, interacting with those who taught English as a second language, those who taught Chinese to English-speaking students, and those engaged in sociolinguistic research. He was asked to give a talk about the social significance of English teaching in China which he illustrated with examples of their work at Nankai University. Dr. Labov soon put William in touch with Dr. Wang, the editor of the

Journal of Chinese Linguistics, a publication of the University of California at Berkeley. By the time William graduated in the spring of 1977, with Phi Beta Kappa honors, he had been offered a job at Berkeley's Center for Chinese Studies.

William's transition to life in Berkeley was aided by his work, analyzing Chinese dialects, writing articles on linguistics, and later taking courses in psycholinguistics. Some of his articles were published in the *Journal of Chinese Linguistics.* But what became more demanding of his time was the increasing number of academic exchanges between China and the United States.

While William worked, Grace spent the time alone putting down in writing as much of her life story as she could. In this work she had the assistance of her cousins' daughter, Eleanor McCallie, who lived in San Francisco and often came to stay with her while William was away. Grace wrote to Tom and Mary Hills: "I can say I am quite busy now. I am trying to get down as much of my story as possible, but it's not fast work . . . Willy and Eleanor are really keeping my nose to the grindstone writing my 'history.' Every time Eleanor sees me, she says, 'How much have you written?' and I feel very guilty whenever I can't report some progress. And Willy's the same. I feel very reprehensible if I sit down with an Agatha Christie or some such escapist literature."

During the times when William was traveling, Eleanor often stayed with Grace and had conversations, like the following, about Grace's life in China and the United States:

"Grace, I can understand why you stayed in China with your husband when the Communists came. But when he died, didn't you think about coming home?"

"People tried to talk me into returning then, but I wouldn't think of it. I thought it would be too hard on the children. China was their home. People thought I couldn't stand it, that I couldn't survive."

"Why did they think that?"

"Because I wasn't used to it. I had always had a rather high standard of living, three servants and so forth. How could I survive if I lived like an ordinary Chinese? The place we moved to—it was very primitive and . . . well, it was harsh for me, very harsh—no kitchen, no bathroom, no running water, no heating—but I welcomed harshness then. My husband's death knocked the foundations of the world right out from under me. So I didn't care how hard it was or what I had to do. I wanted to get away from everything that was familiar, to live in an entirely different place and with entirely different people."

"But you were a foreigner. Didn't the people resent you?"

"I thought they would resent me. The people were just ordinary workers and they were so kind to me. When our neighbor saw that I didn't know how to handle the stove, she said she would help—and she did everything for me. It was *the* nicest place I have ever lived in my life. Nini still lives there and you can see from Nini's letter after the earthquake, what an organized society can be—not the 'regimented' society that scares the 'free' West, but one with a sense of security and connection with people. It creates a confident spirit. You can see that spirit in Nini's letter."

"But Grace," Eleanor pushed further, "you sometimes complain of lack of space in this apartment in Berkeley. How could you endure such a small place then?"

"It is different in China. You can't use the same standard that you do here. In China there isn't such a great store in privacy. Our doors were always open and children of other families would just come in, running in and out, asking for this or that—a drink of water, something to eat, what time is it? If we had guests and we didn't have places to sit, we'd just go next door and get a chair and haul it over. They did the same. I think you can see that for me then—when you have had a terrible loss, when you are stricken—that kind of atmosphere is marvelous. It's healing, you know. It saved my life."

Grace continued without prompting: "People are closer in China. There is nothing you can't talk about. Everyone listens to each other. That way your own problems don't seem so overwhelming. I didn't know about any of this until after my husband died. Everything was new then. It gives you a kind of security—to be connected. Here it is easy to feel alone and isolated."

"He's gone so much now," Grace said, thinking about William. "Even when he's in town, he's not here. I never really know what he is doing unless I ask questions. It makes me feel like I'm nosy. It wasn't like that in China. We were always busy together . . . we knew everything about each other, about our work, about our friends . . . I knew his friends well. They were part of the family. It's not that way here."

"But Grace," Eleanor interrupted, "you know that Willy's work, the recognition he is getting—reflects on you. It is your achievement, too."

Then her irrepressible humor came out again, "The only useful thing I can do here is write down what I used to do there." She laughed, then continued reflecting. "In China— even when I was in the hospital—I was in the middle of things. Even when I was old, I felt I was making a contribution. . . . In China *lau tai tai* is a term of respect. But here being called 'old lady' is an insult."

THE AFTERSHOCKS OF THE earthquake and the arrest of those associated with the Gang of Four took a great toll on Tianjin. The situation in Tianjin had grown worse even though it was getting better in the rest of the country. Nini explained in letters that the mayor of Tianjin had been in the clique of the Gang of Four and struggling for power and, consequently, many things weren't getting done. For example, Nini reported, they didn't have any electricity for a long time after the earthquake. Nini put up a big fight for it and even wrote to the newspaper. At that time the newspapers were beginning to investigate what was happening and to print letters and stories from citizens. As a result the leadership was beginning to be afraid of the newspapers. She wrote letters to the electric company and to the building company as well. Nini said that everyone had worked very hard to recover from the earthquake. She and En-hua had moved back to the house even though the construction was still incomplete and everything was covered in dust.

By February, in time for Chinese New Year, Nini wrote that the electricity was finally restored. By then her building had been repaired and the residents had begun to clean the floors and repaint. Grace and William heard from Ellen that Beijing had not been hit as hard by the earthquake. English was now being taught on TV and Ellen's daughters wanted them to bring a television back.

The terrible dust from the earthquake and the stress and strain of recovery and repairs had caused Nini's asthma to reactivate and made it almost impossible for her to breathe. In June Nini wrote that she was in the hospital and had nearly died. But, she said, things in Tianjin had improved since they had a new mayor who got things done quickly and efficiently. The building was repaired and looked better than it ever had. Nini's little girl was staying with Ellen in Beijing while Nini was hospitalized.

⟶

ON AUGUST 8, 1978, ALMOST a year after they came to Berkeley, William noticed a large, hard lump on Grace's neck. Grace said she had been aware of it but hadn't said anything because she didn't know how her medical care would be covered. She had no employer, no insurance, no social security, and even no record of her birth. She would just wait, she thought, until they returned to China, which she expected to do shortly. But William had signed a contract for another year and she needed medical attention immediately.

Several diagnoses concurred that it was a tumor in her throat. No one seemed quite sure what to do. The large size of the tumor was threatening to close off her throat but surgery did not look advisable; as Grace said, "It would cut off my head." The experts recommended radiation accompanied by a drug, still undergoing research trials, which was supposed to increase the susceptibility of cells to radiation. Because this drug was experimental, William was asked to sign papers giving permission.

William wrote to Nini and Ellen to come as soon as possible.

Treatments began just before Labor Day weekend. Grace wrote to
Tom and Mary Hills on September 9, 1978:

> The treatments are indeed causing improvement. I didn't
> expect anything so fast, but there is quite a definite
> progress for the better. Of course you know radiation
> therapy is very drastic—weakening and exhausting—and
> causes loss of appetite. I'm also taking a special drug that
> makes the tumor cells less resistant to radiation and
> together they seem to be working very fast. The drug is
> likely to cause nausea, but I'm given something to combat
> nausea and haven't so far suffered any. But it is not a very
> pleasant treatment and sometimes I feel very miserable.
>
> I've had eight radiation treatments plus, I think, five drug
> doses, and the doctors and all the radiation staff are
> astonished and pleased with my progress. I don't know if
> Willy told you that I'm being treated at the University of
> San Francisco Medical Center. People out here think it's
> the last word in medicine. The buildings and equipment
> are very, very impressive. So far I've dealt with about three
> doctors, and I was "inspected" by about a dozen young
> doctors one morning! One of my doctors is the No. 1 big
> chief of the oncology department.

Grace's tumor shrank so rapidly that she was considered a "case
to be discussed at the next convention." By the last treatment, she
could scarcely swallow because her saliva glands were burned from
the radiation. Food intake became difficult and other complications
began to emerge. She had not eaten for three weeks and her weight
went down to seventy-five pounds. She was admitted to the hospital again for intravenous feeding.

Ellen and Nini had applied for visas but were still waiting.
Grace's condition deteriorated. She wrote what turned out to be
her last letter to Tom and Mary Hills on December 5, 1978:

> I'm sorry I can't write a long newsy letter. My hands are
> still numb and annoyingly useless—it's difficult to write, to
> button anything, to pick up things, or to manipulate safety

pins. It's terribly frustrating. They [the doctors] say it will go away but it's not leaving fast. I am fairly active—I've been out to dinner and walk around the neighborhood. Ellen and Nini think they are leaving around the 19th—but not positive. I'm quite "writ out" now. My hand hurts. Hope we can manage to get to see you before too long. I remember so much about our time spent together.

Much love,

Grace

IN LATE 1978, DENG Xiaoping, twice purged and twice rehabilitated, became China's new leader. Already, even before Nixon's visit in 1972, the economic and technological pressures to move China toward a more open policy were being felt. Deng supported and immediately set in place a national movement toward "The Four Modernizations" of industry, science, technology and national defense.

The United States and China resumed full diplomatic relations on January 1, 1979. The United States increased its liaison office to a full embassy staff, and requests for visas moved faster. Nini and Ellen's requests were among the first to be approved.

When Deng Xiaoping arrived in Washington D.C. on January 28, 1979, he was greeted by ecstatic crowds and press. He toured Houston, Atlanta, and Seattle, forming new corporate and political ties. Nini and Ellen arrived in the United States in time to hear President Carter's speech welcoming Deng, at the same time that the so-called Maoist Red Guards in Berkeley demonstrated with sticks and banners protesting Deng's "capitalist roader" policies.

William's sisters took over the care of their mother, did all the cooking, cleaning, nursing, and trying to make Grace eat more. Grace's weight was now only sixty-eight pounds. As William said in a letter to his Uncle Tom and Aunt Mary Hills, whom he now called "Juma," an affectionate term in Chinese: "You can positively see through her." She spent her days resting and trying to swallow, and even that was a lot of work, as Grace said, "something every minute."

Given Grace's condition, it may seem strange to describe this as a happy time. There was much chattering in English and Chinese and often laughter as the three grown children, their American cousin Eleanor, and Grace spent their evenings together. One night after dinner, they were sitting around the table talking. Grace was sitting up in her makeshift bed in the dining room, leaning against a pile of pillows, right in the middle of things, where she liked to be.

Two letters had arrived that day from China, both of them with good news. Ellen heard from Rui-sheng that the family had been assigned a larger apartment—two rooms with a kitchen and bath. They had been waiting a long time for this and Ellen was excited. The second letter was from Nankai University informing Grace that she had been promoted to Associate Professor.

Grace was pleased with the news and feeling good. Eleanor asked her Chinese cousins, "What does it mean that Grace has been promoted when she is not there?"

"It means that she has been 'rehabilitated.' Those who were accused of crimes during the Cultural Revolution are being cleared now. It is just the beginning." said William.

Eleanor turned to Nini. "How do you think F. C. would have fared if he had lived during the Cultural Revolution?"

"He would have done as Grace did, given his all to his work. He might have suffered as she did, but still, I can't imagine him preferring to live in the old society—the way China used to be before 1949."

"Changing human beings is the most difficult," Ellen added in her wise way. "That will take generations."

"So what do you do in the meantime?" Eleanor asked.

"Well, what would you do?" Nini asked back. "Would you 'grumble against heaven' because of what has happened to you? Would

you judge other people by your own yardstick? Or would you just
go on living the best you can and do what you have to do?"

A FEW DAYS LATER Grace was completely unable to eat. She was
told to return to the hospital for an operation to insert a feeding
tube, but she was too weak. Alone, in her hospital room at night,
her breathing stopped. A nurse called the family to come immediately. Her three children stood by her—Ellen stroking her fore-
head, Nini touching her feet, and Willy holding her hand—as the
monitor recorded her last heartbeat.

April 26, 1979

Dear Uncle and Juma,

It was very difficult for me to talk to you about the sad
event over the phone this morning. I know how much both
of you felt for her and her children. My mother has always
meant so much to me, not only as a mother, but, as I had to
take care of her, she was also like my child, therefore I feel
a double loss. Although she did not live an easy life, it was a
courageous and interesting one. She not only worked hard
for her family, she also worked hard in doing her job, and
she was loved and respected by many.

My mother always maintained a deep love for her family
and especially for her favorite brother, and she had
transmitted this feeling to her children by telling them
many, many stories, and that is why I felt so much at home
with all of you.

Dear Uncle Tom and Juma, I am only writing a short
note, at this sad time, to say how we, her children,
appreciate the love and kindness you both showed her and
her children. I am enclosing one of the last pictures my
mother took, and one picture of your nephew and two
nieces. We love you. Take care.

Love,

Willy

THE BONE-CHILLING WIND was again gusting over the Great Wall, sweeping down from Siberia across the mountain barriers on its way to the sea. No invaders from the North now swept along with the piercing gale. No red-cheeked army marched triumphantly down Tianjin's empty streets. The image of a lone foreign woman standing at her courtyard gate watching them was now only a phantom memory. Nor was the same frail foreigner holding onto a lamppost as the chilling winds blew across the frozen lotus ponds. On the university grounds, no loudspeakers or large character posters announced the event. Only a small note on the official bulletin board read:

> Associate Professor Grace Divine Liu of the Foreign Language Department of Nankai University, died of illness on the 25th of April, 1979. Professor Grace Liu's memorial will be held on January 12th, 1980, 4:00 P.M. at the Tianjin Hall of Revolutionary Martyrs.

At the proper time, an official ushered the assembled crowd, numbering about eighty, into a large hall where dusty paper flowers on the walls commemorated the dead. On one wall hung a picture of Grace Liu, framed by a wreath of paper flowers and draped in black crepe. The crowd stood before her picture. Her soft gray eyes and her thin face looked down upon them. Crashing sounds of Chinese funeral music came over an intercom. An officiating person read from a list of names of people and organizations that had sent wreaths and condolences.

Then a man rose and stood before the solemn audience. The music stopped. It was Lou Ping, Vice President of Nankai University, the same man who had stood on the stage with Grace Liu twelve years before, who had been forced with her to trudge through dirt and manure, who had been shamed and condemned before the jeering crowd. Now in this silence he gazed at those gathered, both young and old. The room was heavy with the moment. He read from a prepared statement. The assembled crowd listened to the carefully chosen words:

> With profound grief, we deeply mourn Associate Professor Grace Divine Liu of our Foreign Languages Department.
> Grace Divine Liu was an American with Chinese nationality who was born in February 1901 in Chattanooga, Tennessee, the United States. She was educated in Chattanooga, where she also taught high school, and in New York City, where she studied music. In 1932, she married Mr. Liu Fuqi [Fu-chi] who was a graduate of Qinghua University and an overseas student studying in the United States, and then came to China to live. Mr. Liu became the chief engineer at the Tianjin Water Works in 1937 and died of lung cancer in 1955. Grace Liu came to teach in the Foreign Languages Department as an English teacher in 1957 and received her Chinese citizenship the same year. She became a Lecturer in 1960 and was promoted to Associate Professor in 1979. In the fall of 1974 she went to visit her family and to seek medical treatment in the United States. She died on April 25th, 1979, in a hospital in San Francisco. She was seventy-eight.
> Grace Liu loved China. She resolutely supported her husband for devoting his knowledge and talents to the service of the motherland and its people. She broke through many barriers to come to China and willingly united her life with the fate of the Chinese nation. When the American Consulate suggested sending her whole family back to the United States in 1948, she decided to remain in China to welcome the liberation of the whole nation. From the fifties to the sixties, she endured tremendous setbacks in her life: first her husband died and she had difficulty in living, and then she herself suffered a serious illness, but she still consistently did her job well. She wrote many times to both Premier Zhou Enlai and Deputy Premier Chen Yi to report the problems in the teaching of foreign languages and to give her opinions on the subject. At the same time, she was active in writing and published many articles about New China in the progressive publications in the United States, introducing our country's great achievements under socialism. During the Cultural

Revolution, she suffered serious political persecution, but she did not give up.

William stood silently between his two sisters. He could feel Nini's heaviness beside him. Tears welled in her swollen eyes. Her puffy hands were clasped in front of her. She had not been well in the six months since her return to China. He knew that she felt a great loss, not only of her mother but of a vital part of herself. The world she had known was gone. With William remaining in the United States and Ellen in Beijing, there was no one who could share the other side of her. And what of her daughter . . . and Ellen's children, William wondered. They had never really known their grandmother. The world in which Grace lived had changed so much from their own that his sisters could never really explain to their own children this remarkable woman and what she had lived through.

William knew the importance of these words as an official statement of Grace's life, but he was moved by the apparent emotion of the speaker and the crowd. He wondered what would be said of her legacy. Lou Ping continued:

> Grace Liu was conscientious, active, and enthusiastic in her work and made achievements in the studies of modern English and American linguistics and literature. For two decades, she put great effort into the study of the teaching of English and wrote many articles to introduce more advanced theories and methods from abroad, while putting forward many valuable opinions and suggestions. She led the compilation and the editing of textbooks for the teaching of basic English and rigorously trained a group of English teachers. Thus, she made very valuable contributions to the Foreign Language Department of our university. She never ceased to be concerned for the work of the Department; even after she went abroad in '74, she still wrote and mailed books and other materials back to the Department.
>
> While Grace Liu was in the United States, she started to write her memoir, using her personal experience to tell about

the great cultural tradition of China and its achievements in the socialist revolution. Unfortunately, she could not complete this work before she died. We are all deeply impressed by her spirit.

The death of Grace Liu is a great loss to the Foreign Languages Department of Nankai University. We lost a loyal and active teacher and friend. Today, while we are striving to realize our nation's Four Modernizations, to mourn the passing of Grace Liu we must learn from her love of China, her pursuance of truth, and her tenacious revolutionary spirit; we must learn from her scientific attitude of serious pursuit in academic studies and research and the seeking of truth from facts, her diligent and conscientious style of work. We will always remember Grace Liu's profound feelings for China and the active contribution she made to the teaching of English at our university.

Grace Liu, rest in peace!

At the conclusion of the eulogy, the wreath bearing Grace's image was handed to Nini. William carried the rectangular container bearing her ashes. Together they led the crowd to an upper room in the mausoleum where he placed the container into a slot next to F. C.'s. William glanced at his father's name and then at Grace's picture. Could she or F. C. ever have imagined that Grace would be eulogized here at this Hall of Revolutionary Martyrs? That this would be their final resting place?

As the crowd moved back through the great hall and down the steps to the outside, each one spoke words of condolence to the family before departing. Just as he reached the van, William was stopped by a slightly older man with a bold shock of white hair. He shook hands warmly with William. Although the man was Chinese, he spoke to William in fluent English: "I knew your mother during the Japanese Occupation. I was then about twenty years old and I remember you as just a little boy." He chuckled slightly at the memory. "I came to your house to learn English, but your mother discovered it was my dream to be a tenor in the great operas—I never did that but I sang with her. She gave me a book. It was from her teacher Proschowsky, called *The Art of Singing*. I wish I could give it back to you now but it was burned during the Cultural Revolution."

The van began to move. "Your mother was a great lady, . . . always . . . always, she was a lady . . ." His words trailed off as the van lurched forward and the white-haired man was lost to sight, merging with the bundled crowd in the cold wind.

William Liu with Professor Li Jiye, Chairman of the Foreign Language Department, after Grace's Memorial Service, Tianjin, January 1980.

· WILLIAM'S AFTERWORD ·

In mid-August 1979 I watched my sisters Nini and Ellen take off from Tampa Airport, returning home to China. After our mother, Grace, had died that April in Berkeley, California, my sisters and I, with our cousin Eleanor, drove cross-country to visit our American roots in Chattanooga, Tennessee. Nini had been there forty-five years earlier, as an eighteen-month-old baby, when Grace was bidding farewell to her family on her way to China to reunite with her Chinese husband. Now, after visiting my uncle and aunt in Naples, Florida, my sisters were taking our mother's ashes back to China to rejoin her husband for the final time.

After their plane took off, I began driving toward Massachusetts and a new teaching job at Wellesley College. I drove right into a fierce thunderstorm. It was early evening, and the rain and wind were so strong that I had to pull onto the shoulder of the highway. The wind rocked the car and the rain pounded the windshield. When lightning flashed, I could only see a waterfall in every direction, while an impenetrable darkness enveloped the car.

Sitting there in the dark, I felt for the first time in my life completely alone, and, for the first time, I tried to look at my parents not through the eyes of their child, but to see them as a couple who had lived their lives with love and respect: an American woman and a Chinese man who had maintained a deep respect for each other's values, beliefs, and commitments. They came from vastly different backgrounds, from cultures that to others often generated seemingly irreconcilable values. Yet each was able to absorb the excellent qualities of the other into a union that defied the then-prevalent deep-seated prejudice against mixed marriages, the devastation of wars, the turbulence of revolutions, and, ultimately, even death.

The most important legacy my parents gave their children was the loving family they created under the most difficult conditions, which demonstrated to us the power of our combined cultural heritage. On that stormy night, as the intermittent lightning flashes gave me glimpses of the box on the car seat beside me, a box filled with my mother's writings, I reaffirmed my determination to tell their story.

My mother had been writing her memoirs for a couple of years before she died. My cousin, Eleanor McCallie, who had lived with us in Berkeley and helped take care of Mother when she became sick, and I encouraged her to write the story of her life.

Over the years Eleanor and I had made many efforts to continue what Grace had started, but we were never able to find the time to carry it out. Now, with the addition of valuable new material, we have finally gotten the story told.

We both strongly believe that we must let Grace tell her own story, and any other voices we use are intended to represent her attitude and point of view or reflect aspects of her character. We were fortunate that our frirend, Paul Kivel, taped recollections of my sisters Nini and Ellen before they died. I take great comfort in the fact that represented in the book are the voices of both Nini, who at the age of nine was reading English classics and entertaining our bedridden neighbor, Mrs. Holmberg, with Dickens and George Eliot, and whose brilliant intellect set a tough path for me to follow, and Ellen, whose beauty, honesty, and goodness awed many.

With courage and intellectual inquisitiveness, Grace witnessed and took part in gigantic social upheavals. Her strong mental power helped her through many difficult periods that would have been daunting even to someone physically much stronger than she was. People were always surprised that such courage came from a woman scarcely over five feet tall and who often weighed less than a hundred pounds.

Grace was born in 1901 and died in 1979, a life that spanned most of the twentieth century. In the new century, we face a fast-shrinking world with swiftly changing boundaries, with races, cultures, social systems, religious beliefs, and economic interests colliding in rapid succession.

If one slight and fragile woman, under horrendous circumstances, could have the courage to follow her heart, the conviction to stare down prejudices, and the self-sacrificing determination to give all her effort to educate and to foster understanding, is there any reason to doubt that the rest of us can try, in our own ways, to do the same?

· ACKNOWLEDGMENTS ·

We are grateful to many friends and family members for their support, encouragement, and contributions without which this book would be less, if at all. Special thanks must be given to Mary Hills Divine, who saved her sister-in-law's letters for more than fifty years; Elinor Divine Benedict, who has written her own tribute to Grace in poems and read early drafts; and Paul Kivel for recording and transcribing interviews.

The archives of the following institutions contributed: Nankai University, Qing Hua University, Tianjin Water Works, University of California at Berkeley Center for Chinese Studies, Cornell University, New York Public Library, Girls' Preparatory School, and the McCallie School.

28 DATE DUE DAYS